Emotional Histories in the Fight to End Prostitution

History of Emotions

Series Editor: Peter N. Stearns, University Professor in the Department of History at George Mason University, USA and Susan J. Matt Presidential Distinguished Professor of History at Weber State University, USA.

Editorial Board: Rob Boddice, Senior Research Fellow, Academy of Finland Centre of Excellence in the History of Experiences, Tampere University, Finland
Charles Zika, University of Melbourne & Chief Investigator for the Australian Research Council's Centre for the History of Emotions, Australia
Pia Campeggiani, University of Bologna, Italy
Angelika Messner, Kiel University, Germany
Javier Moscoso, Centro de Ciencias Humanas y Sociales, Madrid, Spain

The history of emotions offers a new and vital approach to the study of the past. The field is predicated on the idea that human feelings change over time and they are the product of culture as well as of biology. Bloomsbury's history of emotions series seeks to publish state-of-the-art scholarship on the history of human feelings and emotional experience from antiquity to the present day, and across all seven continents. With a commitment to a greater thematic, geographical and chronological breadth, and a deep commitment to interdisciplinary approaches, it will offer new and innovative titles with convey the rich diversity of emotional cultures.

Published:
Fear in the German-Speaking World, 1600–2000, edited by Thomas Kehoe and Michael Pickering (2020)
Feelings and Work in Modern History, edited by Agnes Arnold-Forster and Alison Moulds (2022)

Forthcoming:
Emotions in the Ottoman Empire, by Nil Tekgül
The Business of Emotion in Modern History, edited by Andrew Popp and Mandy Cooper
The Renaissance of Feeling, by Kirk Essary

Emotional Histories in the Fight to End Prostitution

Emotional Communities 1869 to Today

Michele Renée Greer

BLOOMSBURY ACADEMIC
LONDON • NEW YORK • OXFORD • NEW DELHI • SYDNEY

BLOOMSBURY ACADEMIC
Bloomsbury Publishing Plc
50 Bedford Square, London, WC1B 3DP, UK
1385 Broadway, New York, NY 10018, USA
29 Earlsfort Terrace, Dublin 2, Ireland

BLOOMSBURY, BLOOMSBURY ACADEMIC and the Diana logo
are trademarks of Bloomsbury Publishing Plc

First published in Great Britain 2023
This paperback edition published 2024

Copyright © Michele Renée Greer, 2023

Michele Renée Greer has asserted her right under the Copyright,
Designs and Patents Act, 1988, to be identified as Author of this work.

For legal purposes the Acknowledgments on p. vi constitute
an extension of this copyright page.

Cover image © Jurriaan Brobbel/Alamy Stock Photo

All rights reserved. No part of this publication may be reproduced or transmitted
in any form or by any means, electronic or mechanical, including photocopying,
recording, or any information storage or retrieval system, without prior
permission in writing from the publishers.

Bloomsbury Publishing Plc does not have any control over, or responsibility for,
any third-party websites referred to or in this book. All internet addresses given
in this book were correct at the time of going to press. The author and publisher
regret any inconvenience caused if addresses have changed or sites have
ceased to exist, but can accept no responsibility for any such changes.

A catalogue record for this book is available from the British Library.

A catalog record for this book is available from the Library of Congress.

ISBN: HB: 978-1-3502-7556-0
        PB: 978-1-3502-7559-1
        ePDF: 978-1-3502-7557-7
        eBook: 978-1-3502-7558-4

Series: History of Emotions

Typeset by Integra Software Services Pvt. Ltd.

To find out more about our authors and books visit www.bloomsbury.com
and sign up for our newsletters.

Contents

Acknowledgments	vi
Introduction	1
1 Moral Liberals and the Monstrosities of State Medicine (1869–1880s)	13
2 Purity Crusaders and the Threat of Degeneracy (1880s–1920s)	35
3 Maternal Feminists: From Social Mothers to New Women (1880s–1930s)	53
4 Global Doldrums and National Vestiges (1940s–1960s)	87
5 Radical Feminists and Raging Wounds (1970s–today)	97
6 Social Regulators: Shifting the Burden (1980s–today)	109
7 Survivors: Suffering as Expertise (1980s–today)	133
Conclusion	147
Notes	157
Bibliography	193
Index	218

Acknowledgments

First and foremost, I would like to express my thanks to the editors of this series Peter Stearns and Susan Matt, the anonymous reviewers, as well as the staff at Bloomsbury for this opportunity to publish my work. Through their helpful comments and suggestions, I hope to do even greater justice to those upon whose shoulders I stand with this humble contribution to the history of emotions.

The research and the writing of this work is the culmination of a very long project which began over ten years ago in pursuit of my doctorate at the Université Paris 8 Vincennes-Saint-Denis. As such, I cannot neglect to mention the importance of my supervisor Elsa Dorlin and PhD committee members Camille Froidevaux-Metterie, Bertrand Guillarme, Joyce Outshoorn, and Frédéric Regard in refining my analytical framework and strengthening my arguments. I also wish to extend my appreciation to the staff of various university and public libraries in France, England, and Belgium, most especially the Bibliothèque nationale de France, the Women's Library at the London School of Economics, and the Bibliothèque Royale de Belgique.

Punctuated by a variety of hardships, this investigation into the emotional lives of actors involved in the fight to end prostitution was undertaken alongside my endeavor to manage my own emotions while juggling jobs and staying in a dozen different countries. With that in mind, words fail to express the gratitude I feel for the invaluable support provided by my family and friends in the pursuit of this project, especially Kathleen, Angie, and Vero who assisted in checking the manuscript. Thank you, mom, dad, Aurélie, Dan, Florine, Heather, Ulli, Yuko, for the immeasurable amount of strength and encouragement you have given me and for casting light over the darkest of moments. I am eternally grateful.

Introduction

In 2018, Israel joined the ranks of Sweden (1999), Norway (2009), Iceland (2009), Canada (2014), Northern Ireland (2015), France (2016), and Ireland (2017) by passing a law which aims to end prostitution and protect its victims through directly targeting the male demand which drives it. Commonly referred to as the Nordic Model, this law criminalizes the purchase of sexual services, but not the provision or sale, effectively shifting the burden from prostitute (victim) to john (perpetrator). The specifics vary by country, but often include fines and awareness-building programs for sex buyers, as well as releasing funds to support the overall fight to end prostitution, such as prevention and rehabilitation initiatives. The Nordic Model has thus served to distill what were once divergent abolitionist—or anti-prostitution—activities into a single strategy with a unified purpose both nationally and internationally. Abolitionist feminist groups have aimed to unconditionally qualify prostitution as a gender-based violence, a framing which carries great traction in international public opinion and transnational forums. As a result, influential and passionate abolitionist campaigns have emerged in Germany, Austria, the United Kingdom, Malta, the United States, New Zealand, and Australia.

Of course, equally fervent opposition to abolitionism—commonly known as the sex work lobby—has also emerged and includes actors from the worlds of feminism and commercial sex, as well as from the fields of public health and human rights. As is often the case in social movements, emotions run high on both sides of this debate and are instrumentalized to frame arguments, to construct subjects, and to shape subjectivities in line with resonant ethos. Although the abolitionist lobby currently carries more institutional influence, the sex worker lobby appears to have gained some momentum within the #MeToo movement, with various groups for sexual violence survivors, such as the Survivors' Agenda,[1] calling for the full decriminalization of commercial sex to reduce the vulnerability of sex workers. That said, there is also a growing anti-porn and anti-prostitution contingent within #MeToo.[2] In sum, there is little to suggest that the feminist debate surrounding prostitution will be over anytime soon, and neither will commercial sex be officially and unanimously normalized, condemned, or eradicated by the world's nations.

The key to understanding the ongoing fight to end prostitution, as well as the opposing views on prostitution within feminism that it reveals, lies in the abolitionist movement's past. Today's Nordic Model campaign can be traced back to the moral crusade waged by British social reformer and liberal feminist Josephine Butler from 1869 to repeal the Contagious Diseases Acts. In an effort to curb rising levels of venereal disease, these forced the registration and examination of prostitutes by speculum in garrison towns in the British Empire and its overseas territories. Outraged by the infringement of human (and particularly female) dignity and the clear double moral standard on sexuality it buttressed by ignoring male clients, Josephine Butler and her supporters established a national society to fight the government's regulation of prostitution. In a nod to the movement to abolish the slave trade—a movement to which many of their supporters had relational and ideological ties—the freshly dubbed "New Abolitionists" launched their campaign to end the state's regulation of prostitution beyond the borders of Great Britain in 1875. This extension albeit came at a price, as the already chameleon-like discourse of abolitionists had morphed and was distorted by new actors to fit the increasingly nationalist, conservative, and reactionary climate of the latter part of the long nineteenth century.

A Contested Genealogy

Various scholars have pointed to the significance of the historical British repeal campaign in the development of the women's rights movement.[3] In this book, I support this argument by doing what few have done and tackle both early and late phases of abolitionism from a historical epistemological perspective to glean a better understanding of its role in the development and evolution of feminist protest politics. This genealogy, especially concerning prostitution, is indeed a matter of debate. Take, for instance, the book *The Pimping of Prostitution: Abolishing the Sex Work Myth* penned by British journalist and abolitionist feminist activist Julie Bindel which exposes the results of a two-year investigation of the international sex work industry. Typifying the current abolitionist position and advocacy style, the book opens by tracing—as many others have done before—the contemporary movement's origins to the repeal campaign launched by Josephine Butler to end the state's regulation of prostitution in the late nineteenth century. Julie Bindel explains:

> Butler was ahead of her time in that she firmly placed the blame for the abuse of the women in prostitution, and for the existence of the sex trade, on the shoulders of men: something that many feminists today are reluctant to do.[4]

Yet, the extent to which Josephine Butler would view the abolitionist movement today as the inheritor of her mantle is debatable, as anthropologist and sex workers' rights advocate Laura Agustin challenges in her review of *The Pimping of Prostitution*:

> Bindel feels Josephine Butler would be on her side? I feel she'd be on mine. [...] Butler saw how few alternatives women had to achieve economic independence and did not advocate they should be deprived of the possibility of selling sex to survive.[5]

Unsurprisingly, since its publication in 2017, *The Pimping of Prostitution* has polarized readers and academics alike who have either applauded it as "a thorough refutation of the myths peddled by the pro-prostitution lobby" or criticized it for its "extreme level of dogmatism and lack of charity to any other viewpoint."[6] On the one hand, this book preserves the trend of expertise-based advocacy which has become characteristic of radical feminist causes, as exemplified by works such as Kathleen Barry's *Female Sexual Slavery* or Janice Raymond's *Not a Choice, Not a Job: Exposing the Myths about Prostitution and the Global Sex Trade*. On the other hand, dismissive of abolitionist opponents which include sex workers' rights advocacy groups and non-governmental organizations like Amnesty International, it presents a one-sided argument blending affective and scientific discourses to forge what French sociologist Lilian Mathieu has called the *style abolitionniste*[7] ("abolitionist style"). It is used by activists to develop their own credibility as experts in defense of the major tenets of contemporary abolitionism that all manifestations of sex work are forms of sexual enslavement and violence against women; that government must work to eradicate prostitution, not normalize it as the pimp lobby of the so-called sex workers' rights movement would argue; and that the best way to achieve this is to end demand through criminalizing the purchase—not the selling—of sexual services.

Emotional Histories: Emotional Communities and Styles

It is this abolitionist style—together with the group subjectivity and knowledge it shapes, fosters, and communicates in newsletters, meeting minutes, letters of correspondence with fellow supporters and opponents, public lectures and addresses, and assorted advocacy materials—that is taken as subject matter in this present book. When looked at from a historical epistemological perspective, the genealogical line drawn between the past and present abolitionist crusades is actually quite muddled. Abolitionism is revealed to have been heavily influenced internally by the situated interests of its dissimilar actors and externally by concurrent campaigns and ethos, both congruent and oppositional. To render this heterogeneity more approachable, this book investigates the movement through the lens of its emotional communities to weave together a narrative of abolitionist emotional histories. An emotional community, as developed by history of emotions scholar Barbara Rosenwein, is characterized by individuals "adher[ing] to the same norms of expression and valu[ing]—or devalu[ing]—the same or related emotions."[8] In other words, it is a group that shares similar emotional styles. Comparable to the notion of habitus, an emotional style encompasses "the experience, fostering, and display of emotions," following the theoretical development of Benno Gammerl, and oscillates "between discursive patterns and embodied practices as well as between common scripts and specific appropriations."[9] This highlights the multiplicity of emotions and how they operate in relation to each other. As conceptual devices, "emotional community" and "emotional style" are dynamic, malleable, porous, and easily pluralized. This allows for an investigation of emotional praxis beyond the rigid designative boundaries of an individual or group, or of a geographical area or period. In fact, many emotional communities may exist within a given social group and individuals may—and often do—flow between them, adapting to the appropriate modes of emotional expression. This book identifies a few key abolitionist emotional communities and their characteristic emotional styles, thus revolving around the retelling of their emotional histories. Not only will the emotional communities' origins be traced but also their overlaps, their rivalries, their negotiations, and their battles with pre-existing social structures—such as gender or class—among themselves, and with other contemporaneous emotional communities and styles. These emotional histories will paint a more nuanced view of the abolitionist movement, as well as shed more light on the genealogies of feminist protest politics and cis-gendered female victimhood.[10]

The study of emotions offers a great deal due to their intersubjectivity and unboundedness which allow them, like any other cultural construct, to move, to transform, to change in use and meaning, as well as to acquire historicity. Together with the neurosciences, the field of the history of emotions has provided sufficient evidence that emotions are involved in basically everything that we think and do. Emotions also interact with social norms by contributing to their enforcement and maintenance. Negative feelings like shame, guilt, or embarrassment are experienced when deviant behavior is met with punishing feelings of anger, disgust, or hostility, whereas positive feelings like happiness, pride, or excitement are felt when conformity is rewarded with gratitude, admiration, or honor. That these are constantly shaped by culture and society makes them dynamic, highly situational, and constitutive of emotional histories. Some scholars, like Monique Scheer, have even conceptualized emotions as tools of social practice which are wielded by group and individual agents.[11]

Since emotions are forms of knowledge constituted about the external world, they are largely contingent upon the sociocultural settings in which an agent is situated. As such, emotional practices transmit information which has been informed by a specific interpretation of this world and the things within it, potentially shaping, re-enforcing, or challenging the subjectivities of an emoting agent and his or her audience alike. This occurs through the performative dimension of emotion in particular, which Sara Ahmed explains through the example of disgust: with his or her emotive speech act (e.g., "That's disgusting!"), an agent generates the very object that he or she names, and this often in line with the given norms and conventions of speech in order for "disgust" to be successfully conveyed and understood by an audience.[12] In fact, an audience predisposed to the same worldviews and of a similar subjectivity as the emoting agent will find more resonance with his or her emotional performance of disgust than one that is not.

Emotional practices aiming, for instance, to qualify something as disgusting are integral to constructing and communicating group knowledge, which may later be transformed into explicit and institutionalized ideologies, practices, propositions, and policies.[13] That group knowledge becomes the dominant mainstream knowledge is arguably the ultimate goal of any social protest movement, social action itself being by definition acts of an agent based on his or her knowledge of the social world to transform that world.[14] That the emotive speech act is embedded in the social often makes it perlocutionary—having an effect or consequence on the audience—granting it sociopolitical transformative potential. However, as Pierre Bourdieu[15] as well as Michel

Foucault[16] have demonstrated, the emancipatory potential of speech is hindered by its enunciation in the social which subjects the content to mediation by expert authorities and inscription into dominant regimes. In this respect, emotional practices communicating group knowledge can be viewed as emotion work aiming to promote their claims as natural and universal in negotiation or even in competition with existing structures.

Because emotions involve a stance on and a way of perceiving the world, they are intentional and necessarily directed towards other things—both material and immaterial. Nowhere is this clearer than in political protest, where actors converge upon a common political object, constitute dynamic and culturally contingent emotional norms around different objects and subjects, and establish a shared emotional style which reinforces belonging within a group, shapes collective subjectivity, and orients collective action. Bearing this in mind, an epistemological tracing of abolitionist emotional communities also contributes to a better understanding of the role played by emotion in the production of group knowledge, but, moreover, gender-based knowledge. This is especially visible in the transnational activism for women's rights—for which "violence against women" has become the cornerstone—where once-peripheral feminist knowledges based on what had contemporaneously been considered to be uniquely female emotive capacities (for instance, for compassion) and emotional experiences (for instance, of victimhood) have risen in esteem and legitimacy to become dominant discourses, and this of course at the expense of alternative knowledges.

As James Jasper and co-authors Michael Young and Elke Zuern have recently demonstrated in their publication on public characters, politics—whether it be protest politics or electoral politics—is a pursuit of power which hinges on one's ability to persuade the public by favorably deploying not just resources but also by mobilizing the right impressions, emotions, and moral sentiments.[17] Character work is an invaluable tool, as they argue, for creating reputations which may inspire admiration for heroes, pity for victims, fear and loathing for villains, or ridicule and contempt for minions.[18] Take, for instance, the politics of reputation at work in the beforementioned contemporary use of Josephine Butler. Her dedication and audacity actually saw her shaped rather early by actors of the British repeal campaign into a heroic and almost mythical figure whose exploits were marked by the melodramatic—a key register in this age of sensationalism. She was thus described as a gentle woman emboldened by the righteousness of her cause, but heavily outmatched in battling "gigantic evil."[19] Her own memoirs *Personal Reminiscences of a Great Crusade*, L. Hay-Cooper's biography *Josephine Butler and Her Work for Social Purity* published by the Society for Promoting Christian Knowledge in 1922, and *Josephine Butler: Flame of Fire* commissioned by the Josephine Butler Society in 1963 are but a few examples which propagated her legacy as a British heroine and often in the service of specific groups. For instance, the biography from the Society for Promoting Christian Knowledge is written in an evangelical register and thus opens by describing her as God's vessel:

> Josephine Butler was an instrument consummately fashioned for the service of humanity. Every circumstance of her life and personality fitted her to meet her singular and heroic destiny.[20]

It is thus unsurprising that the contemporary abolitionist movement would also highlight her work, presenting her as a figure of collective abolitionist pride. Alongside Julie Bindel's beforementioned comments one might add the post inspired by Jane Jordan's biography on the Nordic Model Now's webpage entitled "Josephine Butler: Pioneering Feminist Activist" that adopts a much more revolutionary tone. For instance, the article highlights the audaciousness of her work—explaining how she not only went to brothels to speak with prostitutes, but she also took in women and girls trying to escape the life into her own home—and looks at her causes from a radical and intersectional feminist perspective:

> It is impossible to over-emphasise [sic] the boldness, courage and generosity of taking these women into her house. It defied all the social norms of the era and could have ruined her husband's career, and the health and standing of the whole family, including the servants.[21]

Character work such as this does much in telling audiences how to feel about the subjects involved in often brief yet effective ways. A simple narrative, for instance, employing resonant keywords or tropes, can forge a hero whose feats of courage against villains or exemplary shows of compassion for victims are meant to inspire confidence as well as action.[22]

To glean a better understanding of the emotional histories in the fight to end prostitution, it is first necessary to tackle the complexity of the abolitionist movement's long history. As such, all but one of the core chapters of this book are dedicated to the examination of a different emotional community in a loosely chronological manner with a strategic focus on key events and dominant actors. As voiced by British newspaper editor and abolitionist William T. Stead and many of his contemporaries, the twentieth century at the turn of which abolitionism emerged was the century of internationalism.[23] The globalization which accompanied colonial expansion, economic interconnectedness, and migration created possibilities for the expansion and internationalization of various local social reform projects. As a result, the geographical scope of this book strives to be international despite focusing on dominant abolitionist campaigns at the national level when they were taken as models for the larger movement, as well as highlighting local emotional cultures or attitudes which impressed upon different prevailing abolitionist emotional communities at a given time. Each chapter aims to illustrate the workings of emotion as political practice, not only in designating and empowering individuals (like Josephine Butler) or groups (like the European Women's Lobby) as entrepreneurs of meaning and intentionality on behalf of a given collective, but also in producing and shaping discourses which are then carried out in the social field across various distances, via diverse communication technologies, and for different aims.

Structure of the Book

The first three chapters trace the origins, emergence, and evolution of three emotional communities from the early phase of the abolitionist movement from 1869 to the 1930s: the Moral Liberals, the Purity Reformers, and the Maternal Feminists. The Moral Liberals of Chapter 1 appeared at the outset of the abolitionist movement in the campaign to repeal the Contagious Diseases' Acts in Great Britain. The chapter thus tends to focus on the British repeal campaign from its first years through to its extension and internationalization in 1875. This is indeed when this emotional community was most prominent and active, playing a leading role in driving the campaign to reach its peak in the 1880s. Given opportunity by antislavery activism and voluntarist philanthropy cultivated in the decades before, the Moral Liberals emerged when Josephine Butler and other female campaigners joined forces with like-minded male peers as well as members of the working class, whose fears of the encroaching powers of the state, medicine, and police were already piqued by mounting legislation targeting their bodies. This chapter looks at the defining emotional styles of Moral Liberals—from anti-statist distrust of the police to abhorrence of scientific medicine, from liberal benevolence to nationalist pride—while also investigating their origins and instrumentalized uses in imbuing their campaign and their supporters with epistemic value. There is a special focus on Moral Liberals' narratives of medical rape which—appealing to the taste for the melodramatic and sensationalist already cultivated amongst the Victorian public—aimed at provoking a moral shock, as well as publicizing the inefficiency, unconstitutionality, and immorality of these medico-police measures to regulate prostitution.

Moral shock appears as an equally important device in the next chapter on Purity Crusaders. It tracks the emergence of this emotional community in the 1880s with the inclusion of more conservative actors from the adjacent movement for social purity. They would eventually jump to prominence amid a moral panic on white slavery which struck Western countries in 1883. Their sensationalizing of emotions, notably fear, to cultivate a hatred of sin and a desire for reprimand tied them closer to governmental authorities. This alliance with statis powers aided their rise to prominence, making this emotional community a formidable rival of other abolitionist emotional communities at the turn of the twentieth century. Their origins and emotional styles are particularly investigated in relation to broader contemporary anxieties related to moral degradation and sexual delinquency, and later—under the influence of social hygiene—widespread degeneracy.

Chapter 3—the last tackling this early phase of abolitionism—treats the emotional community of Maternal Feminists, which was inherently tied to other feminist mobilizations of the period, from anti-vivisection to suffragism, both nationally and abroad. Maternal Feminists are seen instrumentalizing contemporary socially constructed and essentialized notions of gender to not only challenge the foundations of state-regulated prostitution but also to make a case for the recognition of their own legitimate and indispensable role in public affairs. This chapter focuses on their wielding of gendered emotions as expertise. For instance, the esteem of motherly love in contrast to fatherly care emerged as part of an emancipatory strategy calling for the reform, if not for the upheaval, of the situation of women that was rooted in women's differing nature. The foundations of this emotional community in the liberal tradition are explored, as well as its engagement with the dominant discursive frames of nationalism, imperialism, and later eugenics.

Chapter 4 departs from the focus on emotional communities and instead looks at the prevailing emotional patterns and attitudes shaping the context in which the abolitionist movement waned at the international level in the postwar era. While this global doldrum was mostly caused by a shift in the interwar period among abolitionist movement actors from targeting regulated prostitution to targeting trafficking and their increasingly divergent interpretations of prostitution, the upheaval caused by war shifted nation's concerns. New ways of understanding society and the individual therein fueled by the psychological turn are central to this chapter's development. Rising political passions would converge in various rights-based claims of recognition or identity movements. It is within this dynamic setting that the vestiges of abolitionism on the national level, evolving and adapting to local contexts, would reignite in the radicalization of the second-wave feminist movement in the 1970s.

The last three chapters focus on the remobilization of the abolitionist cause in the 1980s and 1990s, as prostitution was reframed by new and old abolitionist activists as an international issue on the basis of its connection with trafficking and the systemic gender-based violence inherent to sexual inequality. The emergence of the Radical Feminists is treated in Chapter 5 as an emotional community rooted in the anti-pornography movement. It viewed prostitution as a hallmark of unequal power relations between the sexes and thus abhorred not only its persistence, but its normalization through regulatory systems like those currently found in Germany, Switzerland, and the Netherlands. A miserabilist portrayal of prostitution is central to Radical Feminists' emotional styles involving anger and resentment, with the dehumanized victims of prostitution transformed into commodities on the sexual market becoming decontextualized objects of female suffering.

Next, Chapter 6 on Social Regulators speaks to the rise of this emotional community from the 2000s with a convergence between the few national campaigns—namely in France—which had survived the eclipse of the earlier abolitionist movement and Radical Feminists from the United States and Sweden under the so-called Swedish example of prostitution, later referred to as the Nordic Model. Social Regulators formed around this desire to shift the burden away from prostitutes, the victims, to the johns, the perpetrators. However, rather than seeking simply to create rules and punish those who do not follow them, Social Regulators value rules, especially the shame, guilt, and fear of humiliation which are incurred when they are broken. Rules are thus seen as serving to inculcate moral norms whose regulatory effects will lead to positive change on all levels of society. This is indeed the sense of duty shared by Social Regulators and one that is amplified in regional politics, as the focus on recent abolitionist lobbying in Europe demonstrates here.

Finally, Chapter 7 tackles the rise of a new actor in the movement and thus of a new emotional community: Survivors. Survivors are an emotional community whose convergence is necessarily the result of a shared and yet individually lived injury caused by experience in prostitution. This chapter explores how, by coming forward and exposing their stories to public scrutiny, Survivors can face their shame and sense of loss and transform into a

1

Moral Liberals and the Monstrosities of State Medicine (1869–1880s)

The British Contagious Diseases Acts of 1864, 1866, and 1869, which collectively became the offending object upon which the first of the abolitionist emotional communities—including that of the Moral Liberals—would converge, were fashioned amid anxieties surrounding the health and security of the nation which had been triggered by the rising levels of venereal disease in Britain's army and navy. These Acts were largely inspired by the popular French or continental system developed by French hygienist Alexandre Parent-Duchâtelet in 1804[1] which saw the mandatory licensing of women suspected of being in prostitution with the police, their inspection for syphilis by speculum, and their sequestration and treatment within lock hospitals if found to be infected. As a member of the Paris *Conseil de salubrité* ("hygiene council") which since its establishment in 1802 pioneered modern European notions of public health as a state duty and citizen's right, Alexandre Parent-Duchâtelet quickly emerged as the primary reference on prostitution and its regulation. Yet this exchange of scientific knowledge also served to escalate anxieties surrounding biological contagion and to build an obsessive fear of syphilis, which was framed as the most serious, dangerous, and dreaded of all the illnesses that could affect the human species.[2]

Such widespread concerns about the proliferation of venereal disease, moral and physical degeneration, and weakened national security made sexuality a key contemporary public issue for many nations. Applying an approach imbued with scientism—a belief that true knowledge can only be achieved using empirical or scientifically observable methods[3]—physicians like the British William Acton developed new medicalized understandings of sexuality, linking dysfunctional, deviant, and criminal sexualities in particular to emergent hereditary theories. "[C]onsorting with prostitutes," William Acton argued, "is one of the very worst sins, both in nature and result, which man can commit."[4] Yet his study on prostitution in Great Britain—employing the same socio-scientific methods combining archival research, fieldwork interviews, and statistical analyses as Alexandre Parent-Duchâtelet—framed the prostitute less in terms of her deviant sexuality than as a victim of economic necessity. For him, the degrading conditions of life for the urban poor saw many women turn temporarily to prostitution, as he demonstrated in his monograph first published in 1857 under the title *Prostitution Considered in its Moral, Social, and Sanitary Aspects*. Regardless, both physicians reflect the contemporary tendency of state medicine—at home but also in the British colonies[5]—to stress the moral, social, and cultural dimensions of medical conditions.

William Acton was the medical authority behind the drafting of the British Contagious Diseases Acts. Like Alexandre Parent-Duchâtelet, he stressed the role of the prostitute as the main diffusor of venereal disease and that biological contagion held devastating consequences for the health and stability of society as a whole, not just their male consorts. He thus outlined a schema for regulating women in prostitution—first in garrison towns, then nationwide—which was heavily inspired by the French system as well as his own training in Paris at Hôpital du Midi under the French venereologist Philippe Ricord, a specialist in syphilis and an advocate for the systematic use of the speculum in diagnosing venereal disease in women.[6] The result was thus the translation of the French system's rationale and practices into British legislature. Yet, while involving the same administrative practices, the Contagious Diseases Acts differed from the French system in its rendering of prostitution into an official and legalized institution, instead of a formally tolerated practice. Prostitutes had already been viewed as a nuisance to public order in earlier solicitation laws (the Vagrancy Act of 1824 and the Metropolitan Police Act of 1839) which subjected "any common prostitute"—the ambiguities of this term developed further later—to fines and imprisonment for "behaving in a riotous or indecent manner."[7] The recognition of prostitution was an essential component for William Acton, who believed only the full exposure of the issue would allow for its better treatment.[8] Qualifying prostitution as "a social plague that cannot be got rid of,"[9] he argued that "it is better to recognize what we cannot prevent, and to regulate it rather than leave it to itself [...],"[10] reflecting contemporary understandings of "nature" as negatively effecting behavior and requiring control. Of course, this purported "full" exposure and recognition of the issue was in truth only partial—it was only working-class or foreign women who were monitored, registered, and examined, and not their male clients or wealthier counterparts. Instead, firmly institutionalized in the Contagious Diseases Acts, prostitutes represented a homogeneous social category, and their bodies were constructed as exclusively female and working-class or foreign/colonial sources of disease which jeopardized Great Britain's project of empire and threatened its future with moral and physical degeneracy.

Righteous Indignation against Oppression and Injustice

Resistance to the Contagious Diseases Acts in Great Britain was organized by middle-class liberals and nonconformists in 1869, when the third act extended the reach of the state's regulatory device. The righteous indignation triggered by this fresh assault on the personal dignity of female members of the working class gave rise to the first of the early abolitionist emotional communities: the Moral Liberals. As a powerful and mobilizing sentiment, righteous indignation sat at the heart of this group's emotional styles and helped propel the repeal campaign from its humble beginnings in petition writing to an abolitionist federation of national branches holding international congresses across Europe by the 1880s.[11] Importantly, the British repeal campaign's spread followed largely the same paths and involved the same networks of actors as those to end the slave trade and slavery decades before, contributing to the abolitionist movement's dissemination, but also to the continued influence of this emotional community into the early 1900s. As such, the Moral Liberal emotional styles are culturally and historically contingent. This is most especially true of its righteous indignation.[12]

Set in opposition against the blind animalistic rage or fury many—especially in Great Britain—attributed to the French Revolution, contemporaries believed righteous indignation to be a legitimate and virtuous form of anger.[13] A strong reactive feeling caused by "disapprobation of what is flagitious in character or conduct,"[14] as one dictionary puts it, indignation holds arguable worth as a tool of social practice for identifying and rooting out that which is detrimental to society. In fact, even before her crusade against regulationism had begun, Josephine Butler herself espoused the usefulness of indignation as a sort of lens of truth in a world full of sin to her niece in 1867:

> The loneliness of heart, the burning indignations [met] with no sympathy [...] I do beg you dear not to put away the indignation—nay, even cherish it. Cherish every feeling of anger against sin & wrong, as well as deep compassion for sinners [...] keep up your secret mental protest against conventionality, luxury & selfishness, & against the shallow theories by [which] people soothe their consciences.[15]

Clearly, she sees indignation—and compassionate love—as intrinsically connected to Christian sensibility in such a way that not only makes it righteous but also a duty. Such an emotion is clearly motivated by morality and thus to go against it or to try and modify it would be a sin, as she writes, "don't give in to thinking that others are right & you are wrong, but be silent, & bide your time."[16] Already deep in her charitable work with prostitutes at this time, she testifies to a recent, more generalized shift in public opinion:

> I am so glad that I did not let my painful & indignant convictions grow weak. [...] the principles & truths which we have clung to in silence so long are now asserting themselves, & proving themselves even in the presence of the sceptical [sic] world to be the very truth [...][17]

This rising tide of public moralism she perceived here is likely what emboldened her crusade against the Contagious Diseases Acts two years later, the motivations for which she explains in a journal entry:

> Nothing so wears me out, body and soul, as anger, fruitless anger; and this thing fills me with such an anger, and even hatred, that I fear to face it. [...] I pray Thee, O God, to give me a deep, well-governed, and lifelong hatred of all such injustice, tyranny, and cruelty; and at the same time, give me that divine compassion which is willing to live and suffer long for love to souls [...] If doubt were gone, and I felt sure He means me to rise in revolt and rebellion (for that it must be) against men, even against our rulers, then I would do it with zeal, however repulsive to others may seem the task.[18]

The righteous indignation felt in Josephine Butler's words which would form the basis of the Moral Liberals' advocacy platform originates from one of the first instances of a widespread, public humanitarian sentiment appearing in Western society: the antislavery movement. The movement began as a largely Quaker initiative at the turn of the nineteenth century which stretched across the Atlantic. Petitioners employing Enlightenment-inspired, evangelical, and moralist framings of the slave trade and slavery demanded that the American and British governments end these inhumane practices inflicting suffering upon "[...] fellow-creatures, entitled to natural rights of mankind."[19] This simultaneously presented a moral and physical barrier to the spiritual awakening of the slaves and threatened the eternal salvation of the sinning slave trader or owner.[20] The early campaign to end the slave trade and slavery demonstrated a zeal—predominantly evangelical, but also secular—for public moralism which would also mark all emotional communities of the early abolitionist movement.

In the early 1800s the practice of holding indignation meetings where people could publicly express their "anger at what is regarded as unworthy or wrongful"[21] in new laws or policies appeared in the United States and spread in the subsequent decades to the English-speaking world. Righteous indignation[22] was thus established as a conventional emotion wielded to pass judgment on governmental actions and to create standards of behavior for all of society. This emotion formerly directed at the government for upholding the inhumane and sinful practice of slavery was subsequently mobilized by Moral Liberal repeal campaigners against the state's regulation of prostitution on the same basis of it threatening not only the morality of the individuals involved but also that of the nation itself. For instance, William T. Stead explained to his readers in the *Pall Mall Gazette* that it was impossible to not speak about the regulation system (in this case in British Egypt)—which he skillfully illustrates through an accumulation of adjectives like "horrible," "degrading," "odious," "hideous"— without "fierce indignation."

> The responsibility rests on us all. The crime is national. It calls for national reparation. [...] it is the duty of all who wish to cleanse England's name and England's fame from this foulest of blots, to take prompt, effective, and concerted action.[23]

As can be seen here, Moral Liberal repeal campaigners used the same themes blending moralism with evangelism, nationalism, liberalism, and humanitarianism to create parallels between slavery and prostitution, as well as the slave and the prostitute.

Although not a concern held by most Moral Liberals, it is notable that some like Josephine Butler placed a special emphasis on the moral redeemability of the prostitute herself. In opposition to the longstanding societal view of her deprived moral status as a fallen woman—a "bad" object evoking negative emotions such as disgust, hatred, and fear—the aim was to transform the prostitute into an object of compassion whose suffering was worthy of inciting anger. Yet, this transformation relied on her becoming an object of suffering, or more precisely still, an object of undeserved suffering, a victim—already established and popularized by the antislavery movement. Key to this emotional practice was the emergence of what historian Bryccan Carey has dubbed "a sentimental rhetoric of antislavery"[24] in the late 1700s. Hinged on the rhetorician's belief in the power of sympathy to elicit public awareness in this nascent age of sensibility, this strategy of persuasion through an affective, as well as affecting, mode of expression—such as in the form of a sentimental hero—appears in abolitionist novels, letters, speeches, pamphlets, and other forms of propaganda.[25] To achieve similar ends, Moral Liberals focused firstly on narratives demonstrating the violence suffered by the prostitute, and secondly on her blamelessness through her portrayal as voiceless, passive, and defeated by forces beyond her control. For instance, writing about child prostitution on the Continent, Josephine Butler explains how they are mistreated to the point that they are worn out by the age of 13 or 16:

> Quick murder with dagger or revolver would be mercy and gentleness compared with the slow and agonizing two years' dying to which these beings are doomed.[26]

As Judith Walkowitz has maintained, repeal campaigners "found it politically expedient to depict 'fallen women' as passive victims of evil machinations."[27] Much like slaves in antislavery, prostitutes were recast by Moral Liberals as lacking due to nature or circumstance and in need of being raised to a good standing by their compassionate moral betters, forming similar victim-objects to operate within a renewed Christian moral economy of reciprocal duties and obligations,[28] as well as an emotional economy of compassion. Thus, mobilizing the past emotions of the antislavery movement—and most notably righteous indignation—to render their positions self-evident held obvious advantages for early (as well as current-day) abolitionists, all the while reproducing the infantilization of victims.

Although detailed accounts and depictions of the suffering of slaves were used to elicit public sympathy and righteous indignation, Christopher Brown, a key reference on antislavery, has shown that most campaigners were motivated more by "self-regarding, self-concerned, and even self-validating impulses"[29] than by altruism. In light of such a description, a parallel can be drawn between the ambitions of antislavery and those of a "status movement,"[30] as conceptualized by Joseph Gusfield in his seminal work on the American temperance movement which has informed the study of moral crusades in general. Antislavery activists' desire to raise or defend their own prestige translated into a wish to elevate public morals in a way that was closely tied to changing conceptualizations of colonialism and contributed to the elaboration of a new morally defined, yet paternalistic, model of empire. Sara Ahmed's thought-provoking discussion of utilitarian justifications of empire in *The Promise of Happiness* highlights how paternalist notions informed an imperialist-humanitarian duty narrated through "the language of philanthropy: the love of the people becomes the will to augment happiness [...] to relieve others from suffering."[31] This "philanthropic gift" when imagined in terms of civility, operated in a grammar of force:

Human happiness is increased though the courts (law/justice), knowledge (reason), and manners (culture/habits). Civilization is imagined first as what is brought to 'their doors' and second as an irresistible moral pressure. [...] Empire becomes a gift that cannot be refused, a forced gift.³²

This is particularly evident in James Mill's—notably John Stewart Mill's father—*History of British India* which Sara Ahmed describes as aiming to show "the unhappiness of un-British India as a way of defending the happiness of the colonial end."³³ His governance strategy is thus one that assimilates India to the British model of civility, as the local institutions were to his mind an impossible foundation for the establishment of an ideal and just government. This philanthropic gift—a forced relief from suffering—became a moral duty of those deemed morally superior or more civilized, as well as a defining element of modern society.³⁴

An example of this moralism informing the project of a public, conscientious reckoning can be seen in William Wilberforce's now-famous speech on the slave trade delivered in the House of Commons in 1789.³⁵ First, employing the rhetorical technique of *captatio benevolentiae*, he humbles himself magnanimously before his audience, speaking to his "weakness" and "inadequacy" to promote such an imperative cause:

> When I consider the magnitude of the subject which I am to bring before the House—a subject, in which the interests, not of this country, nor of Europe alone, but of the whole world, and of posterity, are involved: and when I think, at the same time, on the weakness of the advocate who has undertaken this great cause—when these reflections press upon my mind, it is impossible for me not to feel both terrified and concerned at my own inadequacy to such a task [...] I take courage—I determine to forget all my other fears, and I march forward with a firmer step in the full assurance that my cause will bear me out [...]³⁶

Then, using the authority he has established as a moral superior, he identifies the sin and qualifies it as causing collective guilt from which none, himself included, are exempt:

> I mean not to accuse any one, but to take the shame upon myself, in common, indeed, with the whole parliament of Great Britain, for having suffered this horrid trade to be carried on under their authority. We are all guilty—we ought all to plead guilty, and not to exculpate ourselves by throwing the blame on others [...]³⁷

His aim was to see the country repent for being the active agent behind the suffering of slaves and thereby remove the stain from its very moral character (note the clear rhetorical parallels to William T. Stead's words from 1887 cited earlier). But it was also to see that it assumes its paternalist responsibilities as an imperial power by establishing a "Christian moral economy centered on reciprocal duties and obligations"[38] between a backwards colonialized population who was not quite equal to white Christian Europeans.[39] Such notions would not only affect the later phases of the antislavery movement in more nationalist and imperialist ways, but they would also find a home in the social purity movement and the emotional community of Purity Crusaders discussed next.

In sum, by tuning into the righteous indignation of the antislavery movement, Moral Liberals were able to employ a superior set of values which combined the mindsets of liberal nationalism and religious moralism, as well as warranted their attitude of self-righteousness. Yet it also might have served to bypass the negative social connotations of the subjects at the heart of their campaign: prostitution, sexuality, and venereal disease. Arguably more so than in the other contemporary movements, female repeal campaigners struggled to publicly discuss and assert their authority on taboo subjects such as prostitution, sexuality, venereal disease, and gynecology in opposition to male authorities. This was also true within the Moral Liberal emotional community and the campaign itself. Its founding group, the National Association for the Repeal of the Contagious Diseases Acts, excluded women from its ranks, requiring Josephine Butler to set up a Ladies' National Association with suffragette and fellow women's education advocate Elizabeth Wolstenholme Elmy in 1869. To the fascination or embarrassment of many, the Ladies' National Association—representing female Moral Liberals— not only wrote publicly about these shameful and stigmatized subjects in petition and letter-writing campaigns but also spoke about them in public talks with potential sympathizers and in the ladies' gallery during repeal debates held at the House of Commons.

Depending on their public, Josephine Butler and other Ladies' National Association members framed these arguments in numerous ways and using different sentimental registers—some of which will be treated in other chapters—not only to justify this awkward revolt of women, as one Member of Parliament called it,[40] but also to incite others to join their cause. Likening prostitution to slavery was thus part of a rhetorical strategy to not only stimulate righteous indignation but also to shift from stigmatization to compassion and shame to pride. It is also significant that respected British feminist advocate for antislavery Harriet Martineau gave early impetus to anti-regulationism by writing a series of letters against the Contagious Diseases Acts which appeared in the *Daily News* and co-signed with Josephine Butler the petition "Remonstrance against the Conspiracy of Silence" directed at the London Press.[41] In so doing, Harriet Martineau not only helped challenge the taboo surrounding such subjects for public discussion but also created an important ideological link between the campaigns. Furthermore, by identifying repeal campaigners as "New Abolitionists," which Josephine Butler did in an 1875 publication marking the internationalization of her mission, a new Moral Liberal emotional history was written. Their actions were linked to the abolitionists who decades earlier had successfully waged war against the slave trade and slavery in Great Britain and abroad, encapsulating one of the greatest humanitarian mobilizations to date and a symbol of pride and heroic triumph in British social memory—this reputation established as early as 1808.[42]

Distrust of Government and Fear of its Police

At the turn of the nineteenth century, righteous indignation was understood as anger "mingled with contempt, disgust, or abhorrence"[43] which necessarily delineated who or what was at fault or to blame. How this constructed objects of scorn can be seen in Josephine Butler's recounting of an abolitionist meeting held in Paris during which a man began to argue in favor of regulation, but then was interrupted "by the furious burst of scorn and anger which preceded from all the women and almost all the men."[44] To her pleasant surprise, the opponent's voice was drowned out by a "storm of righteous indignation"[45] in the form of hisses, moans, and protests. Yet this scorn was often foregrounded by other feelings, which in the case of Moral Liberals were distrust of governmental authorities and great alarm at the extension of their powers through minions such as the police.

Liberalism, utilitarianism, and evangelical egalitarianism contributed heavily to shaping Moral Liberals' understandings and diagnoses of the problem with the Contagious Diseases Acts, as well as their construction of scorned objects. The state's regulation of prostitution was thus targeted as a violation of personal civil liberties, due to its compulsory registration, inspection, and sequestering, but also for its institutionalization of a sexual moral bias, as women alone fell under its reach. Father of liberalism John Stuart Mill was even involved in the campaign, and thus it is no surprise that Moral Liberals sought to limit the law in order to ensure the liberty—or the absence of constraints—of an individual's free-willed self-regarding action. Thus, the Moral Liberals argued, "Parliament in making the Contagious Diseases Acts, has invaded and trampled on the liberties of the people."[46] An important proof provided here was the arbitrary nature of its all-important term "common prostitute" delineating the very subject of regulation: without a clear definition or indicators, an agent of the *police des mœurs* ("vice police") could justifiably arrest anyone he suspected of prostitution. As the Ladies' National Association decries in *The Lady's Appeal and Protest*, this directly affronts the notion of Habeas Corpus, a mainstay of English law since its guarantee by *Magna Carta*:

> [...] no English subject can be arrested, subjected to outrage, or imprisoned either with or without their consent, on a mere suspicion without proof, or on mere hearsay evidence, without any public trial, without being confronted with the witnesses for the prosecution, without any magistrate's warrant.[47]

Often women were forced to submit to medical control no matter what but could attempt a lengthy bureaucratic appeal process to have their names removed from the police registry for future internal exams organized at the behest of the surgeon. Amendments made in 1866 provided for a process by which women could make a written appeal demanding their release from a lock hospital, exception from mandatory examination, or removal of her name from the registry. However, this did not guarantee that any reimbursement of related costs or fines would be made. Failure to not voluntarily submit to such exams would result in being compelled, fined, or imprisoned. Thus, as the Ladies' National Association bemoaned, "the legal safeguards hitherto enjoyed by women in common with men" were removed by the Acts, placing "their reputation, their freedom, and their persons absolutely in the power of the police."[48] As John Stuart Mill wrote in a letter from 1870, the coercive nature of regulation was what made it inherently antagonistic to civil liberty:

> I do not think the abuses of power by the police mere accidents which could be prevented. I think them the necessary consequences of any attempt to carry out such a plan thoroughly. If once examination is made other than voluntary the police must try to prevent evasion of it, and this at once opens the door to innocent mistakes on the part of the police, and makes it necessary to entrust them with power over women which no men are fit to have.[49]

The absence of a clear definition of this term "common prostitute" meant that in the designated garrison towns, any woman suspected of prostitution could be—as one repeal leaflet asserted—"in flagrant defiance of the British Constitution [...] dealt with as guilty, unless she can prove her own innocence."[50] By providing such arbitrary powers to the police and surgeons, as argued by John Stuart Mill,[51] all women were rendered vulnerable to abuse and violation. In 1875, the apparent suicide of a widowed professional singer and actress Jenny Percy from Aldershot accused of being a common prostitute, hounded by the *police des mœurs*, and threatened with forcible internal examination appeared as an exemplary demonstration of the dangers of such a scheme. The case was heavily publicized by Moral Liberals to demonstrate these dangers of the Contagious Diseases Acts, to enflame the sensibilities of the public to garner support, especially among the working class, as well as to break the English press's silence on their cause.[52]

By challenging the policy of targeting only the female actors in prostitution, Moral Liberals also levied the harm principle against the Contagious Diseases Acts by which "the only purpose for which power can be rightfully exercised over any member of a civilized community, against his will, is to prevent harm to others."[53] By ignoring these "male accomplices" of "female sinners," the Acts were rendered not only inefficient but illogical given that it was male vice which sustained prostitution. Pointing to the legalized double standard of morality by which men were exonerated and women were given the full blame, Josephine Butler decried this inequality before the law as part of a history of oppression against this "fallen class of women" in an address given in 1871:

> [It] is for the most part a history of alternate patronising [*sic*] and punishing. Their best repressive measures have been almost exclusively directed against one sex. They have seldom practically acknowledged the fact that these female sinners have in every case male accomplices; and therefore they have failed to put down the evil.[54]

Making an analogy of prostitution with the slave trade, she continued to explain:

> As well might you attempt to do away with the slave trade by making it penal to be a slave. If we had punished every slave who was bought and sold, and if we had left the buyers untouched, we should never have got rid of the slave trade.[55]

Such discourse often appearing amongst Moral Liberals had emancipatory potential by challenging the Acts' underpinning rationale according to which male sexuality was permissible whereas female sexuality was condemnable. Therefore, rejecting "the false and misleading idea that the essence of right and wrong is in some way dependent on sex,"[56] she insisted on a single standard of morality—that is, of sexual restraint within and abstinence outside of marriage—as an essential factor in establishing and maintaining social purity. It is in this way that Moral Liberals were also aiming for moral revival, and not just safeguards against despotism.

Despotism was, of course, a central fear of Moral Liberals and one that was most directly embodied by the *police des mœurs*—an object of distain against which they levied hostility in their speeches and writings. Seen as hypocritical and arbitrary, they were frequently highlighted as the morally failing male agents of this injustice and bore the brunt of Moral Liberal anti-statist righteous indignation. In France, once the British repeal campaign—and its emotional communities—extended abroad in 1875, *La Lanterne* under the initiative of Yves Guyot launched a crusade against the *police des mœurs,* publicizing shocking stories of arbitrary arrests and forced false testimonies[57] to mobilize the public to call for their abolition. Fellow scathing critic of their ambiguous and arbitrary practices, Republican Senator René Bérenger also referred to such publicized scandals as an outrage. His solution, however, reflects some variations in approach—and sees him more characterizable as a Purity Crusader. He put forward a proposal to penalize prostitutes for solicitation, arguing that it would afford them the protections of being in the *droit commun* ("common law") and placing their registration out of the hands of these unscrupulous police officers and into those of the judiciary.[58]

Alongside contempt, the *police des mœurs* also evoked feelings of xenophobic anxiety and paranoia. To Moral Liberals in the British repeal campaign, this "spy police" as they were often called dressed in plain clothing was another appendage through which government was becoming increasingly secretive, intrusive, and repressive. This undermined the liberal and individualist values which the British had held as a matter of national pride and superiority to others, as well as an indication of their national stability compared to those on the Continent.[59] Josephine Butler voiced this concern, claiming that London was in danger of sliding towards "an occult and immoral tyranny"[60] by adopting foreign practices of espionage and

> the same vast police machinery which […] stands a powerful engine for political purposes, ready to the hand of any future autocrat or political party who may yield to the strong temptation of making such a use of it.[61]

Little by little, she claimed, the government was lowering the people's resistance to having their lives controlled by the state, and there was reason to distrust and be afraid. The medico-police regulation scheme was often referred to in Moral Liberal discourses as a foreign practice characterized by a centralized bureaucracy—described by Josephine Butler in *Government by Police* (1879) as "a hydra-head"[62]—and the secret police which, originating in ancient Rome and France, was "the cancer which eats into the vitals of society, a pollution of which Great Britain may be proud of having escaped."[63] Such character work often ironically employs analogies of contagious disease to the corrupting continental practices of immorality and despotism entailed in the French system. For instance, Josephine Butler writes to friends on the importance of protecting the integrity of the nation by taking the campaign abroad to proactively stop the disease at its source:

> If we left the Continent unmoved and unhelped, we should not be safe for a year on our own soil. Whence did this particular evil come to us? Did it not come from the Continent? And what would hinder the infection from again invading us?[64]

Nationalistic pride was also instrumentalized in this Moral Liberal emotional style as a rallying call to "[carry] the war into the enemy's country" using incendiary language. In Josephine Butler's memoirs *Personal Reminiscences of a Great Crusade* recounting the movement's internationalization, England is portrayed as the sole resistance standing in the way of a relentless evil host advancing from abroad:

> [T]hey have hitherto got all they wanted, until they touched the sacred soil of England. From the moment when that desecration was known opposition commenced.[65]

Implicit in this description of coming to the nation's defense is the portrayal of the abolitionist cause as heroic, but also it aims to incense feelings of patriotic duty.

It is worth mentioning that anti-aristocratic sentiment was also a part of the Moral Liberals' emotional culture, especially in its capacity to support a shared identity amongst campaigners through constructing clearly defined notions of an "us" and a "them." In fact, Josephine Butler in particular used the term "aristocratic" as a signifier for all minions—from government officials to johns. The importance of this lies in the extension of the British repeal campaign to members of the working class which brought diversity to its predominantly middle-class liberal and nonconformist ranks. Demonstrating an anti-aristocratic sentiment typical of Moral Liberals, Josephine Butler bemoaned the complacency and selfishness of the upper class, whose privileged status made them blind to political and social affairs which did not affect them directly. As she alleges, they had made clear that the regulation of prostitution was "no question of theirs":

> To them this legislation involved no present and immediate diminution of freedom for themselves [...] But when we turned to the humbler classes we found that they knew that it is a question for them, and that they, more intelligent

in this than the upper classes, knew that it was also a question for this whole country of England, whose political liberty depends on the preservation of the rights of all.[66]

This aggrandizing of the lower classes as "humbler," "more intelligent" than the aristocracy acted in service of reinforcing a coalition between the working and middle classes, who shared not only social and political interests, but were much more socially conscious of the issues facing the nation. Josephine Butler was not alone in emphasizing her middle-class roots and lower-class experiences while portraying the elite as completely foreign and "other," as she wrote to one of her opponents, a well-known British positivist:

> I am ashamed of my countrymen. It is a subject which justifies a little anger if any subject ever did. I have lived among the middle and lower classes. I know nothing of fashionable society or aristocracy or grand London people. The few times I have been among them, I found they did not understand my language, nor I theirs.[67]

Within this indignity or shame, as she calls it, felt towards the aristocracy lies a feeling of superiority and a sense of legitimate authority that surpassed the Old Regime with its corrupt and conservative politics.

The distrust of the government and fear of the police felt amongst the Moral Liberals also operated—albeit differently—within its working-class contingent. In fact, the repeal campaign found resonance amongst working-class men, with Josephine Butler even assisting in the establishment of the Working Men's National League in Liverpool in 1875.[68] As explained earlier, the Contagious Diseases Acts were almost exclusively directed at the lower classes as it was their bodies which were considered dangerous and requiring legislation for increased monitoring and control. The police targeted exclusively poor and working-class women as they were more likely to be circulating unchaperoned, but also as they were, in fact, more likely to be prostitutes. As William Acton had noticed in his beforementioned study, working-class women temporarily resorted to prostitution as a necessary survival strategy amongst worse alternatives. Indeed, the sexual discrimination seen in the wage labor market created by laissez-faire capitalism often made it impossible for working-class women to make ends meet. Thus, the working class had a vested interest in the repeal campaign—in defense of themselves, their families, their daughters, their wives, their sisters, and so on. Thus, forming a diverse coalition, the Moral Liberals, while certainly aiming for widespread moral revival, also exemplify a contemporary trend to speak up on matters concerning the body—especially in the context of creeping state intervention through coercive health legislation. Thus, the bodies of prostitutes emerge here as the battleground for competing discourses regarding sexuality and health, often acting as a catalyst for discussing the bodies of other "Others"—sexed, classed, raced—in the face of new regimes emerging in the fields of public health and scientific medicine.

Abhorrence of Scientific Medicine

The abolitionist emotional communities in this early phase of the abolitionist movement took different and constitutive stances to state medicine, whose tenets fanned an obsessive fear of biological contagion and thus venereal disease, leading to the passing of the Contagious Diseases Acts. In the case of the Moral Liberal repeal campaigners, this stance was hostile. The origins of this hostility or even abhorrence of scientific medicine lie in the fact that the Contagious Diseases Acts were just one result of an alliance between state, medical, and police powers forged in the mid-nineteenth century to better manage societal issues through the regulation of bodies in an expanding British Empire. The growing need for state intervention in health matters—especially with the cholera epidemics of 1832, 1848, and 1854—led to government extending medical practitioners' role and authority through the creation of numerous posts in public office, for instance, that of Medical Officer of Health for London in 1848. Despite a certain inefficiency due to difficulties in centralizing public health organisms, a series of public health reforms from 1854 to 1871—creating, for instance, the Medical Department of the Privy Council in 1859[69]—led to the increased professionalization and institutionalization of medicine. As these physicians were developing an important scientific authority—in collusion as well as in competition with that of female philanthropy which is discussed in a later chapter—over societal affairs, they were also assisting the state in constructing its biopolitics. This, as demonstrated by the public health initiatives of this period, targeted the bodies of the lower classes, particularly the urban poor. The strong working-class presence in the repeal campaign was in large part due to the instrumentalization of their pre-existing suspicion of state medicine by middle-class Moral Liberal campaigners. Their populist rhetoric decried the exploitative economic system and increasingly repressive measures and described medical scientists as aristocrats—despite most coming from the middle class—to unite the lower and middle classes for the cause.[70]

Moral Liberals campaigning to end the state's regulation of prostitution aimed to find resonance in the raging contemporary campaign against compulsory smallpox vaccination which incited the largest medical resistance campaign ever seen in Europe and which lasted until the turn of the century.[71] This acted as an early example of how scientism framed institutional understandings and practices related to organizing and treating society, its individuals, and its issues. Smallpox, a highly contagious disease caused by the variola virus represented a major threat to the public health with a mortality rate of 30 percent and carrying long-term afflictions for its survivors. Appearing around the same time as the Contagious Diseases Acts, the first act in 1853 required the vaccination of children under three months old but lacked the mechanisms to enforce compliance; this was remedied in 1867 with the appointment of public district vaccinators and in 1871 by adding fines. Importantly, as Nadja Durbach demonstrates, different visions of the body emerged. The one of state medicine saw the body as a threat and source of biological contagion and the one of anti-vaccination supporters saw it as highly vulnerable to contamination and violation.[72] For instance, in the case of the latter, many feared "pollution" through vaccines derived from pustules on animals or inferior people. The former of course contributed to the logic underpinning the British Contagious Diseases Acts in which the bodies of the working poor—contagious, filthy, and dangerous—became the target par excellence for state medicine's schemes. The ethical problem apparent in such a demeaning and monolithic portrayal of the working poor by state medicine is just one reason for the Moral Liberals' mistrust of scientific medicine's moral and ethical standards. William Acton himself in the second edition of *Prostitution* responds to the repeal campaigners' righteous indignation by arguing that any civil rights infringement by the law in compulsory registration, examination, or vaccination is justifiable as it is for the greater good. He writes, "personal liberty and personal rights must be in all cases subservient to the public welfare."[73]

It is in this way that scientific medicine represented a new regime of modern science which, inherently distinct from religion if not a replacement for it, presented challenges to providential or theological mindsets describing social problems like disease or crime as God-willed. In fact, the relationship between religion and scientific naturalism was quite complex at this time: the growing preeminence of French experimental medical and physiological practices fed a real and imagined connection between scientific materialism with radical politics and atheism which many wished to break.[74] Evolutionary theory in particular was believed by many to be fundamentally at odds with the contemporary evangelical view of humanity and its relationship with the divine. This was well-demonstrated by the public debate held at Oxford in 1860 setting Darwinist Dr. Thomas Huxley against William Wilberforce's son Bishop Samuel Wilberforce during which the former famously responded thusly to a jab made by the latter about his kinship with an ape:

> I asserted—and I repeat—that a man has no reason to be ashamed of having an ape for his grandfather. If there were an ancestor whom I should feel shame in recalling, it would be a MAN, a man of restless and versatile intellect, who, not content with an equivocal success in his own sphere of activity, plunges into scientific questions with which he has no real acquaintance, only to obscure them by an aimless rhetoric, and distract the attention of his hearers from the real point at issue by eloquent digressions, and skilled appeals to religious prejudice.[75]

Although the accounts of this debate—no official transcript exists—have recently been proven inaccurate and part of Darwinist myth-building,[76] it does show how conflicts between science and religion were framed by contemporaries of the British repeal campaign and the early abolitionist movement. In fact, the latter part of this quote employs a typically recurring argument used by supporters of scientific medicine to silence their opponents, including Moral Liberals: they were not scientists and thus had no legitimate authority to question scientific truths; they lacked objectivity due to religious and/or gender-based sentimentality. Instead, supporters of scientific medicine argued that social problems were resolvable if rationality and scientific knowledge were supported by government and put to the task of providing prescriptive solutions. As such, the emergent ideology of scientism saw science itself evolve from a simple knowledge of the existing world to an actual generator of values and practices for the improvement of society and the well-being of bodies.[77]

Resistance to scientism seen in the anti-vaccination movement, the anti-vivisection movement—yet another contemporaneous political cause—and the British repeal movement thus occurred for various reasons, including the beforementioned fear of bodily contamination or pollution, as well as a distrust in state doctors, whose incompetency, lack of moral scruples, and fatal errors were well-publicized by the press.[78] Indeed, scientific medicine lacked any uniform system of regulation or single licensing body before the Medical Act of 1858 which distinguished between qualified and unqualified practitioners. The notion of charlatanism persisted long after in popular culture and thus it was frequently evoked by scientific medicine's opponents to render their claims dubious. This indeed appears often in the Moral Liberals' activism, buttressing their claims of the regulatory, medical, and police measures of the Contagious Diseases Acts as inefficient, arbitrary, as well as immoral.

To abhor state medicine, that is, to regard it "with horror or detestation,"[79] was a Moral Liberal emotional practice which operated together with righteous indignation to not only denounce the state's regulation of prostitution but also to identify—and construct—a clear culprit. A strategy par excellence used to demonstrate the immorality of scientific medicine was to expose the suffering endured by those women—some as young as 13 years old[80]—suspected of prostitution and targeted for forced examination by speculum. Aiming to cultivate an abhorrence of scientific medicine and enflame their audience's righteous indignation, these tales of "medical rape" were recounted by Moral Liberals during public meetings and in letters published in the press. For instance:

> These are the words I hear so often: 'It is such awful work; the attitude they push us into first is so disgusting and so painful, and then these monstrous instruments—often they use several. They seem to tear the passage open first with their hands and examine us, and then they thrust in instruments, and they pull them out and push them in, and they turn and twist them about; and if you cry out they stifle you with a towel over your face.'[81]

Some more graphic accounts of medical rape were given, although most like the above tended to speak euphemistically of the "violation" or "destruction" of the female body. The exams were, in fact, brutal, painful, and unsafe.[82] Typically tied down with her legs clamped open, the suspected prostitute was inspected inexpertly, risking not only infection due to the use of unclean instruments but also misdiagnosis which would see her locked in a hospital without recourse.

Nonetheless, female campaigners in particular were already stepping well beyond the limits of contemporary conventions by speaking on such subjects as prostitution, sex, venereal disease, and internal exams. Thus, drawing both positive and negative attention to the abolitionist cause, medical rape and its medical scientist perpetrators were described in sensationalized or even fetishized ways so as to operate well within existing emotional economies, such as the forementioned one proffered by antislavery campaigners which sought compassion for innocent victims of suffering. Note, for example, what Josephine Butler described in her private letter to Dr. William Carter as the "peculiar (& most useful for *us*)" case of "an innocent little country girl" named Adeline Tanner who was duped into prostitution abroad by a false suitor, but then returned to England a virgin.[83] This story was indeed useful not only because this victim was unsuccessfully forced into sin due to her being physically unable to have intercourse as the result of some anatomical defect and could only be faulted for her naivety. It also involved grueling ordeals of physical torture as the young woman was moved from brothel to hospital, and finally to prison, where she was violently torn into by men at the brothel and by doctors with their instruments *"to be made larger"* which left her traumatized, "like a child [...] like a crushed worm, hopeless, sullen, & at times quite wandering in mind."[84]

Prior to the British repeal campaign, it is important to note that the Victorian public had developed a taste for the melodramatic. For instance, rooted in the rise of the culture of sensibility in the eighteenth century, the sensation novel—like Wilkie Collins's *The Woman in White* (1860) or Mary Elizabeth Braddon's *Lady Audley's Secret* (1862)—peaked in the 1860s.[85] This ethos—reflecting various nameless contemporary anxieties—greatly influenced political expression thereafter. Thus, the theme of rape was arguably prime for use as an advocacy device since the Indian Mutiny in 1857 during which horrific accounts of the systematic rape and murder of innocent English women by Indian sepoys circulated and captured the public's attention, inspiring artwork such as the famous *In Memoriam*. The painting centers on the helpless, innocent white women and children awaiting their ravaging and violent deaths at the hands of the brown-skinned barbarians barely visible to the left; however, in the foreground one catches a glimpse through the window of British soldiers, illuminated as if sent by God himself, coming to rescue. The scene speaks to the construction of rape as a fetish object of male imperialist shame which aimed to mobilize nationalistic notions of male chivalry to protect English womanhood—what Jenny Sharpe has called "an important cultural signifier of a colonial hierarchy of race"[86]—through what was to be an extremely violent counterinsurgency by the British.

The narratives of medical rape recounted by Moral Liberals centered on the speculum. This metal instrument used for spreading the vaginal cavity open to make internal inspection easier represented a strong symbol for the ways in which women's bodies had been invaded by men.[87] As discussed earlier, the rationale behind the Contagious Diseases Acts was rooted in the predominantly male medical scientific authority which had developed around issues related to public health. Its main referent, Dr. William Acton, had been instilled with a strong belief in the necessity of systematically using the speculum in diagnosing venereal disease in women during his time with Dr. Philippe Ricord in Paris. Yet in the early 1800s, modern gynecological practices involving the speculum—which had been re-discovered by French physician Joseph Récarrier in 1801 and introduced into the regulation of prostitution from 1810[88]—remained controversial amongst doctors for fear of its insertion into the womb causing moral debasement or emotional distress. For the treatment of hysteria or "womb disease," for instance, some suggested the use of the speculum had degrading effects on the patient's morality, reducing them to lustful temptresses.[89] For the wider public, the phallic-shaped speculum—whose use was sensationalized through demonstrations or accounts detailing how it was inserted[90] and then opened within the vaginal cavity—helped visualize medical rape and materialize the fear of scientific medicine's increasing willingness to encroach upon the perceived sanctity of the body.

It is in this way that the fetishization of the perpetrator of medical rape emerged from the contemporary anxieties surrounding dangerous forms of sexuality, as well as the growing power and influence of "amoral" modern science in social affairs. The distinctions between those in the medical profession—physiologist, police surgeon, family physician—were erased in Moral Liberal (but also Maternal Feminist, as described later) depictions of medical rape. At worst, driven by what Josephine Butler called "medical lust,"[91] doctors were portrayed as sinister monsters who, as French abolitionist and nonconformist Émilie de Morsier accused, "in the name of science, rape virgins to make them prostitutes!"[92] That modern scientific practices were corrupting doctors' moral sense, making them more susceptible to depravity and indifferent to the suffering of their patient, was propelled in particular by Dr. Elizabeth Blackwell, a notable figure in both abolitionism and moral purity, but also a leader in the anti-vivisection movement.[93] She even correlated the increase in surgery—especially "ovariotomy" on women—with the spread of animal experimentation in modern laboratory science:

> The practice of recklessly sacrificing animal life for the gratification, either of curiosity, excitement, or cruelty, tends inevitably to create a habit of mind which affects injuriously all our relations with inferior or helpless classes of creatures. […] The hardening effect of vivisection is distinctly recognised [sic] in the Profession, although often excused under the abused term 'scientific.'[94]

At best, doctors were an object of fear: emotionally deviant, hard-hearted, and willfully ignorant of their patient's suffering. For instance, Josephine Butler contrasts her own hot righteous indignation—the keystone of Moral Liberals' emotional culture—with the police doctors' cold detachedness, writing how "one of the things that has made my heart on fire with anger of late" is that the words "from the victims of the Acts, the suffering women" attesting to the pain caused by examination do not hold weight compared to the medical opinion, as "[d]octors say in the coolest manner that the process is not painful."[95]

This emphasis on the invisible suffering of the victim (their emotional pain, their wounded souls) stressed the importance of immateriality, imbuing medical rape with value within the evangelical moral economy which resonated most with the nonconformist contingent of Moral Liberals. Yet this emphasis also testifies to an acknowledgment of what Georges Vigarello has called the moral violence of sexual violence through his study of contemporary French law, first against children and then against adult women (respectively *la loi de 1832* and *l'arrêt Dubas de 1857*), which created an important precedent for the legal recognition of abuse-related psychological trauma.[96] Moreover, the attachment of medical rape to notions of objectification and dehumanization reflects an interaction of the similarly invisible harms of structural and symbolic violence. As suggested by repeal supporter Dr. J. J. G. Wilkinson in his 1870 pamphlet, the medical rape by speculum was voyeuristic:

> And remember that the steel, that common infector, is indiscriminately put in not to cure disease but to spy it. Not examination of sick women in your game, but espionage of enslaved wombs.[97]

This "espionage" echoes Michel Foucault's concept of the medical gaze[98] resulting from the eighteenth-century epistemological break in scientific medicine in favor of the empirical knowledge regime which is underpinned by a dogmatic belief in the absolute truth being that which is visible. Referring to the biomedical paradigm of body-as-machine,[99] the doctor abstracts his patient's suffering and reframes the subject uniquely in terms of his or her problem or dysfunction—here, infection with venereal disease. This dividing practice entails the dehumanization of the subject by the scientific power, turning the human into subject. Female and animal bodies were subjects par excellence of the medical tradition of biological determinism in respect of their opposition to the perceived male body norm. This also entailed structural violence as the practices of the dominant power transformed the bodies into objects and disregarded their immaterial worth. Consequently, medical rape—a physical, but also a psychological and spiritual violation—made women "no longer women," as Josephine Butler decried, "but bits of numbered, inspected, and ticketed human flesh, flung by Government into the public market."[100]

In both the anti-regulation and anti-vivisection causes—whose memberships overlapped, namely the Maternal Feminists discussed later—the instrumentalization of rape to mobilize righteous indignation met with the challenge of the lack of consideration accorded to the victims: fallen women commonly seen as absent shame and moral dignity, and animals ruled as lower beings less capable of feeling pain. Employing instead the more humanitarian economy of compassion established during the antislavery movement, the depictions of victims focused on their humanity[101] and capacity to feel both emotional and physical pain, as Josephine Butler attests: "Scarcely ever have I heard the horrid process mentioned except with a blush, or an averted face, or a spasm of shame in the face."[102] Thus, the construction of both the helpless and innocent prostitute as an object of compassion and the sadistic and perverse doctor as an object of fear for all, not just for prostitutes, were arguably important to the successful use of medical rape in Moral Liberals' activism.

2

Purity Crusaders and the Threat of Degeneracy (1880s–1920s)

Despite contributing to its eventual fragmentation and dissolution in the 1930s, the internationalization and extension of the British repeal campaign was necessary to its survival. The globalization which accompanied colonial expansion, economic interconnectedness, and international migration created possibilities for the expansion and internationalization of prostitution markets—particularly through its institutionalization and regulation as provided for in the French system.[1] With prostitution problematized as an international issue of concern, it was of strategic interest to the Moral Liberals to take their cause abroad to oppose the dominant discourses of state medicine. While the Liberals' defeat to the Conservatives in the 1874 general election and the loss of their representative's seat in Parliament may have also contributed to the campaign's focus abroad, it was framed by repeal campaigners for the British public as a defensive measure in a reasoning—also seen in the anti-vivisection and antislavery campaigns—underpinned by nationalistic and xenophobic notions. Such sentiments and anxieties about national security also gave strength to a new emotional community of Purity Crusaders which would rise in prominence within the movement to abolish state-regulated prostitution—initially allies to the Moral Liberals, but later their rivals.

Adopting the same mantle of supreme moral authority seen in the British-led international campaign to abolish the slave trade and slavery, the fight to repeal the Contagious Diseases Acts was thus upscaled in 1875, passing through missionary channels and networks forged decades before, employing analogous tactics and practices, and relying on the same rationales. Published the following year, the strategically named book *The New Abolitionists* opens its account of this mission with a seminal meeting at York that marked these first steps taken beyond the borders of England prompted by a sudden awareness that "a large and powerful organization on the continent" aimed to create an international regulatory system for prostitution "which should bring the whole world within its scope."[2] Faced with this impending threat, Josephine Butler—a "frail but courageous"[3] child of God—is described as leading the charge in this David-and-Goliath fight against demonized governments, *police des mœurs*, and men of science in the defense of the dishonored and victimized prostitute. Armed with a list of fellow evangelicals and others who may be sympathetic to her cause, she began her first tour in France—the stronghold of this French regulatory system—before continuing to Italy and Switzerland, arranging public meetings and helping local entrepreneurs establish national societies with connections to her newly created British, Continental and General Federation for the Abolition of the Government Regulation of Vice, renamed the International Abolitionist Federation in 1898.

Finding early support amongst nonconformists, social radicals, liberals, and feminists—especially those affiliated with the International Council of Women and the International Women's Suffrage Alliance—national abolitionist committees demonstrating Moral Liberal emotional styles were established in countries like France, Germany, Italy, Switzerland, Belgium, and the Netherlands.[4] They kept in touch and shared information with the British executive committee through regular correspondence, production of reports, and attendance of congresses and assemblies—some of which were excerpted and reproduced in the International Abolitionist Federation's journal *Le Bulletin Continental*. These practices helped distribute and reinforce common positions—heavily informed by Moral Liberals and Maternal Feminists from the Ladies' National Association—on prostitution amongst its members: the state's regulation of prostitution encouraged vice and punished its victim while legalizing a double standard of morality between the sexes and failing to lessen the prevalence of venereal disease.

In 1883 the Contagious Diseases Acts were suspended in Great Britain and finally abolished in 1886—with India exempted until 1895. Doubt had been sufficiently shed upon the effectiveness of the French system in controlling venereal disease, for which better understandings of pathologies were improving both diagnosis and treatment. Entering what Josephine Butler hoped would be "a second chapter of our great Abolitionist Crusade,"[5] the Ladies' National Association launched a new campaign in India while repeal efforts on the Continent were continued through the Executive Committee of the International Abolitionist Federation which continued to coordinate and correspond with the national sections. Yet, the International Abolitionist Federation's many political and denominational cleavages, as well as local impediments to feminist projects, had begun to undermine their efforts. Abolitionist objectives of eliminating the state regulation of prostitution, the double moral standard, and forced internal exams by police doctors set by Moral Liberals and Maternal Feminists became overshadowed by the ambitions of the greater social purity movement. Comprising the emotional community of Purity Reformers, this component shifted the international abolitionist movement's purpose, strategies, and goals increasingly towards strengthening governmental and legal authorities to ameliorate the nation's morals and effectively, as historian Alan Hunt put it, "chain the devil of impurity in a large number of men and women by fear of law."[6]

White Slavery and Sensationalizing Fear

The rise in importance of the Purity Crusaders within abolitionism was made possible through their role played in triggering a moral panic on "white slavery"—the sex trafficking of white, non-foreign girls and women—which struck in the early 1880s. A key moment in this moral panic was the publication of the English missionary and purity reformer Alfred Dyer's *The European Slave Trade in English Girls* which told the sensationalized account of his rescue of four young British women from their entrapment "infinitely more cruel and revolting than negro servitude"[7] in a state-registered brothel in Brussels. Investigative journalist William T. Stead's shocking account of child prostitution and trafficking in a series appearing in the *Pall Mall Gazette* starring himself and two women working undercover as prostitutes threw fuel on this fire in 1885. Entitled "The Maiden Tribute of Modern Babylon: The Report of the Secret Commission"—a melodramatic use of Greek and Christian mythologies—the public was engrossed by this series which aimed to reveal filth and perversion in the city of London. Complete with lurid sub-headings like "A Child of 13 Bought for £5," "Strapping girls down," and "I Order Five Virgins," it was imbued with the sensationalist, moralist, and anti-aristocratic tones popular at the time. Receiving some help from the Salvation Army's Bramwell Booth and Josephine Butler herself, William T. Stead recounts his purchase of a 13-year-old girl named Eliza Armstrong from her desperate parents, the verification of her virginity by a specialist, and then her drugging and transport to a brothel in France. He was later tried and found guilty of kidnapping, serving to bring more attention to the scandal and stir up further outrage both in England and abroad. Other sensationalized tales regarding the practices of the sex trade circulated, from unscrupulous brothel owners keeping prostitutes perpetually in debt to "little children, English girls from 10 to 14 years of age, who have been stolen, kidnapped, betrayed, carried off from English country villages"[8] to be held captive in foreign brothels. The slavery frame already instrumentalized by Moral Liberals to evoke feelings of compassion and righteous indignation at the oppression of prostitutes by the regulatory system was thus extended to include the system of prostitution itself, namely the trafficker and the brothel owner. These feelings appearing in religious and nationalist registers incited the public to end what Purity Crusader Alfred Dyer dramatically qualified as "the systematic abduction and enslavement of our countrywomen"[9] and prompted both statist and non-statist initiatives on national and international levels. The result of this mobilization was a vibrant international anti-trafficking movement which lasted until the interwar period, and which drastically shifted the abolitionist movement's membership, rationales, strategies, and goals.

In the early moments of this moral panic, the Moral Liberals of the International Abolitionist Federation were quick to causally connect the international traffic in women and girls to the state's regulation of prostitution, marking an important and long-lasting shift in abolitionist group knowledge by which the regulation system created a demand for female bodies which were commodified for consumption like chattel.[10] As reformers from the social purity movement promoted a Purity Crusader's influence and component, the International Abolitionist Federation's understanding of culpability expanded beyond the government, the police, and the aristocracy to increasingly include those profiting from prostitution and trafficking: brothel owners, procurers, traffickers, clients. Writing to the editor of the *Shield* in 1880, Josephine Butler echoes Alfred Dyer's language to describe the "horrors" of female slavery she witnessed on the Continent, but especially those perpetrating it:

> [...] what state of degradation must be to which the men of a country have sunk who can require and take a vile advantage of the forcible subjection by money grasping traders of terrified little girls to the service of the brutal lusts of male animals, men sunk in vice, diseased, cynical, worn out, old enough often to be these children's fathers or grandfathers. [...] when you add to sexual vice, organized cruelty, rape, and murder, you double and treble its enormity, and you invite a curse upon your nation.[11]

Josephine Butler's choice of vocabulary to describe these reprobates—"degradation," "sunk," "brutal," "animals"—instrumentalizes the contemporary preoccupation with civilizational progress and degeneration to spell out the doom of the country, as well as typifies the resonating discourses of the time. As

Mary Ann Irwin[12] has suggested, "white slavery" acted as a signifier of multiple nameless fears and anxieties in relation to imperial wars, revolutionary politics, economic recession, immigration, and so on, converging with the contemporary obsessive fears of societal demoralization and degeneration.

Moral purity thus became tied to national security and stability,[13] as white Western girls and young women in particular emerged as symbols of the weak nation in need of safeguarding. Ways to achieve this were becoming increasingly bent towards penal measures, such as the dissuasion or punishment of (would-be) attackers through limits on immigration, increased policing, and tougher penalties, as well as protective ones. For instance, in one pamphlet, after first explaining that the demand for English girls and children in brothels were higher than all the others, Josephine Butler argued for stronger legal protections in Great Britain against child abduction.[14] However, the measures taken up and fueled on the national and international levels by Purity Crusaders of the social purity movement brought abolitionism closer to the conservative, carceral, and statist powers Moral Liberals had claimed to distrust. Moral Liberal and Maternal Feminist Josephine Butler herself acknowledged this shift and initially—as suggested in the abovementioned quotes—encouraged it, temporarily also taking on the mantle of the Purity Crusader:

> It is evident that there is a growing feeling in the country, of a determination to obtain from Parliament some protection for children and young persons. The "traffic" in connection with Belgium has opened the eyes of the community to some of the crying defects in our laws.[15]

Joining the Purity Crusader ranks—or at least adopting their sensationalist and moralist registers—was a surefire way to effectively drum up widespread concern amongst the public and mobilize the authorities to finally take action. For instance, the attempts to raise the age of consent in Great Britain from age 13 to age 16 had been ineffective until the scandal caused by William T. Stead's *The Maiden Tribute of Modern Babylon* series. An immediate result of its publication was the Criminal Law Amendment Act passed in 1885 which granted new legal powers to authorities to prevent the sexual exploitation of children. Yet it also further policed deviant sexualities, namely by criminalizing sex work and extending the laws against male homosexuality which would land Oscar Wilde in prison a decade later.

This Act also established the National Vigilance Association whose mandate was "to enforce and improve the laws for the repression of criminal vice and public immorality, to check the causes of vice, and to protect minors."[16] It englobed existing organizations and groups working towards social purity, giving the movement—and the Purity Crusader emotional community—an enormous boost. Just a few years later during an international white slavery congress, the National Vigilance Association set up the International Bureau for the Suppression of the White Slave Traffic. Under the influence of the National Vigilance Association's own secretary, William Alexander Coote, the International Bureau would represent and nourish the Purity Crusader component in abolitionism, eventually becoming a major rival of the International Abolitionist Federation and other contemporary abolitionist emotional communities.[17] Structured very much like Josephine Butler's Federation, it employed similar means: heading crusading missions on the European continent, seeking out and communicating with supporters, founding local committees, organizing international congresses and lectures, and disseminating pamphlets and petitions. This organization tended to be more paternalist, elitist, and xenophobic. Seeing more success than the International Abolitionist Federation, it appealed to states' agendas by framing the issue of prostitution within nationalistic terms by often calling for exclusionary and suppressive measures for controlling trafficking and prostitution. Branches emerged throughout Europe and in some colonies; by the twentieth century, most committees were governmental, with some in countries like Germany, Spain, Portugal, and Hungary even headed by state officials. This close affiliation with state authorities helped the International Bureau shape international legal and policing[18] guidelines between 1885 and 1912 to prevent procurement and trafficking for sexual exploitation by protecting naïve young women from traffickers. Apart from making strides in international law and establishing legal definitions of keys terms—such as the trafficking victim—the International Bureau's efforts helped formalize and institutionalize the relationship between governments and these new international voluntary associations.

A Curse upon the Nation: Fear of Divine Retribution

In order to better understand the emotional styles of the Purity Reformers and their contributions to abolitionism and its emotional histories, it is important to unpack this emotional community's connections to past campaigns for the improvement of public morality rooted in paternalism and providentialism. Be it natural or divine, belief in providence was popular. It underpinned various crusades to improve public morality for the sake of the nation centuries before finding expression in the emotional styles of the Purity Crusaders. In the Christian tradition, providentialism refers to seeing God as directly involved in human events and divine government as the tool for enacting his plans.[19] This also found its translation into secular thought, namely in Adam Smith's famous invisible hand, buttressing notions of laissez-faire economics and also the imperial civilizing mission. Another prevalent—sometimes parallel—variant of providentialism, however, held that there was a direct connection between morality and fortune, so that the wicked suffered punishments while the devout received blessings. With the rise of the notion of predestination in Protestant theology which placed a greater importance on God's omnipotent power and on personal introspection, this latter interpretation of divine providence took precedence in England. For instance, influential contemporary British thinkers thought that mass poverty, epidemic disease, or crop failure were forms of divine retribution. What historian F. D. Roberts has dubbed an English brand of providentialism became fixed in popular thought in England through events like the Restoration of the Anglican king Charles II to the throne in 1660, the Glorious Revolution of 1688–1699 which overthrew the Catholic king James II, the thwarted Jacobite rising of 1745–1746, and the defeat of Napoleon in 1815.[20] Indeed, this view of providentialism often manifested in a nationalist register and was even diffused from the pulpits, as demonstrated by this sermon given by influential Church of England clergyman Claudius Buchanan comparing the English to the Israelites:

> As a nation cannot be punished as a nation in the next world for its iniquity, it must be punished in this world [...] From the fury of these desolating judgments we have hitherto been preserved [...] it should seem as if God had selected this nation, as formerly his chosen people Israel [...][21]

Thus, if the receipt of blessings on the state-level was predicated on public virtue, it justified placing an emphasis on more paternalistic philanthropic ventures—for instance, teaching sexual abstinence—instead of tackling the root socio-economic causes for poverty and other social troubles.

The forerunner to the social purity movement was the Reformation of Manners. This movement starting at the turn of the eighteenth century saw not only a series of moral panics aiming to control sexuality but also led to the construction of British masculinity through a religious and civic humanist lens. As Stephen H. Gregg has shown, reformers mobilized an image of the nation "as a fortress-isle, hedged around by God's especial care but under threat of immoral invasion often figured in metaphors of plague."[22] One particular "threat" of infection was the transgression of gender roles, namely the assessment that British men would become effeminate[23] through debauchery and luxury, and that women's wanton and assertive sexuality would go uncontrolled.[24] As one influential preacher Edward Stillingfleet stated in his sermon, *Reformation of Manners, the true way of Honouring God*:

> [T]he Sins of a Nation do naturally tend to the Weakness and Dishonour of it [...] Who can deny that Luxury and Debauchery, and all sorts Intemperance, not only sink the Reputation of a People, but effeminates and softens them.[25]

Note that reformers placed value on purity (both physical and spiritual) and sexual separation—for instance, men's abstinence leagues were popular during this time—as civic duties to the nation. Anxieties surrounding uncontrolled female sexuality were enflamed through shocking revelations of young men being victimized by sexually assertive women.[26] As such, the theme of sexual victimization was rampant and reflected a distinctively misogynist feature:

> The mouth of a strange woman is a deep pit; those that are abhorred of the Lord shall fall into it [...] her house inclineth unto death; none that go unto her return again.[27]

Moreover, movement discourses, according to Margaret Hunt's thought-provoking study,[28] tended to reflect a belief in retribution for such sexual infractions, either directly by God—such as in the case of Sodom and Gomorrah—or indirectly through weakening the integrity of social institutions which conservatives and paternalists held dear, such as marriage, and thus cause social dissolution. The latter was also a tendency of Counter-Reformation and post-Enlightenment thought beyond Great Britain's borders.

Despite it being less impactful as its initiatives eventually disappeared or were incorporated into other reform movements, the later phase of the Reformation of Manners was significant for bearing witness to the foundation of the Proclamation Society in 1789 by William Wilberforce—a key figure in British antislavery and humanitarianism. It would become the Society for the Suppression of Vice in 1802 and then be absorbed into the National Vigilance Association upon the latter's foundation in 1885. In a late eighteenth-century context marked by industrial and political revolutions, the Proclamation Society's work is significant in its demonstration of a shift in contemporary moral entrepreneurs' focus from sexuality to blasphemy and obscenity[29]—most particularly amongst the urban poor. It took an anti-materialist stance against "that increasing wealth, luxury, and refinement [...] attended with a decay in religion and morals"[30] while also displaying repressive, reactionary conservatism. Such notions appear most especially in activism for the prevention of cruelty against animals which was contemporaneous to the antislavery movement, involved the same actors, and followed the same pattern. This is to say that the animal welfare movement, even after becoming international under the impetus of heterogeneous actors of both secular and religious persuasions, continued to take the advocacy work of the British campaign as its standard.[31] Coordinated by the Society for the Prevention of Cruelty to Animals which William Wilberforce helped to establish in London in 1824, early campaigners understood cruelty against animals as socially disruptive or deviant, drawing a connection between one's violence towards animals and one's propensity of violence towards humans. It was thus something to at least disfavor and at most fear. For instance, one of the earliest targets of activists was blood-sports like bearbaiting or bullbaiting which were viewed by them as dangerous not only for causing moral debasement but also for stirring the blood lust of the lower classes. This was a frightening thought that resonated with the persistent anxieties felt by the upper classes over the influence of radicalism coming from post-revolutionary France. Looking at an early debate initiated in the British House of Commons in 1802 regarding bullbaiting, William Wilberforce and his supporters qualified the practice as "hurtful to morality [fostering] every bad and barbarous principle of our nature."[32] By this logic, abolishing this "practice which degraded human nature to a level with the brutes"[33] involving "[a] bull, that honest, harmless, useful animal" would thereby be in service of raising lower-class morality and thus overall public virtue. Yet, there was a clear faction of those who qualified it as cultural sports heritage of the working class, as Mr. Courtenay remarked:

> [B]ull-baiting was the great support of the constitution in church and state, and that the generosity, courage, and humanity of the lower ranks of the community solely originated from this heroic and laudable species of entertainment, which had distinguished both the dogs and men of this country from the earliest records of history.[34]

It was an amusement they "were entitled to" and, at best, it was a distraction which "saved [them] from all the horrors of Jacobinism and fanaticism." They mocked animal welfare campaigners as either "influenced by a species of philosophy dictated by their wives"[35] or religious zealots who wished to "force [the poor] to pass their time in chaunting at conventicles [chanting at small nonconformist meetings]."[36] Regardless, this moralist rhetoric reflected class-based and nationalist notions of superiority which were increasingly nuanced by a new evolutionist logic which recast old hierarchies between races, nations, classes, sexes, species, and so on—a phenomenon which would prove widespread and recurrent in other contemporary campaigns. As Rob Boddice posits, Darwinian evolutionist thought served to buttress the idea that white, upper-class educated men deserved their sense of superiority by virtue of good breeding.[37]

In many ways, the obsessive fear surrounding venereal disease which drove the passing of the Contagious Diseases Acts in the first place was combined with providential anxieties to become an obsessive fear of divine or natural retribution within the Purity Crusader emotional community. From the more religious providential perspective, what was at stake was the moral degradation of society and the resultant wrath of God. Combined later with the social hygienic perspective, society risked degeneracy, or becoming arrested or devolved. In both perspectives, the Purity Crusaders' fears and anxieties were translated into emotional styles directed toward the nation, society, the lower classes, and women and girls. The creation of rules to control the latter two seemed not only necessary, but urgent to safeguard them against evil and to avoid a divine reckoning. As such, aiming to combat immoral conduct and encourage sexual purity, Purity Crusaders focused on a wide range of tasks, from prosecuting those selling lewd books, photographs, and other paraphernalia[38] to working with local authorities to shut down music halls, gambling houses, and brothels. This repression negatively impacted the working prostitute who was forced to the streets. This caused a certain amount of backlash, most openly seen in the garrison town of Aldershot. Resisting a campaign driven by the National Vigilance Association to close brothels in 1888, prostitutes protested and marched, causing a media sensation.[39] Of the hundreds made homeless and offered protection and rehabilitation by the National Vigilance Association, reportedly only one accepted it. As *Personal Rights Journal* asked in January 1889:

> It is difficult to say whether the bravery of a powerful society, cramming homeless and helpless girls into a hospital where surgical outrage […] awaits them, or the eccentricity of those who were not willing to accept such protection, is the more remarkable. We should like to know what became of the remainder of the 400, and also whether the one lamb 'willing' to be led to the slaughter was led by the gentle hands of the Aldershot police.[40]

Contrary to Josephine Butler who spoke often of the prostitute's moral redeemability, many social purity reformers viewed the unrepentant prostitute as unworthy of compassion and did not shy away from supporting punitive measures. For instance, the severe police repression of prostitutes and abuse of their civil liberties in London from 1901 to 1906 was led by the National Vigilance Association and the newly established Public Morality Council, whose Watch Committee included feminists Lady Isabel Somerset, Millicent Fawcett, and Florence Booth.[41] This tendency towards repressive legislation indeed led Josephine Butler to speak out against social purity in 1897, although she remained part of the National Vigilance Association only by name.

> Beware of "Purity Societies" [...] ready to accept and endorse any amount of inequality in the laws, any amount of coercive degrading treatment of their fellow creatures in the fatuous belief that you can oblige human beings to be moral by force [...][42]

The divide between Moral Liberal and Purity Crusaders' sensibilities is clear here, but most especially in the former viewing despotism as the enemy and the latter believing it to be vice.

As one contemporary newspaper described it, the National Vigilance Association believed that "[p]revention is better than cure," thus "look[ing] to the destruction of the causes of temptation"[43] was paramount. This similarly framed their view of prostitution, as Purity Crusaders tended to focus on protective measures rather than on rescuing the prostitute from the socioeconomic forces leading to sex work in the first place. Instead, understanding sexual violence as a driver of prostitution—an activity believed to be so revolting it would not be chosen by an individual of sound mind—the vulnerability of women and girls to exploitation became a concern. Some pointed to the unequal relations of power and authority existing between the sexes, such as between servants and masters,[44] but also to female naivety and gullibility making them easy targets of seduction. As such, the course of action most often taken up by Purity Crusaders was legal and paternalist oversight: protective and restrictive legislation was sought; female job advertisements were investigated; borders, railway stations, and ports were policed; and female migration for employment was regulated.[45] This inherently devalued individual personal liberty as it was considered more important to avoid a larger social harm or to oblige the rule-breaker to adopt a better way of life. This is why Purity Crusaders supported the reduced mobility of young women and girls to protect them from falling prey to unscrupulous traffickers and procurers. At the most extreme, they even calling for the detention of those of abnormally low intelligence. Historian Paula Bartkey has well-demonstrated how care initiatives for the feeble-minded were driven by middle-class women-led organizations that were equally concerned about these young women's welfare as their potential immoral impact on society if left to their own devices.⁴⁶ The Travellers' Aid Society, for instance, alongside patrolling stations and ports, directed awareness campaigns at "ignorant country girls" wishing to come to London to discourage them from coming or warn them about the "terrible snares" awaiting them.⁴⁷ British eugenicist Sir James Marchant—National Vigilance Association leader and founder of the National Council of Public Morals, as well as the friend and biographer of Alfred Russel Wallace—for his part labeled the difficulty of safeguarding women from sexual exploitation the "master problem" of the twentieth century in his book of the same name in 1917. Yet his strategy was to effectively banish prostitutes from larger society so as to protect it:

> An individual is trained to personal cleanliness of the soul and thought, but useful and necessary a part of the 'hygienising' [sic] process is to remove the contaminating elements from the reach of the individual [...]⁴⁸

Similar to the Moral Liberals, sentiments of nationalism and xenophobia found expression in the emotional culture of the Purity Reformers, especially in their efforts to fight white slavery. The International Bureau's domestic and international policy work were underpinned by notions of British superiority which tacitly exalted the respectable (male) British citizen and made distinctions between the deserving and the undeserving foreign poor.⁴⁹ For instance, the Royal Commission held on alien immigration in 1903 saw William Alexander Coote testifying on behalf of the National Vigilance Association not only to stories of innocent girls being lured to Buenos Aires where they met their doom—a popular propaganda story—but also to the extraordinary level of licentiousness and perversity embodied by the foreign prostitute:

> She has introduced into England what is called special forms of vice, which even amongst gentlemen would not bear mentioning, but they are some of the most destructive forms of vice, and you must remember that the forms of vice are brought into contact with our young men [...] Our English girls simply do not understand that sort of thing.⁵⁰

The resulting Aliens Act of 1905 limited immigration and allowed for the expulsion of improper and scandalous foreigners which represented an important shift in focus from the protection of English female citizens abroad by controlling migration to the protection of the nation against a female foreign threat.⁵¹ As seen earlier in Josephine Butler's xenophobic framing of the Contagious Diseases Acts using the metaphor of disease in Moral Liberal activist discourse, England had been targeted for contamination by the Continent's "moral filth" and yet this time it was embodied in the mind/body of the foreign prostitute for Purity Crusaders.[52] By the time the Criminal Law Amendment Act was passed in 1912, increasing tensions in Europe on the brink of war saw an increase in xenophobia and conservatism. Propaganda increasingly reinforced an image of an innocent and fragile woman in need of protection against foreign—frequently Jewish[53]—traffickers and brothel-keepers.[54]

Purity Crusaders on the other side of the Atlantic tended to emphasize this foreign aspect, adding a racist dimension and a rigorous campaign to criminalize the entire system of prostitution. In Canada, for instance, racist immigration policies emerged such as the Female Employment Act of 1912 in Saskatchewan which criminalized any immigrant Chinese business owner who hired a white female employee.[55] Likewise in the United States, the moral panic against white slavery—a cultural myth by which no woman would engage in paid sex acts without being actively forced and thus they needed "saving"[56]—served to enact legislation to both monitor and police foreign and non-white communities. For example, after the outbreak of a public scandal surrounding a particular tale of forced prostitution in Chicago, the White-Slave Traffic Act (the Mann Act) was passed in 1910 which outlawed transporting women and girls across state lines for prostitution and created the Federal Bureau of Investigation to assist in the prosecution of such matters. While designed to fight white slavery, it was also used to dissuade interracial relationships through its ambiguous language forbidding transportation for immoral purposes,[57] as seen in the infamous arrest of African-American heavyweight boxer Jack Johnson, the Galveston Giant.

Hate the Sin, Punish the Sinner

The Purity Crusaders' fear of divine or natural rebuke fed into another characteristic feature of their emotional culture: a hatred of sin. They abhorred and were intolerant of it and each of their activities aimed to thoroughly root and snuff it out, lest it spread. Negatively appraised, vice such as "low literature" was seen as an infection, as French pastor and anti-pornography advocate Tommy Fallot proclaimed, emitting "pestilential miasma."[58] A similar sentiment was held for evildoers, as evident in their insistence on punishment and repressive legislation. Such intolerant contempt also translated into spiteful vendettas to see sinners shunned from society, as exemplified by British repeal campaigner and suffragette Millicent Fawcett, who led several campaigns against public figures who she felt had behaved licentiously. For instance, she severely damaged the political career of Conservative Member of Parliament Harry Cust in 1894 for his philandering past—he had initially refused to marry his wife whom he had seduced and impregnated. She told him in a letter that "as a woman I have naturally the strongest feeling against men of known bad character being elected to the House of Commons."[59] This animosity was also felt for prostitutes—the victims of vice according to Moral Liberals—who were considered equally culpable if they refused to change their ways. For instance, Dr. Elizabeth Blackwell wrote in *Medicine and Morality*:

> [...] the tenderest compassion may be shown to the poor creature who ceases to be a prostitute [...] but do nothing to raise the condition of prostitutes as such, any more than you would try to improve the condition of murderers and thieves.[60]

Her words denote a clear worldview informing emotional norms of sympathy for the worthy victim and distain for the willful reprobate, while also affording a certain degree of agency to the prostitute whose reluctance to repent was attributable to a deviant moral character similar to that of "murderers and thieves." Her unsympathetic view of the sinner saw her write in a pamphlet *Wrong and Right Methods of Dealing with Social Evil* that both allowing individuals to police themselves and attempting to regulate them would lead to vice. Her recommended course was to suppress vice through "repressive law, municipal vigilance, and organized beneficence" as "the only righteous method of dealing with vice by means of law."[61] The forced closure of brothels and the eviction of prostitutes into the streets were thus entirely justifiable acts, as well as the arrest of the latter for soliciting.

Purity Crusaders' certainty that sin and sexual deviancy were widespread—a monolithic conceptualization of evil buttressed by vice's tendency to be hidden or done in secret—saw them encourage and support statist instruments for surveying, regulating, and policing the social body.[62] Although the results varied locally,[63] the collaboration between the National Vigilance Association committees and the local police in the closures of brothels is a prime example of this. In fact, English law permitted private individuals to make arrests, as *The Manual of Vigilance Law* schooling National Vigilance Association members in legal matters to assist them in this demonstrates.[64] This additionally attests to the Purity Crusaders' vigilantism and desire to actively participate in policing one's fellowman through private enterprise, as seen in the earlier Movement for the Reformation of Manners.[65] They also employed covert tactics, as demonstrated by Laura Ormiston Chant, editor of *The Vigilance Record* and member of the Social Purity Alliance. Undoubtedly inspired by the beforementioned William T.

Stead's *The Maiden Tribute of Modern Babylon*, she went undercover with fellow suffragette Lady Henry Somerset in 1894 to investigate claims of prostitution and other forms of vice at the large and famous music hall in London's West End, the Empire Theatre of Varieties. Dressed in a disguise, she made observations and conducted interviews with the "very much painted and beautifully dressed"[66] women she found walking unaccompanied on the Empire's promenade. Taking her findings to the London County Council in which she proffered a vision of prostitutes as women victimized by villainous wealthy male patrons, she successfully demanded the closure of the Empire's promenade and sparked a heavily publicized debate. When qualified a prudish meddler and self-serving spy by her critics,[67] she published a response in *Why We Attacked the Empire*. She corrected erroneous understandings of how events had transpired and aimed at providing factual evidence in the form of excerpts of the London County Council's hearing transcripts and press clippings from both sides of the debate. While eloquently written and offering sound arguments, it holds notes of indignant hostility and self-righteousness in the publication; for instance, it is introduced with a letter acerbically signed "A 'Puritan'" which states that

> [...] in all victories there is the sadness of partial defeat in the hatred of some of the defeated, yet such is the righting power of example, custom, and a public conscience that we hope even the haters will be conquered in time, and brought on to the right side.[68]

Her actions, despite being heroic from the Purity Crusader perspective, were not recognized as such by the broader public. Here, her disappointment at the negative reaction is clearly rooted in her certitude of being in the right.

Purity Crusaders' hatred of sin and preoccupation with the causes of vice led to them increasingly seeking explications by appropriating and negotiating social hygienism's scientific discourses. Indeed, contemporary views of science had come to understand nature as an objective reality that was reliably knowable through science and thus capable of being wielded to transform humanity itself.[69] With this, Purity Crusaders formed a new medico-moralized discourse in which Man's animal nature was understood to be reined in—as Charles Darwin's *The Descent of Man* suggests—by his moral faculties. The contemporary notion of the materiality of the mind in the brain turned the body into a "source of truth"[70] rendering class, sex, race, temperament, and moral character visible, paving the way for an increasingly eugenic and hereditary movement trajectory at the turn of the twentieth century. Already a key subject of scientific medical interest in the nineteenth century, the prostitute would appear in the twentieth century as an example of a born delinquent arising from a common degenerative origin, innately deviant and criminal with Cesare Lombroso and Guglielmo Ferrero's work.[71] Thus, a discourse of moral pathology emerged by which immorality was understood as a disease emanating from an aberrant character. Notions of bodies as "against nature" or "contaminating" others through their environmental proximity came to inform legal and social categories of the "degenerate" and the "criminal" developed as modern scientific discourses were increasingly applied to broader understandings of society and populations. By shifting from sinners to degenerates,[72] this effectively created a sliding scale upon which a mind-body can degenerate into moral depravity or evolve into moral superiority. This was taken by Purity Crusaders as a matter of great urgency to set mankind right. For instance, Dr. Elizabeth Blackwell warned against masturbation because of the danger it posed to the young especially as "it is an injury to mind as well as body, through the inseparable union of the moral and physical elements of our constitution."[73] She therefore helped found the Moral Reform Union which emphasized moral education in 1881. Similarly, the Salvation Army's William Booth in his *In Darkest England and the Way Out* spoke of "moral lunatics" who were "carrying with them the contagion of moral leprosy, and multiplying a progeny doomed before its birth to inherit the vices and diseased cravings of their unhappy parents."[74] To combat this degeneracy, Purity Crusaders increasingly distributed handbooks, tracts, pamphlets, and public speeches directed at the lower classes whose sexuality was construed as dangerous and proffered a moral education to children. This experience in public outreach later proved useful to their hygienist allies who would become interested in vulgarizing lessons on sexual education in the interest of public health.

However, educating the public fell short in fulfilling Purity Crusaders' uncompromising standards. Rules were thus held in high regard by Purity Crusaders and characterized their work, creating them according to a black-and-white worldview and punishing those who did not follow them. Such binary views dividing bodies and behaviors as good or evil fueled an authoritative and self-righteous attitude that underpinned their emotional styles. Their strong need to create rules was driven by a dissatisfaction with the existing rules because there was a perceived evil—broadly speaking, vice and sexual delinquency—which they found profoundly disturbing.[75] Nothing could be right until the proper rules were established which would target and correct the evil. Legislation was thus a primordial tool through which state intervention could be utilized to enact and enforce laws that would combat evil and be to the overall benefit of society. Their faith in law and belief that nothing could be right in the world until the proper rules were established saw them targeting sin and its correction through state intervention and legislation. Such attitudes harkened a renewed sense of paternalism which blended notions of a divine, immutable authority and of societal interdependency with liberal imperialism, informing not just abolitionism but also humanitarianism more generally.

If informed by the correct worldview, the social ramifications of law were tremendous, as Dutch abolitionist Pastor H. Pierson argued before his audience during a white slavery conference held in Amsterdam:

> Let us not forget that an imperious, inflexible, even rigorous law is not always an evil, but that—provided it is right—it is actually a blessing, enlightening the conscience, signaling vice, exhorting virtue, bringing the weak to the right path, confirming the strong in their moral convictions, thus tracing with a sure hand for all without exception the line of demarcation between the true and the false, the just and the unjust, the good and evil, the pure and the impure.[76]

William Alexander Coote, for instance, similarly insisted that men could be kept "sober" by simple Act of Parliament:

> While human nature is so weak and yet capable of so much wrong-doing, we must by every means in our power, by the administration of just and equal laws, do all we can to enslave vice and give the utmost liberty and freedom to all that is pure and good.[77]

A clearly fervent and uncompromisingly antagonist position is taken here against "vice" to which mankind, "so weak," was inherently inclined. The correction of perceived evil through rules and laws tended towards prohibition; this suppression of behavior deviating from the Purity Crusaders' ethic by any means was justifiable so long as the ends were met. The National Vigilance Association—again, the Purity Crusader mainstay organization—held the opinion that "no amount of rescue work by itself, however well done, will accomplish the object" as it left evildoers unpunished "to pursue their cruel work on others."[78] This justified their beforementioned collusion with police in the repression of brothels, street prostitution, obscene publications, and so on. Increasingly severe punishments were sought,[79] as demonstrated in the 1898 extension of the 1824 Vagrancy Act which permitted flogging a man "in any place persistently [who] solicits or importunes for immoral purposes" to be applied to male prostitutes and pimps by making "living on the earnings of prostitution" a punishable offense.[80]

The need to create and enforce rules directly resulted in an esteem for knowledge. As such, Purity Crusaders cultivated various sorts of expertise.

Joseph Gusfield looking at Max Weber's distinction between fact and value argues that moral crusaders did not view science as merely a means to achieve ends and values supplied by other institutions and elites.[81] It was also a value in itself, a process of searching for knowledge which gave meaning to existence or, in this case, purpose to the crusade. Purity Crusaders' range of activities brought them into contact with law, police procedure, community[82] and international politics, medical and social sciences, and so on. In her crusade against the Empire, Laura Ormiston Chant employed both the techniques of investigative journalism and of social philanthropy to acquire insider knowledge about prostitution on the promenade. Their development of professionalized expertise gave value to their work both to their own eyes and to that of outsiders, prone to belittle Purity Crusaders as "meddlesome bigots" and "hysterical women"[83] and to discount their claims. The appropriation and use of modern science by the predominantly fervently religious Purity Crusaders was made possible through the emergence of a more tenable understanding of Darwinism by the 1870s. Initially, Darwin's theory of evolution was understood as a threat to the axioms of Christianity—namely that of intelligent design—thus the religious response was initially hostile. Yet in treating the evolution of morality in man and higher animals in *The Descent of Man*, Charles Darwin saw the most important shared instinct being what he called sympathy or other-regarding emotions: just as intellect increased through natural selection—unequally of course—so did the capacity for "love, sympathy and self-command."[84] These qualities being highly valued by Purity Crusaders, Darwinian discourses of heredity and degeneration were added to those of sin and God's wrath in the moralizing initiatives.[85]

3

Maternal Feminists: From Social Mothers to New Women (1880s–1930s)

Developing alongside—and in many respects overlapping—the emotional communities of Moral Liberals and Purity Crusaders, Maternal Feminists also represented a significant component of this first phase of the abolitionist movement, originating in Great Britain before spreading to the Continent and across the Atlantic to mix with similar domestic components. As an emotional community, it is inherently tied to other feminist or women-led mobilizations of the period, from antislavery and anti-vivisection to suffragism, both on the local level and internationally. Like other campaigns they were involved in, Maternal Feminists instrumentalized the contemporary socially constructed and essentialized notions of gender to not only challenge the foundations of state-regulated prostitution but also to make a case for the recognition of their own legitimate and indispensable role in public affairs. However, the dissimilar settings in which local repeal campaigns were taking place—from the dominant political culture to the public and political status of women—also made it necessary to negotiate at the local level what was meant by Josephine Butler's rallying words to her fellow Maternal Feminists: "We revolt!"[1] For instance, in Switzerland, abolitionists like Marie Humbert-Droz (*les Amies de la jeune fille*) and Betsy Cellerier (*l'Association du Sou*) focused primarily on rescue work—framing their advocacy as efforts of protection and socially conscious voluntarism rather than as political projects for the liberation of women.

Feminism[2]—a dynamic concept of diverse origins, developments, and uses by feminists, opponents, and past and present scholars alike—emerged as a social project for equality between the sexes in the United States and Europe around the mid-1800s. By the turn of the century, feminist discourses shifted more towards one of female emancipation from male privilege and control, feeding a women's collective identity and consciousness, as well as a transnational women's rights movement. This is especially true of the women's suffrage campaign, a predominantly Anglo-American initiative emerging out of the antislavery movement which led the fight for women to have a voice and role in public matters. And yet as the scholarship on first-wave feminism has shown,[3] feminist mobilizations—of which the abolitionist movement was one—were far from homogenous: actor discourses demonstrate various cleavages from political leanings (liberal or conservative) to fundamental understandings of society. There were also discursive paradoxes, as identified by Nancy Cott, which continue to define elements of feminism today:

> Feminism asks for sexual equality that includes sexual difference. It aims for individual freedoms by mobilizing sex solidarity. It posits that women recognize their unity while it stands for diversity among women. It requires gender consciousness for its basis and yet calls for the elimination of prescribed gender roles.[4]

Therefore, from its start, the extent to which women's activism in social reform efforts actually challenged the status quo between the sexes was variable. For instance, in the United States the connection between the antislavery movement and the development of feminism is clear. The exclusion of Lucretia Mott, Elizabeth Cady Stanton, and other female American delegates from the World Antislavery Convention held in London in 1840 had the immediate impact of creating a parallel between the oppression of slaves and that of women. It sparked a local women's rights movement which culminated eight years later in the first National Women's Rights Convention, whose *The Declaration of Sentiments* declared:

> The history of mankind is a history of repeated injuries and usurpations on the part of man toward woman, having in direct object the establishment of an absolute tyranny over her.[5]

In contrast, the greater tendency of British feminists was to emphasize a gender-based sympathy as motivation behind their advocacy which aimed to see enslaved women share their own "privileged status" in the antislavery movement. Mirroring the broader antislavery movement's Christian moralist frame, they tended to emphasize the suffering of a voiceless, passive victim whose "proper station as a Daughter, a Wife, and a Mother,"[6] as one abolitionist petition writes, was interrupted by the harmful institution of slavery. Such understandings of victimhood, as demonstrated in the earlier chapter on Moral Liberals, were transferred to the prostitute in the British repeal campaign.

In fact, truly radical feminist notions were rather marginal at this time and instead feminist activists tended to employ either liberal frames against state despotism, medico-police tyranny, and for equality before the law, or those emerging from the social purity movement. As such, the chameleon-like discourses employed by and the diversity within its own ranks became increasingly problematic for Maternal Feminists in the midst of social purity's ascendance, the white slavery panic, and a progressively tension-filled geopolitical scene seeing nations growing anxious over the security of their borders and the health of their soldiers. The International Abolitionist Federation—the organization most representative of this emotional community—was struggling to maintain a common vision, not to mention one that remained faithful to Josephine Butler. While aiming to be secular and non-partisan, the International Abolitionist Federation demonstrated quite strong Protestant, feminist, and socialist elements which limited the impact of its national and international efforts and alienated certain constituencies. This was the scene in Germany, for instance, where a local split between liberal and conservative abolitionists[7]—or even between Moral Liberals and Purity Reformers—on the contentious issue of criminalizing prostitutes. This argument even spilled over into the International Abolitionist Federation and contributed to a constitutional change granting national sections more autonomy in 1901.[8] To the dismay of German liberal abolitionists like Minna Cauer and Anna Pappritz who saw the state's intervention in sexual matters as a civil rights' violation, German conservative abolitionists like Hanna Bieber-Böhm believed the body to be first and foremost God's creation, thus rendering illicit sexuality a criminal offense which necessitated the compulsory internment and re-education of any male or female offenders.[9] Likewise in France, Josephine Butler's early repeal campaign involving Protestant Maternal Feminists like Émilie de Morsier and Sarah Monod had limited support despite causing a stir with Yves Guyot's lengthy study of the *police des mœurs* in *La Prostitution* (1882). The movement was criticized for being un-French and too British—incidentally one of the reasons for abolitionism's failure in Italy as well.[10] Instead, the dominant local ethos of imperialist nationalism and conservative Catholicism proved more in tune with social purity which came to be embodied by neo-regulationist and major player in the Purity Crusader emotional community in France, the beforementioned Senator René Bérenger. Derisorily called "*Père la pudeur*," he was involved in various causes calling on the French government and later the international community to establish tougher laws: pimps and procurers, prostitutes, pornography, white slavery, and child prostitution. He was instrumental in establishing a close relationship between the French government, French neo-regulationists, and the International Bureau—later continued by Marcelle Legrand Falco and her *Union temporaire contre la prostitution réglementée et la traite des femmes*—which would thrive till the Second World War.

Despite the difficulties faced by Maternal Feminists, as Anne Summers[11] has argued, this crusade against the Contagious Diseases Acts and its challenge to the double moral standard provided a model for others where the local women's movement was only just beginning and influenced a new generation of feminists—of "New Women." In an era characterized by scientific and technological advances, emancipation movements, expansive empires, aggressive nationalism, and political revolutions, feminists were one of many new constituencies that emerged whose worldviews often challenged and clashed with those of the incumbent elite. It is important to bear in mind that they emerged, while not exclusively, from the mobilizations of the newly empowered middle class to solve societal problems. Heavily informed by classical liberalism, social Christianity, and scientism, these middle-class social reformers formed local and international voluntary associations, of which women were often active participants. Wielding various framings of issues and prescriptive strategies, they fought for social reform movements and left lasting effects on the construction of social problems and of state intervention both in regulating citizens' behavior and in ensuring citizens' welfare. They also paved the way for the inclusion of civil society expertise in matters of global governance. These social reformers, new and old alike, increasingly took their battle to the international stage where a new space was being erected which presented feminists in particular with new possibilities for placing pressure on national politics to affect social change. Feminists would thus find a foothold in this new space from which transnational civil society would emerge in the postwar period.

Fatherly Care versus Motherly Love

Lying at the heart of the Maternal Feminist emotional community was the esteem and defense of feminine expertise in matters of the body. Underpinning the very legislature which triggered its creation and what has been called "the western world's first feminine revolt"[12] was the looming threat posed by the surge in cases of venereal disease to the health and military might of the nation. This issue raised alarms throughout the Western world in a context of growing imperialist nationalism and conflict which centered on controlling the bodies of the poor. A rich corpus[13] exists on the sociocultural construction of the body. It well demonstrates how the body itself produces certain kinds of knowledge and discourses which are subject to shifts and changes given that its boundaries are policed by dynamic notions of hygiene and cleanliness. Initial conceptualizations of disease and illness were heavily influenced by moralism and providentialism, as seen earlier, with these being understood as a manifestation of God's divine wrath punishing the sinner and with convalescence as being hinged on repentance and salvation. The immateriality of the soul was prioritized over the materiality of the body—a system of values which had dominated religious discourses since the Middle Ages. By contrast, contemporary progressive reformers sought to establish a proactive stance by establishing a preventative form of state social medicine in which, however, competing discourses were often negotiated. For instance, while acting as President of the Health Section discussing sanitary legislation, evangelical reformer Lord Shaftesbury stated in 1858:

> Our great object should be to do all we can to remove the obstructions which stand in the way of such worship and of the body's fitness for its great purpose. If St. Paul, calling our bodies the temples of the Holy Ghost, said that they ought not to be contaminated by sin, we also say that our bodies, the temples of the Holy Ghost, ought not to be corrupted by preventible [sic] disease, degraded by avoidable filth, and disabled for His service by unnecessary suffering.[14]

This quote is interesting for placing the body's health at the same level of importance as the soul's purity. Similarly, the early dominant discourse of state social medicine was decidedly a blend of the medical and the moral. The works of naturalists like Charles Darwin placed an emphasis on mankind's kinship with animals that arguably reduced the perceivable distance between civilized man and his more primitive past of brutish beast. This rendered the self-control and mastery over society's primal instincts all the more imperative for its very maintenance—as also seen in the beforementioned animal welfare movement—but also constructed a more animalistic and feral representation of the urban poor. The revulsion felt for the poor, for instance, seen here in the words of John Liddle, the medical officer of health for Whitechapel, centers around their "offensive" lack of hygiene:

> They merely pass dirty linen through very dirty water. The smell of the linen itself, when so washed, is very offensive, and must have an injurious affect upon the health of the occupants. The filth of their dwellings is excessive, so is their personal filth. When they attend my surgery, I am always obliged to have the door open. When I am coming downstairs from the parlour [sic], I know at a distance of a flight of stairs whether there are any poor patients in the surgery.[15]

Filth, dirt, and excrement were popular motifs in medico-moral discourses, both representing a visible material manifestation of miasma—bad airs widely regarded as the cause of disease and illness—and sin. Understandings of their interplay were defined by the belief that pestilence and moral depravity lessened the body's resistance and thus contributed to greater degrees of contagion.[16] As Frank Mort in his exemplary study focused on the constructed notions of sexuality during this period has rightly argued, discursive polarities were made between the urban poor and their middle-class social commentators along the lines of "physical health/non-health, virtue/vice, cleanliness/filth, morality/depravity, civilization/animality."[17]

When resistance to the Contagious Diseases Acts was organized by Josephine Butler, it in many ways, as Mort argues,[18] represented the collapse of the medico-moral alliance between female social reformers and state medical reformers wielding contrasting forms of knowledge and authority. In essence, fatherly care—initially characterized by paternalism, but later framed as masculine scientific objectivity—was pit against motherly love—initially demarcated by feminine dispositions to morality and later to more biologically female ones to maternity. Derived from the Latin adjective *paternus* meaning "fatherly" or "of father," paternalism in Western Europe at the dawn of modernity was centered on notions of a divine, immutable authority and of societal interdependency. Often buttressed by theological arguments, paternalism informed patriarchal systems, most importantly that of monarchical absolutism, which was in practice from the medieval era until the late nineteenth century. Other paternalist authorities were validated using similar principles: the pope over the faithful; the landlord over peasants; the father over family members. Alongside establishing hierarchies, paternalism—as F. D. Roberts demonstrates in *Paternalism in Early Victorian England*—entailed numerous social attitudes which informed different norms and practices. These namely prescribed duties to which both the patriarch and his subject were beholden; for instance, the clergy had moral superintendence over parishioners in that they were expected to educate them enough to read the catechism to learn obedience, humility, sobriety, and proper conduct.[19] More generally, fatherly love as benevolent control was expected of the patriarch while obedient reverence was due from his subject. The maintenance of this sacred hierarchy based on fatherly love and the dutiful performance of each of their role were what was believed to best manage society.

However, intellectual[20] and industrial revolutions brought this paternalist governance and status quo of the Old Regime into question. In France, the Age of Reason and Enlightenment saw the emergence of radicalism based on notions of rights and liberties, triggering political revolution. By most emblematically beheading their king, France saw the paternal authority give violent way to the fraternal—that is, the authority of bonds between non-kin men. The adoption of the *Déclaration universelle des droits de l'homme* and of universal male suffrage in 1792, as well as the abolition of slavery in French colonies in 1794 in the wake of the French Revolution introduced democratic notions to Europe—despite the latter two being later retracted. French radicalism, but also rising utopian anti-classist ideologies spurred local challenges to traditional political and religious institutions—for instance, Thomas Paine in Great Britain—but also reactionary conservatism and repression.

Likewise, the industrial revolution in Europe saw industrialism emerge as an ideology upon which, as French philosopher Saint-Simon famously put it, the whole of society was based.[21] This is not to say that the paternalist ethos was entirely eclipsed; it found translation, for instance, into new Napoleonic law by reasserting the rights of employers, husbands, and fathers at the expense of workers, wives, and children, thereby into industrial relations. Historian Donald Reid demonstrates this well by explaining the shift in usage from the Old Regime term *"maître"* to *"patron"*—the Latin word for father—by the 1830s as "the transformation of a system of institutionalized inequality" into an employer-employee relationship of "deference and clientage."[22] Yet as the forerunner of industrialization which began in the late 1700s and peaked in the 1850s, England was most effected by the correlated social, political, demographic, and economic changes. The hegemony of its aristocrats and landed elite waned in favor of a rising urban middle class whose new forms of wealth eventually transformed into political power. While the unregulated wage labor system and laissez-faire economic model were profitable for some, those in the lower classes faced poor working and living conditions in the cities or pauperization in the countryside. Early attempts to develop welfare schemes, such as the 1795 Speenhamland system, proved inefficient and even exacerbated poverty. Thus, by the 1830s[23] the multitude of social problems was becoming more and more difficult to ignore; thousands of men, women, and children were dying each year due to malnutrition, exposure, contaminated food or water, industrial accidents, or overwork.

The social policy reform initiatives which emerged to deal with these issues—especially those pursued by middle-class pro-industrialists and liberals like John Stuart Mill—were greatly influenced by utilitarianism. As initially set out by philosophical radical Jeremy Bentham, its basic tenet was that achieving the greatest happiness for the greatest number was the only measure of right and wrong.²⁴ As such, he and his followers—notably Edwin Chadwick—sought to streamline policy with the aim of increasing global happiness. The result of this was the establishment of a sort of welfare capitalism which ultimately buttressed the laissez-faire system, but also of repressive policies against those demonstrating socially harmful behaviors—the criminal, the pauper, the prostitute. For instance, Jeremy Bentham drafted a number of tracts on poor law reform outlining a panopticon scheme in which a National Charity Company would be formed to manage a chain of industry houses where the poor—and their offspring—would be put to work. Such ideas inspired the repressive 1834 Poor Law Amendment which reformed Elizabethan workhouses by making the living and working conditions terrible to discourage people from staying there.

Opponents to Benthamite utilitarianism like Thomas Carlyle, John Ruskin, and Charles Dickens were also more critical of industrialization, looking rather at the deplorable situation of the urban poor as reflecting the degraded moral condition of the country itself. Most notable in this regard were the social reform initiatives led by a group calling themselves Young England. As recounted by Stewart Jay Brown, this assembly of young Anglican laymen—mostly Cambridge-educated aristocrats—endeavored for policy based on Christian paternalism and a stronger monarchy, as inspired by an idealized vision of medieval society.²⁵ Nostalgia for the "simpler" time of pre-industrial society was tangible, as expressed in this verse written by Lord John Manners in 1841:

> Each knew his place—king, peasant or priest
> The greatest owed connexion [sic] with the least
> From rank to rank the generous feeling ran
> And linked society as man to man.²⁶

Most notably promoted by Tory politician and later prime minister Benjamin Disraeli, Young England bemoaned the deterioration of pastoral Britain and blamed such atrocities on the newly wealthy for being "rootless, mobile, free of obligations and knowing no duties."²⁷ Yet, state intervention was not Young England's goal; instead they relied on the beforementioned belief that the best way to manage society was through fatherly care, or "vertical personal relations, in mutual obligation and loyalty, in control and dependence [...]."²⁸ Thus, they ultimately provided few real radical policy solutions to challenge the laissez-faire system and improve the lot of the working classes. This can be explained on the one hand by their devolved interests in property rights and regional affairs, entailing a reluctance to centralize government. On the other hand, a mainstay of this conservative paternalist ethos was the belief in poverty being an inevitable aspect of the natural order. This natural order having been created by God, it was not for the paternal authority to challenge one's appointed place in the hierarchy, but rather to fulfill their required duty of fatherly care to the lower orders by seeing to their moral and religious improvement, as well as lessening their suffering.[29]

Such notions helped buttress voluntarism[30] which emerged as an important value in the new laissez-faire society underpinned by Christian paternalism, providentialism, and a morality of self-reliance. Women found an important role to play in voluntarism and soon cultivated a public expertise rooted in motherly love. Of course, the effects of industrialization on the public lives of women were experienced differently according to class. In the lower classes, the occupational shift from agriculture to factory employment saw women's— not to mention children's—wages taking on a new significance in the urban household and, later, their inclusion in labor movement and trade union politics. Amongst the burgeoning middle-class eager to distinguish themselves from the ornamental womanhood of the aristocracy, women found fresh opportunities in philanthropy at home and mission work abroad in new industrial and imperial contexts. Josephine Butler and many other Maternal Feminists had already engaged in charitable work to fight the suffering of others in women's shelters and poor houses before becoming involved with abolitionism. Female voluntarism was even encouraged by the public authorities, as Eileen Janes Yeo has shown in her study on what she calls "social motherhood"[31] when censuses in 1851 and 1861 revealed a surplus of women, contributing to anxieties over spinsterhood. A new openness to seeing these women occupied or even employed in positions qualifying them as "social mothers" is a vital shift which made later female-dominated social movements, such as that against the state regulation of prostitution, possible. Social mothers were thus important early figures in the Maternal Feminist emotional community and their motherly love.

The mid to late nineteenth century saw the pinnacle of social mothers' voluntarism which had become increasingly controlled by its evangelical component and institutionalized through the rise of societies dealing with specific issues from vagrancy (such as the Charitable Night Refuge or the Mendicity Society) to prostitution (such as the Magdalen houses or the Rescue Society). Within these associations, women were able to carve out their own feminine civilizing mission by playing to their presumably innate maternal strengths of tolerance, love, self-sacrifice, devotedness, and hope—a gender-specific emotional expertise. As a major figure of Christian philanthropy, William Wilberforce is attributed with saying:

> How can we ever think that the female sex is inferior when we see the essential responsibility God has given women in this world?[32]

His valuation of woman draws from contemporary conceptualizations of sexual difference and most demonstrably that of women as morally superior. As popularly exemplified by Coventry Patmore's poem *The Angel in the House*, the Victorian feminine ideal was a woman not only submissive to her husband but also one who "loves with love that cannot tire."[33] Representing the immaterial, woman disposes of more instinctive, intuitive forms of knowledge, as William Wilberforce continues:

> [Women's] sensitivity to spiritual concerns seems to be far more innate and natural than a man's. Mothers and wives often are the medium for our intercourse with the heavenly world, the faithful repositories of spiritual knowledge and wisdom.[34]

And these mothers and wives instrumentalized these notions to extend the limits of the domestic realm to include increasingly more public areas of concern. They consoled, advised, and cared for the poor godless, friendless wretches in prison, workhouses, asylums, and slums; they preached to and converted the heathen woman—largely inaccessible to male missionaries yet the crux of the missionary project. For instance, Ellen Ranyard founded the London Bible and Domestic Female Mission in 1857 which initially involved organizing visits to the homes of the poor to read and discuss the Bible but later evolved to training the so-called Bible women in nursing.[35] The Queen herself aided in this by providing an example of how one could be both the pinnacle of domesticity and a female public persona.[36] This popular acceptance of women having public lives within these parameters is evidenced by the inclusion of philanthropic heroines in novels by contemporary authors like Elizabeth Gaskell (herself a philanthropist), Charlotte Bronte, and Charles Dickens.[37]

A propeller of the Maternal Feminist emotional community, this distinctively feminine philanthropic expertise of motherly love, granting women more freedom of action and yet supporting the limiting contemporary notions of gender, developed in close relationship to that of an increasingly professionalized male medical expertise. Initially, both were allied in initiatives targeting public morals and public health as essentially one and the same. This break, once again marked in the case of Great Britain by the passing of the Contagious Diseases Acts, can in many ways be attributed to the rise of naturalism. A more universalized vision of humankind—and thus an argument for sexual equality—encouraged by the liberal imperialist model of empire was upheaved not only by this model of empire's failure but also by the emergence of scientific and technological advances.[38] New sociological and anthropological approaches emerged to provide scientifically based explanations of cultural differences which by the late nineteenth century were employed less to justify Empire rather than to act as "alibis for the *fait accompli*."[39] These provided biologically rooted understandings of human difference, as well as paved the way for state biopolitics. As such, the liberal imperialist discourse shifted from universalism to cultural relativism, albeit maintaining a Eurocentric bias. Thus, the colonial Other was conceptualized through the essentialization of differences, primarily along the lines of religion, sex, and race.

Scientists employed empirical and objective methods to produce culturally contingent, and thus subjective, scientific knowledge which replicated, reinforced, and even exaggerated understandings of the Victorian status quo in the contemporary context of patriarchy, laissez-faire capitalism, and imperialism. The assumed inferiority of women to men was nothing new; however, advances in science provided ways to "prove" it, for instance, through a comparative study of men and women's average brain weights in which the latter fell short by about five ounces, empirically attesting to their substandard intellect.[40] These scientific discourses on sex, class, and race upheld the very hierarchies that those publicly calling for the emancipation of slaves and the liberation of women—or at least the extension of their rights—were aiming to dismantle. For instance, British anthropologist James McGrigor Allan, an opponent to women's suffrage, argued that menses not only rendered women invalid by causing them to "suffer under a languor and depression which disqualify them for thought or action," but that this "periodical illness" also turned them into dangerous primal beasts:

> The greater number of capricious acts of tyranny and blood, ordered, or personally committed by women possessed of despotic power, might be thus explained, and testify to the folly of trusting any woman with arbitrary authority.[41]

Sexual difference became thus a scientific subject matter par excellence as the evidence in support of male superiority mounted, taking various forms, and pointing out physiological or "material" differences in body size, musculature, pulse, respiration, center of gravity, brain size, and so on.

Yet the "woman question" was also an entry point for using scientific discourse to create an exclusory ideal of manliness and virility that extended well beyond the issue of sex. As historian Rob Boddice well summarizes in his study of the brain debate dominating the mid-1800s:

> It was not merely the setting of male minds against the minds of women; on the contrary, it was the setting of the best and most manly male minds against the minds of all other men, women, racial others, children and animals.[42]

Already a century earlier, the "virile man," as depicted by naturalists Buffon and Burdach, was seen to reign over all of Creation—other men, women, children, and beasts. The bodies of women and non-European men were studied in depth as "others," their "lack" providing an important contrast to the virile manly body ideal which attested to his superiority. For instance, Buffon wrote in his *Natural History* that the native American males lacked virility and held "no ardour for the female,"[43] as evidenced by their lack of beard or body hair and "small and feeble"[44] reproductive organs. Thus, this notion that both man and animal species can actually degenerate over generations had already been popularized by Buffon when Charles Darwin's hereditary and evolutionary discourse—infused with Joseph-Arthur de Gobineau's racial theory—began to be applied to understandings of human society among Europe's intellectual elite by the late 1870s. Scientism and the reconstrued notion of sympathy in the midst of degeneration fears being detailed in the following section, it suffices to say that Charles Darwin's own cousin Francis Galton coined the term "eugenics" to proffer a new interpretation of the moral imperatives of Darwinian theories which had already been raised by Herbert Spencer's social Darwinism. Understanding that social hierarchy of bodies by which some were biologically better equipped for survival than others, a worldview emerged which became totally determined by heredity. While this concept would eventually be utilized by some Maternal Feminists to argue for more freedoms and equality in marriage, it first called for the defense of social mothers' emotional expertise.

Female Duties in Forging National Subjectivities

As described in the previous chapters, in many ways, the regulation system established in Great Britain, on the Continent, and in the colonies, and the notions of gender it buttressed, embodied a reaffirmation of traditional values related to marriage, family life, class hierarchy, male superiority, sexuality, and sexual separation which had been eroded by the social and cultural disruptions associated with this age of industry, empire, and revolution. For instance, its construction of male virility lay on a naturalist representation of the male animal as in need of being able to periodically expulse his semen—a wholly irrepressible desire and inherent to his nature.[45] Thus, it was expected for male "nature" to occasionally predominate over his "civilization," making his virility both a biological and a social threat, and the guarantee of an outlet for these passions a necessary evil. In order to safeguard the honor of the respectable and culturally conformed "wife/mother," a morally irredeemable prostitute was necessary. W. E. H. Lecky's *History of European Morals from Augustus to Charlemagne* (1897) even argued that the maintenance of a pure, happy home laid on the existence of prostitutes:

> But for her, the unchallenged purity of countless happy homes would be polluted, and not a few who, in the pride of their untempted [sic] chastity, think of her with an indignant shudder, would have known the agony of remorse and of despair. On that one degraded and ignoble form are concentrated the passions that might have filled the world with shame. She remains, while creeds and civilisations [sic] rise and fall, the eternal priestess of humanity, blasted for the sins of the people.[46]

This role of the prostitute was even considered by the state to entail a vital form of female labor in the imperial context of empire-building and colonization, as prostitution served the needs of laborers, soldiers, and so on.[47]

The regulation system thus institutionalized not only this biased view of permissible male and condemnable female sexuality but also of two classes of women. One the one hand, there was the fallen woman—as Josephine Butler lamented[48]—ostracized from regular society, "doomed to death, hurled to despair" for the sole purpose of serving a man as he "sow[ed] his wild oats." On the other hand, the "protected and refined" woman, ignorant of the world and "kept strictly and almost forcibly guarded in domestic purity." Indignantly rejecting this double moral standard, Maternal Feminists insisted on the need to promote a single standard of morality—that is, of sexual restraint within and abstinence outside of marriage—which implicitly centered on male vice as the problem and the tempering influence of female docility as the solution. In fact, because women were seen as having little to no sex drive compared to men who were virile and competitive by nature, this contributed to the notion of spiritual womanhood by which women were believed to have a greater moral power and emotional capacity. This is indeed why Maternal Feminists pointed to their duty to forge national subjectivity, borrowing dominant discursive frames of nationalism, imperialism, and later eugenics to construct a uniquely feminine civilizing mission.

From the outset, the British repeal campaign was closely aligned with notions of moral purity and religious revival. Josephine Butler, while encouraging the same moralist and conservative values of self-restraint, put forth a vision for the moral regeneration of the nation which was intrinsically bound to women's public participation in society and politics.[49] As Chieko Ichikawa suggests, by recasting the maternal figure as militant moral guardian, Josephine Butler was "envisioning a new role for women as reformers and regulators of social norms" due to seeing "the male-dominated social system, based on the sexual double standard, as the root cause of gender oppression and 'national ruin.'"[50] The Contagious Diseases Acts were a clear example of what the horrifying consequences of this failure to do so: "If only women had been consulted!"[51] Josephine Butler bemoans in her most widely translated and circulated tract *Une voix dans le désert* ("A voice in the desert")[52] which was originally written in French and subsequently translated into other languages of the Continent including German, Italian, Spanish, Dutch, and Danish. Evoking the public's memory of the slave trade which had been engraved into the budding British and international humanitarian tradition, a frequent tactic—as seen with the Moral Liberals—was to draw an analogy between prostitution and slavery in the International Abolitionist Federation's texts. Both victims—slave and prostitute—were stripped of bodily and moral dignity by a state-supported system, effectively dragging the whole nation into sin and despair. Compared to men's indifference or ignorance, Maternal Feminists saw women as taking the side of "the weak, the oppressed" against this "masculine despotism."[53] Not only did this play to their "natural" strengths—women presumed to have a heightened sensitivity to injustice and inclination to care for the less fortunate— but the framing of the prostitute as female slave—the victim of forces beyond her control—meant that someone had to speak for her, a voice in the desert, as it were:

> [T]he hour of emancipation is near. What was lacking until now was the voice that gave the signal. The oppressed women had to find an organ in a person of their sex. It is she who comes to announce deliverance and salvation.[54]

In a letter to Monsieur Aimé Humbert in 1875 about the publication of this very tract, Josephine Butler defends sentimentality against material science in very gendered terms:

> I care little that men accuse me, as you say, of mere sentiment, and of carrying away my hearers by feeling rather than by facts and logic. [...] sentiment itself is after all a fact and a power when it expresses the deepest intuitions of the human soul. [...][55]

She goes on to explain that her cry of "one woman speaking for tens of thousands of women [...] a cry of pain, a cry for justice, and for a return to God's laws in place of these brutally impure laws invented and imposed by man [...] the cry of the revolted woman against her oppressor, and to her God"—while imperfect and "not the cry of a statistician or a medical expert"—is needed far more "than any reasoned-out argument."[56]

In line with French male feminist Ernest Legouvé's notion of "*l'égalité dans la différence*"[57] ("equality in difference") which characterized early European feminism,[58] Maternal Feminists instrumentalized the contemporary socially constructed and essentialized notions of gender to not only challenge the foundations of state-regulated prostitution but also to make a case for the recognition of their own legitimate and indispensable role in public affairs. This emancipatory strategy calling for a reform of the situation of women was rooted in women's differing nature. Women were born nurturers and educators by nature, biologically disposed "to foster, to cherish, to take the part of the weak, to train, to guide, to have a care for individuals, to discern the small seeds of a great future, to warm and cherish those seeds into fulness of life,"[59] as Josephine Butler wrote in *The Education and Employment of Women*. Such maternal features were further developed through a woman fulfilling her ultimate destiny by becoming a "mother" domestically or extra-domestically, resulting, in a scientific knowledge of social motherhood equal to that of other natural and male sciences. In *Le Féminisme*, Ghénia Avril de Sainte-Croix cites sociologist Jacques Lourbet, who argued that women's subservience in society had been at the great detriment to the evolution of the race:

> Woman has to grow, to magnify her role of mother, to raise it to abstraction because until now she has remained the mother too exclusively focused on the concrete. She must be interested in all that is human, be penetrated by great scientific laws, in order to rectify her instinctive genius, enrich her mind to balance with the treasures of her heart [...] And after having enlarged her consciousness and convinced herself that her essential and inescapable function is to be a mother, [...] she will create the science of education. She will no longer be just the mother around the cradle.[60]

The high esteem for women's natural maternal role was contrasted with the unnatural role of prostitute in which woman was twice the victim: firstly, of male vice and secondly, of the double moral standard. Indignantly, Maternal Feminists insisted on the need to promote a single standard of morality—that is, of sexual restraint within and abstinence outside of marriage—which implicitly centered on male vice as the problem and the tempering influence of female docility as the solution. In fact, with a few exceptions,[61] women were seen as having little to no sex drive compared to men who were virile and competitive by nature. This contributed to the notion of "spiritual womanhood"[62] by which women were believed to have a greater moral power and emotional capacity.

Maternal Feminists centered their arguments for a women's civilizing mission extending beyond the family home on the basis of these attributes, as Maria G. Grey's *Address to Women of All Classes* in January 1886 conveys:

> The power God has given us is power over the hearts of men—the power of the mother, the power of the wife, the power of our womanhood over manhood. [...] It is time that our womanhood should rouse itself to do that part of the work which only the woman's influence over home and society can do [...][63]

These words echo those of early British radical feminist figure Mary Wollstonecraft who in *A Vindication of the Rights of Woman* (1792)[64] called for women's emancipation based on their necessary contribution to societal advancement. Prescribed and circumscribed by their domestic identity, these female duties corresponded to "a gender-specific civic ideal."[65] By not allowing her the liberty to live out her choice of vocation—"'I serve,'" as Josephine Butler later wrote about women, "will always be one of her favourite [sic] mottos"[66]— man was acting in disservice to God, family, society, and nation. Maternal Feminists called attention to this by angrily pointing out the ineptitude of male legislators who ineffectively diagnosed the social problem of prostitution, as Josephine Butler quips through a telling analogy of prostitution with the slave trade. Due to their false focus on legislating "physical facts" not "moral agents," the "unchristian" and despotic system instituted by the Contagious Diseases Acts was just one example of the male authority's increasing encroachment on, and consequential moral contamination of,[67] intimate affairs, as Josephine Butler wrote in an address in 1871:

> Their heavy-handed legislation is applied now not only to matters of imperial interest, but to everything which most nearly concerns our conscience and feelings. It seems to me that we women shall soon have to fight for the last inch of ground left us; — not for our civil rights only, but for our hearths, our homes, our beds, our babies, our very persons. The crudeness of intellect of some of our young male legislators needs to be corrected by the wisdom of the thoughtful matrons of England.[68]

Such sentiments were echoed by Elizabeth Wolstenholme Elmy in *Women and Legislation* (1896): "Surely, sometimes it must occur even to the dullest of men, how unfitted they are to legislate or to administer in matters exclusively affecting women."[69] These combative and self-righteous words frame Maternal Feminists as warring mothers called to a sort of "holy rebellion,"[70] extending their maternal authority beyond the domestic sphere as a moral crusade to subvert the sinful male political authority to spur the moral regeneration of the British nation, as similarly seen in the antislavery and animal welfare movements.

Thus, overlapping with the moralizing discourse and attitude of self-righteousness found in the emotional community of Moral Liberals and mingling with contemporary notions of sexual difference, motherly compassion—born of motherly love—formed a cornerstone of the Maternal Feminist emotional repertoire. Of course, this emotional style depended on character work to designate the prostitute as the target of their compassion, a victim of undeserved suffering and a moral being worthy of love. Once again referring to the contemporary stigma and shame attached to the subjects of their protest—sex, sexuality, venereal disease—abolitionists required a special strategy for women to justify their public protest of the government's regulation of prostitution.

Emphasizing their maternal and spiritual qualities, Maternal Feminists were thus justified to act on the basis of their innate compassion and motherly love which made them more attuned to the suffering of others. This strategy—as well as representing yet another example of how fatherly care and masculine scientific rationality were set against motherly love and feminine sentimentality—was most clear in the controversy over vivisection. This was a contemporary protest movement and considered a common cause by many Maternal Feminists, thus it intertwined with abolitionist discourse both directly and indirectly. By the mid-1800s, major developments and advances in physiological and laboratory medicine on the Continent led to its domestic institutionalization and international diffusion. The British translation of the French system to regulate prostitution into the Contagious Diseases Acts is but one example of this spirit of internationalism and the circulation of knowledge and ideas. Thus, an increase in the practice of vivisection occurred in Great Britain, pioneered with the publication of the *Handbook for the Physiological Laboratory in Britain* in 1873. Admonishment from medical practitioners and the public alike at the institutionalization of such practices spurred a Royal Commission on the Practice of Subjecting Live Animals to Experiments for Scientific Purposes which led to the Cruelty to Animals Act of 1876 allowing experimentation to continue under certain restrictions.

Opposition to vivisection organized and formalized at this time with the founding of the Victoria Street Society—now the National Anti-Vivisection Society—in 1875 by Frances Power Cobbe. For most female campaigners, the appeal of the animal cause lay in it easily being construed as an extension of the domestic sphere—like other contemporary and related movements—of which the family pet had very much become a part. As abolitionist purity campaigner and anti-vivisector Dr. Elizabeth Blackwell argued: "The profound depth of maternity in women extends not only to the relations of marriage, but to all the weak or suffering wherever found."[71] Indeed, what could be more vulnerable than a voiceless, friendless, powerless animal? This hints at anthropomorphism—or a willingness to see animals as having moral and emotional faculties comparable to humans—which can be seen to various degrees amongst anti-vivisection discourse. For instance, some like Frances Power Cobbe tended to focus more on the demoralizing effect of vivisection on the vivisector and society as a whole. Either way, it was common to view the moral superiority of women as uniquely qualifying them as sort of whistleblowers, bringing science into account and insisting that humans had a moral duty to all those with the capacity to suffer.[72] Such essentialist constructions of an innocent, helpless, feminized victim became important signifiers for the patriarchal oppression of women which would resonate over the decades in feminist currents. The status quo was criticized through challenging the institutionalization of various dualisms (e.g., whore–virgin, science–nature, materiality–immateriality, barbarism–civilization, intuition–rationality, emotion–reason) which marginalized women and animals alike as unvalued "Others" to the male standard. Initially mobilizing against male-dominated medical science but eventually in all aspects of society, an immaterialist-theosophist feminist ethos arose which placed a high value on feminine qualities such as intuition or spiritual knowledge in contrast to masculine ones of intellect and rationality.

The effort to end this "cruel and dastardly wrong done to the weakest creatures—to speechless and most defenceless [sic] creatures,"[73] as campaigner Mrs. Charles Mallet described it, was taken up mostly by women, making it inherently tied to sexual politics despite female anti-vivisectors having divergent opinions on suffrage and women's liberation. By the early twentieth century, an ethos had pervaded the suffrage movement within which a sort of vegetarian feminism emerged, particularly amongst its more left-wing and socialist currents. A number of suffrage leaders followed meatless diets and encouraged others to do so, especially when imprisoned because, as the Vegetarian Society's journal from April 1907 attests, "the ordinary mixed prison food that is supplied is not of the most palatable kind [and] the food supplied to vegetarians is nicer in every way."[74] While the visible links between the early women's movement and vegetarianism may be explained in many ways—such as the influence of the contemporaneous food reform movement which claimed that switching to a meatless diet could remedy illnesses such as rheumatism or tuberculosis—Lea

Leneman has identified two dominant motivations.[75] The first is the desire for empowerment, as vegetarianism provided women with a means to create a new, more feminized, and more compassionate world, even when they were confined to the domestic sphere. By refusing to eat or even cook meat, women were engaging, as British suffragette, anti-vivisector, and theosophist Charlotte Despard explained, their "awakened instinct which feels the call of the sub-human, which says:—'I am the voice of the voiceless. Through me the dumb shall speak,'" as part of "a modern phenomenon that cannot be denied."[76] The second is that of compassion brought about by the animal's shared suffering. This is best demonstrated by Lady Constance Lytton of the Women's Social and Political Union, who recounted *In Prisons and Prisoners* an encounter she witnessed between a group of villagers and a sheep which had escaped *en route* to the slaughterhouse. "With growing fear and distress," she wrote, "the sheep ran about more clumsily and became a source of amusement to the onlookers, who laughed and jeered at it."[77] She continued:

> But on seeing this sheep it seemed to reveal to me for the first time the position of women throughout the world. I realised [sic] how often women are held in contempt as beings outside the pale of human dignity, excluded or confined, laughed at and insulted because of conditions in themselves for which they are not responsible, but which are due to fundamental injustices with regard to them, and to the mistakes of a civilisation [sic] in the shaping of which they have had no free share.[78]

As apparent here, some women activists made a symbolic connection between the vivisected animal and the female body as fellow victims of patriarchal oppression, abuse, and sexual violence. This was most blatant during the radical period of the suffrage movement decades later, when imprisoned suffragettes threatening hunger strikes were force-fed using a stomach tube and pump—technologies developed through animal experimentation in laboratory medicine.[79] Multiple suffragette testimonials of this torture were circulated and sensationalized, leading, for instance, to American feminist Djuna Barnes's own voluntary submission to force-feeding in order to share this experience—"the bravest of [her] sex"—which she described as a "brutal usurpation of [her] own functions."[80] The discursive framing of these lewd practices likened it to a sort of medical rape, which also appeared in abolitionist advocacy discourses, as seen in the Moral Liberal emotional community, to describe the gynecological examination of prostitutes.

There was thus a subversive feminist facet underpinning this tactic for shedding light on the male violence inflicted upon the female (or feminized animal) body given that rape was first set out in British law to protect male property rights,[81] to be evidenced by male testimony, and to be ruled upon by male arbitrators.[82] Unless the accuser was under the age of 10, rape was viewed as a necessarily physically violent act which beheld her to examination by a medical authority in order for him to provide evidence in the court of law. While opinions on rape—as on sexuality—varied amongst the medical community, proof of rape typically included signs of penetration (e.g., a broken hymen), but most significantly signs of dissent (e.g., bruises showing visible signs of resistance). Some like Scottish gynecologist Dr. Lawson Tait, who believed that the rape law needed to be amended to protect men, were of an even more extreme opinion:

> When a full-grown healthy woman makes a charge of a completely effected assault against one man, the charge ought to be presumed to be false, unless the woman was first stupefied by drugs. I am perfectly satisfied that no man can effect a felonious purpose on a woman in possession of her senses without her consent. Assault her he may, but effect entrance he cannot [...][83]

Due to this difficulty in proving rape, only extremely violent and repugnant rapes ever came to trial, for instance, those involving young girls or pregnant women, or the transmission of venereal disease.[84] In the late nineteenth century, with essentialized notions of male aggressivity and female passivity gaining scientific credence and the rise of "civilizing" values of self-restraint and compassion towards the weak, there was a shift towards seeing rape as a crime of interpersonal violence; however, women's lack of sovereignty over their own bodies was maintained by exempting martial rape in law—left unremedied in Great Britain until 1991. Thus, in many ways, the use of medical rape could be construed as women's revendication and appropriation of rape as a male violence against a female body testified to by a female mouthpiece. For instance, as one prostitute was quoted by Josephine Butler as saying:

> It is men, men, men, from the first to the last that we have to do with! To please a man I did wrong at first, then I was flung about from man to man, then men police lay hands on us—by men we are examined, handled, doctored and messed on with. In the hospital it is a man again who makes prayers and reads the Bible for us. We are had up before Magistrates who are men, and we never get out of the hands of men till we die![85]

Moral Liberals and Maternal Feminists overlap in their moral and affective consideration of the prostitute-victim, especially when considered from the perspective of the advocacy tool of equating internal examination for venereal disease by police doctors to medical rape. Josephine Butler's early campaign discourses especially demonstrate these links, as they focused on the violation of specifically women's rights and employed a rhetoric which opposed the patriarchal subordination of women in society. In the famous manifesto *The Ladies' Appeal and Protest* published in the *Daily News* in 1870 and signed by 124 women, she and others attacked the Contagious Diseases Acts as being immoral, unconstitutional, and unjust by forcing degrading internal medical exams upon "the sex who are the victims of a vice, and [leaving] unpunished the sex who are the main cause."[86] Like many other female repeal campaigners against the Contagious Diseases Acts, she was involved in various early feminist causes such as suffrage, property rights for married women, and access to higher education,[87] spurred by a maternal feminism which was deeply infused with evangelical and Victorian gender values. Thus, while her crusade against the Contagious Diseases Acts falls under the broader social purity movement which saw mostly female activists targeting vices such as prostitution, alcohol, birth contraception, and pornography from the 1860s, it also represents a milestone in early Victorian, and even European, feminism. Not only did repeal campaigners claim sisterhood with these socially stigmatized and oppressed women, but they also audaciously challenged the long-established patriarchal notions of sexual difference, namely the double moral standard by which the sexuality of men was excused and that of women was condemned.

Maternal Feminists' civilizing mission was also executed through philanthropic engagement and social activism locally and abroad, with a focus on their fellow mothers amongst the lower classes and colonies whom they often called sisters. In her memoirs, Josephine explains how she had been approached by a group of medical men to fight the Contagious Diseases Acts, recognizing

> that the persons most insulted by the Napoleonic system with which our legislators of that day had become enamoured [sic], being women, these women must find representatives of their own sex to protest against and to claim a practical repentance from the Parliament and the Government which had flung this insult in their face.[88]

While such terminology speaks to a feeling of feminist comradery, the extent to which Maternal Feminists saw their sisters as equals is rendered debatable by the power relations inherent within the former framing the latter as victims whom they had to speak out for on their behalf. Even Josephine Butler—although arguably for strategic purposes—equated Indian women to the vivisectors' pitiful and agency-deprived animal subjects:

> They are indeed between the upper and nether millstone, helpless, voiceless, hopeless. Their helplessness appeals to the heart, somewhat in the same way in which the helplessness and suffering of a dumb animal does, under the knife of the vivisector.[89]

Likewise, this use of melodramatic and sentimental registers is exemplified by this story from French nonconformist and Moral Liberal Émilie de Morsier on her visit to a brothel in Paris during which she pretended to not speak French:

> [...] when, upon leaving, I approach these poor wretches, and, seized with immense pity, I take their hands while saying some affectionate words which were translated, they looked at me with an expression of astonishment, gratitude and sadness that I will never forget. It was as if the soul of the woman, attracted by sympathy, sought to free herself for a moment from this foul environment, and cried to me: 'I live again!'"[90]

She goes on to explain that "women of heart"[91]—naming Josephine Butler, Elizabeth Fry, and Florence Nightingale—alone have this ability to find "moral possibilities"[92] amongst such beings, making a case for women's place in the public sphere, especially given that the laboratory animal and the working-class prostitute were constructed in terms of their weakness, their need, and their lack of moral worth.

Alongside this instrumentalization and thus reinforcement of essentialized understandings of sex and gender, "recourse to melodrama," as Judith Walkowitz has pointed out, was "a contradictory political strategy for feminists."[93] It offered women the unique role of passive victim of a seemingly omnipotent male offender, thereby decontextualizing and homogenizing accounts of violence, as well as its actors, to fit and better circulate within the existing economy of sensationalized—and sexualized—violence. The opportunities for these women to negotiate their own subordination in social protest often hinged on the continued subordination of a female Other. As such, Maternal Feminists tended to reproduce and thus strengthen existing class or racial inequalities while positioning themselves as uniquely qualified as custodians of their infantilized sisters. These sisters faced a moral pressure to receive this compassionate assistance, this forced gift of elevation in moral dignity and protection. Moreover, the connection between humanitarianism and imperialism especially demonstrates how notions of empire offered opportunities for Maternal Feminists to extend their authority in the interest not only of morally elevating the nation but also the empire. Thus, this self-serving interest in promoting female duties to national subjectivities increasingly took the shape of Great Britain's status among nations with the rise of nationalism in imperial culture of the twentieth century.[94]

This nationalist discourse became progressively a racialized one with the rise of Darwin-inspired eugenics and the expansion of the state into private affairs with the amalgamation of disease with poverty, immorality, crime, and prostitution. Many Maternal Feminists found opportunities for increased marital and reproductive rights through a kind of social hygiene feminism which championed nuanced understandings of motherhood and marriage as sacred institutions through the prism of hereditary. In fact, looking at contemporary feminist fiction, Angelique Richardson shows how "eugenic love"[95] was often portrayed by its female advocates as an expression of old-fashioned maternal self-sacrifice, the mother's idealized devotion to her children extrapolated to the level of nation and empire as a new feminine civilizing mission. Yet it was also essential for men to change their behavior, something that Josephine Butler—and to a certain extent Purity Crusaders, albeit mostly through force and under threat of punishment—had emphasized in challenging the common assumptions surrounding male sexuality as uncontrollable.

Feminist Anger and the Degenerative Threat of Male Sexuality

An important evolution in the emotional repertoire of Maternal Feminists was the gradual transformation of feelings of righteous indignation—increasingly claimed as gender-specific in women repeal campaigners' politicization of their emotional expertise and merging with their more personal feelings of frustration and resentment—into feminist anger. In other words, while women-led campaigns on behalf of a suffering Other—prostitute or animal— were exercising emotional practices of righteous anger and feminine solidarity, groundwork was being laid for publicly addressing their own suffering and oppression. The height of this can be seen in the radicalized branch of the women's suffrage movement represented by the campaigns of the Women's Social and Political Union between 1910 and 1914. In *The Strange Death of Liberal England*, near-contemporary historian George Dangerfield speaks about this rise of "Harpies" to avenge "the unlived female life"[96] born of the Victorian cult of domesticity. The Women's Rebellion, he criticized, was "achieved in disorder, arrogance, and outrage. It was melodramatic, it was hysterical, it was in a hurry."[97] While demonstrating a strong disapprobation of the suffragettes' shows of feminist anger—such as the argument of the broken windowpane—which he reductively interpreted as women trying to assert their masculinity, he did acknowledge that "the disconcerting vehemence" arose from "the depths of a female soul" reacting to "a collection of neglected instincts, hopes, hatreds, and desires."[98]

In fact, just how directly feminists' angry feelings were aimed at men and patriarchal institutions varied, along with the method. For instance, a sort of intellectualized feminist anger—and one which Virginia Woolf would famously trace among women writers in *A Room of One's Own* (1929) while thinking back "through our mothers"—can be seen in Anna Pappritz's satirical essay "Herrenmoral." Written in 1903, it describes male morality as driving the creation of a mass brothel outside of Berlin in which all women are divided between those who run it and those who sexually service men, who come and go without any responsibility to them nor to the children they father (a criticism of contemporary German Civil Code which effectively did that).[99]

The evolution of feminist anger is most noticeable (and direct) within the emotional culture of the new generation of Maternal Feminists who benefited from the example of female leadership and militancy provided by the early repeal campaign—for instance, Josephine Butler's portrait was regularly sold at women's suffrage meetings as a pioneering feminist icon[100]—as well as the gender-based solidarity it aroused and politicized. For some, the abolitionist crusade represented their first venture in feminist protest politics, such as influential New Woman feminist Sarah Grand who was even expelled from school as a teenager for organizing resistance against the Contagious Diseases Acts in England. In fact, at the turn of the twentieth century, local campaigns in Germany with Anna Pappritz and Katharina Scheven and in France with Ghénia Avril de Sainte-Croix took up Josephine Butler's mantle by targeting the state's regulation of prostitution as a violation of women's civil liberties and fighting against repressive legislation. Yet this new generation faced operating in increasingly globalized and institutionalized contexts as a result of the changing dynamics of both their political cause—the activities of prostitution and its regulation evolving alongside aggressive new imperialist projects—and political spaces. As such, a great variety of new attitudes and ideas strove to find expression in this early phase of feminism, making a single view on a given matter like prostitution difficult to ascribe.[101] Nonetheless, pervasive feelings of frustration and resentment were apparent among Maternal Feminists in response to the overall persistence of female subjugation in custom and in law. Many being social mothers engaged in charitable works to improve the lot of the working class, they experienced first-hand the police oppression which mounted in response to the moral panic on white slavery, as well as to the initiatives of the beforementioned Purity Crusaders.

For instance, Olive Schreiner, a figure of New Woman fiction, in the Men and Women's Club, and in socialist feminism, worked closely with prostitutes in London and at home in South Africa whom she saw as sisters whose lot was a larger symptom of women's lack of economic independence. As she wrote in one of her letters to prominent eugenicist Karl Pearson:

> Sometimes when I have been walking in Gray's Inn Road and seen one of those terrible old women that are so common there, the sense of agonised [sic] oneness with her that I have felt, that she was myself only under different circumstances, has stricken me almost mad.[102]

Her strong convictions even saw her supporting William T. Stead's efforts to increase the age of sexual consent in Great Britain which paradoxically contributed to the increased policing of women which she experienced herself on multiple occasions. She was in fact so angered by a particular encounter when a policeman tried to take her prison while she was walking with a male friend late at night that she wrote about it to the *Daily News* and the *Standard*.[103] Her words admonishing the crude behavior of the policeman and the vulnerability of women inspired William T. Stead to publish correspondence on the subject of these "Male Pests" frightening and angering women in the *Pall Mall Gazette*.[104]

This public demonstration of feminist anger—this self-righteous, gendered outrage emerging from a perceived injustice done to women as a monolithic whole, as a single social class, and directed at patriarchal agents and institutions— is in many ways an outgrowth of the righteous indignation seen amongst the Moral Liberals. Indeed, the liberal ethos underpinned early feminism and women-led campaigns, even as far back as the beforementioned feminist theorist Mary Wollstonecraft.[105] It is also notable that the father of liberalism John Stuart Mill argued in favor of repealing the Contagious Diseases Acts and penned an essay on the moral standing of animals: both campaigns helping to initiate the British suffrage movement.[106] He thereby proffered British feminism a more unequivocal vision of sexual equality by weighing in on the woman question by calling for the establishment of "a system of perfect equality, admitting no power and privilege on the one side, nor disability on the other."[107] His *The Subjection of Women* greatly inspired by his wife Harriet, made strides in the development of a liberal form of feminism in Great Britain by challenging the patriarchy in advocating for the end of "legal subordination of one sex to another"— especially with contemporary marriage laws making wives sexual slaves to their husbands—on the basis of it being "wrong in itself, and now one of the chief hindrances to human improvement."[108]

Josephine Butler's advocacy for women's rights was most definitely centered on decidedly liberal feminist grounds. It is important to remember that she was already in her 40s when started the repeal campaign and arguably had more in common with the previous generation of women antislavery activists than with the new batch of abolitionists emerging at the turn of the century. She was nonetheless daring in her challenge to the sexual status quo which found her directly at odds with conventional notions of female propriety by tackling subjects about which most were too embarrassed to speak. This indeed may explain why the form of anger fostered and nourished in her campaign to repeal the British Contagious Diseases Acts, while self-righteous, moralizing, and religiously inspired (or Moral Liberal), was also unapologetically gendered. Although she, as a bourgeoise, was not in any way threatened by the Contagious Diseases Acts, she was insulted on behalf of all women, as she said in an address to a French audience:

> The degradation for these poor unhappy women is not degradation for them alone; it is a blow to the dignity of every virtuous woman too, it is dishonour [sic] done to me, it is the shaming of every woman in every country of the world. I say it again, and I insist upon it; there is not a pure woman living who does not feel in her heart that the revolting examination which is imposed upon helpless women for the protection of immoral men is insult and violation of her own person.[109]

Here, her claim is that *all* women, irrespective of nationality, moral standing, class, or race, are suffering the same injustice and that men are to blame. Indeed, her desire to end the widespread inequalities existing between the sexes saw her targeting other issues beyond that of prostitution, such as women's unequal access to education and employment opportunities, as well as the law of coverture. Before the repeal campaign, she campaigned Elizabeth Wolstenholme to reform the latter, questioning the right of a married man to the property of his wife upon their marriage and effectively bringing the institution of marriage into the public eye. Other contemporary debates, such as on marital violence surrounding the Offenses Against the Person Act of 1828,[110] strengthened this trend of increasingly challenging the presumed privacy of domestic life, thereby opening it up to scrutiny and providing a target for newly budding manifestations of feminist anger.

For some members of the newer generation of Maternal Feminists, marriage—if not between two equals—thereby came to be understood as just another form of prostitution, or as Mona Caird qualified it in one of her hugely impactful essays, "the greatest evils of modern society had their origin, thousands of years ago, in the dominant abuse of patriarchal life: the custom of woman-purchase."[111] British suffragette and co-founder of the Women's Social and Political Union Christabel Pankhurst likewise argued in *The Great Scourge* (1913) that women should "be warned of the fact that marriage is intensely dangerous, until such time as men's moral standards are completely changed and they become as chaste and clean-living as women."[112] Here, not only are women put forward as the standard for behavior that men should aim to achieve, but venereal disease also emerges as a metaphor for male oppression[113] and a lure for feminist anger. New Women are thus going a step further in the Maternal Feminist call for women to have a place in public life and a role in matters of the body by voicing their frustrations and by placing blame upon the patriarchy. Many of these feminist attitudes and ideas, as Norma Clarke[114] has argued in her analysis of New Women fiction, were dramatized in order to address issues ranging from the stifling narrowness of domestic life to the gap existing between the reality and ideal of marriage. These novels also saw widespread commercial success—for instance, with Sarah Grand's *The Heavenly Twins* (1893) even making the *Overall Best Sellers in the United States* list—which speaks to a popular interest in these intrinsically gendered themes. Most importantly, as Norma Clarke writes, "[t]hrough the legitimate and socially sanctioned moral outrage at venereal disease, women readers were given permission to experience their wide anger at men."[115]

In fact, the turn of the century found the abolitionists with new allies amongst the medical community once the medical surveillance of the French system had proved incapable of managing the spread of venereal disease. Studies revealed the high and widespread prevalence of sexually transmitted diseases, the diversity of their manifestations and infection rates, as well as their devastating transmissible effects, amplifying existing anxieties over the health and sexual behaviors of the nation. This rapprochement was set in motion on the organizational level by two international conferences on the Prophylaxis of Syphilis and of Venereal Diseases held in Brussels in 1899 and 1902, at which abolitionists like Federation president Hendrik Pierson and Hanna Bieber-Böhm were in attendance.[116] Governmental and non-governmental actors mobilized nationally and internationally to set up meetings, congresses, and journals, as well as societies and organizations such as French venerologist and student of Philippe Ricord, Albert Fournier's *Société française de prophylaxie sanitaire et morale* created in 1901 to combat this "true social calamity."[117] Thus, in contrast to the start of the movement, many medical professionals—such as the French social hygienist Louis Fiaux—found themselves aligned with different abolitionist positions.

The generalized anxiety surrounding degeneration and the great scourge of venereal disease created an opportunity for exchange between the new generation of Maternal Feminist abolitionists and social hygiene at the turn of the century, resulting in various degrees of rapprochement and tension. A clear example of this comes from the United States during the Progressive era, when male and female medical professionals and moral reformers joined forces in the American Social Hygiene Association, targeting prostitution and venereal disease. In her study of the social hygiene movement and prostitution in the United States, Kristin Luker explains that prostitution was not conceptualized the same way as in Europe. The nation's development created a situation in which the regulation of "irregular" sexuality occurred locally; the bureaucratic structures to enforce any legislation to regulate prostitution were lacking in the eighteenth and even nineteenth centuries.[118] In Europe, many abolitionists adopted a hostile stance towards venereal disease—channeling the metaphor for feminist anger budding among Maternal Feminists—which saw them engaging with social hygiene's degenerative anxieties. Taking the example of Germany, as Julia Roos[119] has shown, the International Abolitionist Federation's German section leaders Anna Pappritz and Katharina Scheven were active participants in the discussion of anti-venereal disease legislation. Along with many others from the local women's movement, they supported measures to de-stigmatize venereal disease and to offer sufferers better treatment strategies, but also those allowing for compulsory hospitalization and—although more hesitant prior to the First World War—criminalizing infection. As Anna Pappritz expressed in 1916, despite being liberally oriented, she saw this as legitimate "in the face of the great dangers that threaten our people due to venereal contamination."[120] By 1919, the German section was calling for the end of regulationism,[121] but also the compulsory registration and treatment of all venereal disease sufferers—both men and women.[122]

However, in Great Britain, a divide established itself between the "moral" prophylaxis of Josephine Butler's Ladies' National Association—renamed the Association for Moral and Social Hygiene in 1912—and the "social" prophylaxis of the British Social Hygiene Council (formerly the National Council for Combatting Venereal Disease). For instance, the former disagreed with the provision of prophylactic packets including a tube of calomel ointment for syphilis, potassium permanganate solution or tablets for gonorrhea, and cotton swabs for their application to military men, believing it to encourage illicit sexual behavior, whereas the latter regarded it as a modern scientific solution.[123]

The two organizations found themselves in frequent rivalry and the Association for Moral and Social Hygiene had to defend its autonomy by reinforcing the differences in approach. For instance, reacting to her repeated attempts to combine the two organizations in their investigative work on trafficking in India for the League of Nations, one Association for Moral and Social Hygiene member described British Social Hygiene Council and Bureau member Sybil Neville-Rolfe as "seem[ing] to have the feminine equivalent of the Hitler or Mussolini mind in her desire for domination."[124] Such rivalries had never been uncommon, but the new abolitionist generation of Maternal Feminists also found itself operating in new codified spaces for civil society actors who were increasingly required to professionalize in order to have their ownership of an issue recognized by the public, by policymakers, by peers, as a vital element to their success. That is to say, a group's ownership of a social problem lies in its capacity to make its version of reality—i.e., the framing of the problem from its cause to its solution—the only acceptable one.[125]

The shift in medical opinion from looking at the male sex drive as an inevitability and prostitution as necessary to seeing illicit sex as presenting a serious threat to public health and the future of the race had important effects. Firstly, it made both sexual behavior and reproduction objects for scientific rationalization and improvement in the spirit of scientism. This contributed to the establishment of human sciences like psychiatry, sexology, criminal anthropology, theopsy, eugenics, and moreover, promoted the medicalization and pathologizing of deviant sexuality. Secondly, this shift made awareness about venereal disease vital for both sexes in the interest of prevention and early diagnosis, ending "the conspiracy of silence"[126]—as British doctor Sir Malcolm Morris called it in his letter to *The Lancet* in 1913—surrounding such taboo subjects. The frustration felt by medical professionals with the public's ignorance concerning the means of venereal disease infection is tangible in Albert Fournier's *Ligue contre la syphilis* created in 1904. He incredulously gives examples of mothers being infected by the kisses of their sons, wetnurses being infected by congenitally syphilitic infants, and so on:

> One day, one of my clients boasted to me about her baby's wetnurse, 'Imagine,' she told me, 'that she has so much milk, but so much milk, that it often happens to her at the Tuileries, where we go every afternoon, to give the breast to two or three infants that we meet there to calm them.' And as I scolded her for this perilous imprudence, telling her that it was in this way that her nurse was at risk of being infected with syphilis, she replied with the utmost candor: 'Syphilis? But what is syphilis?'[127]

Thirdly, the necessity of sharing medical knowledge of disease to the broader public shaped a masculine scientific and rational language for addressing sexuality and other delicate matters. By becoming a medical subject, sexuality was scientifically mystified by the male elite who established their own dominant expert discourse. This also included deviant forms of sexuality such as pedophilia, which somewhat eroded the notion of personal responsibility for moral conduct. However, this also created a more open sexological discourse[128] which proved especially useful to Maternal Feminists who sought to legitimize their positions as authorities on "womanly" topics, such as female sexuality, marriage, discrimination against illegitimate children and their mothers, or birth contraception. Take, for instance, the widespread popularity and influence of Maternal Feminist Marie Stopes, author of *Married Love* (1918) and *Radiant Motherhood* (1920), as well as founder of the United Kingdom's first instructional clinic for contraception in 1921.

Institutionalizing Feminine Emotional Knowledge

As the rise of eugenics applied scientific discourses to society in ways that reinforced old social and epistemic hierarchies, it also helped create new ones which paradoxically held emancipatory potential for women. For instance, one might argue that the exceptionally feminine propensity for moral purity would warrant women having a central role alongside scientists in transforming the degenerated present into a healthy future. Such arguments were employed to various degrees by Maternal Feminists, especially once science was applied to understandings of reproduction and motherhood which made both an act of public service. For instance, for New Women authors Olive Schreiner and Sarah Grand, low intellect and a propensity towards vice were inherited and thus female financial independence and social equality were paramount to future generations. As Sarah Grand writes in her novel *The Beth Book*:

> Nature decrees the survival of the fittest [...] By the reproduction of the unfit, the strength, the beauty, the morality of the race is undermined, and with them its best chances of happiness.[129]

A "gendered citizenship"[130] was thereby established by Maternal Feminists around responsible motherhood which conferred women with "nobility, prestige, and power" at a time when anxieties over national efficiency and empire were reigning; as Ellice Hopkins incited in her 1886 tract *The Present*

Moral Crisis: An Appeal to Women: "to you, as to woman of old, it is given to save your own nation."[131]

Some Maternal Feminists even stepped into the male-dominated world of science. Women like Drs. Anna Kingsford, Elizabeth Blackwell, and Frances Hoggan aimed to assert the worth but also the necessity of immateriality—notably feminine morality and sentimentality—in overly materialistic science. Yet as Anne Scott has rightly argued in her study of what she calls "purity feminism," the cooption of a discourse of moral purity apparent in this and other women-led movements like abolitionism was as perilous as it was ambiguous for it relied "on intensifying the reason/nature dualism, with an image of the white, English, bourgeois woman standing as bulwark between civilised [sic] man and the dark forces of corporeality."[132]

In fact, the feminist relationship to Darwinism took various forms, especially as eugenics gained credibility. Yet, in contrast to feminism's liberal roots in Mary Wollstonecraft or John Stuart Mill, these perspectives found themselves operating within the same discursive frames of modern science, its reductivism and essentialization of gender proving predominant. For instance, Antoinette Brown Blackwell, co-founder of the American Woman Suffrage Association, challenged in *The Sexes Throughout Nature* the use of the male sex as the idea against which all others were measured; however, she still distinguished between the "greater parental sagacity and affection" of the female mind and the "superior warlike and passional instincts" of the man.[133] Others proved quite radical, like Clémence Royer who as the French translator of Charles Darwin's work took a number of liberties to attack the clergy and the institution of marriage. Adopting a more Lamarckian perspective, she also put forward a darkly racist argument for colonialism and even the extermination of inferior races, maladapted to progress.[134]

Looking closer at the Darwinian theory of evolution, note that it lay on two important mechanisms: that of natural selection by which the fittest of the species survived to pass on their acquired traits to their offspring, and that of sexual selection—that is, the competition between males for females and the mate choice of females. Despite the latter providing for a certain amount of female agency, Darwinian discourses were underpinned by gendered power relations of male force and female inferiority. Demonstrating "greater tenderness and less selfishness,"[135] woman is depicted as passive, sensitive, and altruistic. As he "delights in competition,"[136] man, on the other hand, is inherently aggressive and competitive, struggling to exist and provide for his family in an amoral world. Thus, for Charles Darwin, weighing in on the woman question, it was an inevitable result of the evolutionary process that "man has ultimately become superior to woman"[137] chiefly in terms of "the intellectual powers."[138] While these disparaging remarks as to women's lesser mental capacities and impaired reasoning justified their exclusion from public life, they also emphasized exclusively female capacities which made them innately suited for the domestic sphere. Darwinist evolutionary biologist George John Romanes, for instance, argued that while woman "has been a loser in the intellectual race as regards acquisition, origination, and judgment,"[139] she did have a superior evolution of the "sense-organs."[140] Alongside allowing for a "supremacy of emotion"[141] which may unfortunately manifest itself as hysteria, this also granted woman what he called "the nimbleness of mother-wit"[142] and greater faculties of intuition.

By the early twentieth century, the recognition of feminine emotional knowledge as expertise in philanthropy and social welfare was expanded by more women being admitted into medical schools and by the abovementioned influence of this new generation of Maternal Feminists. This aided in the inclusion of gendered expertise in governmental deliberations. For instance, the British Royal Commission on Venereal Disease held from 1913 to 1916 included physician and gynecologist Dame Mary Scharlieb in their ranks and auditioned Dr. Helen Wilson, honorary Association for Moral and Social Hygiene General Secretary, who was able to weigh in on issues such as compulsory notifications of infection, venereal-diseased patients' care, the social stigma of venereal disease, and the education of hygiene to the public.[143] This acceptance of gendered expertise was furthered in the international domain by the establishment of the League of Nations which, inscribed with the notion of international sovereignty, gave voluntary associations political voice and authority equal to nations. It thus quickly became an important tool for women's organizations through which they could affect change. Contemporary notions of gender prevailing, the League proved especially favorable to women's participation in social problems, of which there were many in the wake of the First World War.

British social reformer and nurse Dame Rachel Crowdy was appointed Chief of the League's Social Section until 1931 and here, unlike other permanent advisory committees, women usually enjoyed equal representation.[144] The Social Section tackled various issues such as child welfare, but the trafficking of women and children quickly developed into one of its central concerns due to the lobbying efforts of actors like the International Bureau, the International Abolitionist Federation, the International Council of Women, and the Association for Moral and Social Hygiene. It was put in charge of the Advisory Committee on the Traffic in Women and Children established in 1921[145] which set to investigating prostitution and its migratory networks, culminating in a large-scale multicontinental study—groundbreaking for its time[146]—headed by Dr. William F. Snow from the American Social Hygiene Association. Subsequent reports published in 1927 and 1932, demonstrated the existence of traffic in women and children, as well as its direct causal link to state-regulated prostitution—a cornerstone of abolitionism since 1885.

Dame Rachel Crowdy's leadership of the Social Section helped advance the abolitionist cause in the Advisory Committee's deliberations between 1921 and 1930, but also in its diverse, sometimes conflictual, facets through her own close relationship to the Association for Moral and Social Hygiene, as well as her appointments of French women's rights activist Ghénia Avril de Sainte-Croix, known for her oratory prowess, and Annie Baker, member of the National Vigilance Association and the International Bureau.[147] Despite demonstrating the divides in abolitionism between those trying to eradicate prostitution by controlling women (Purity Crusaders) and those who sought to abolish it and any other laws targeting prostitutes (Moral Liberals), this congregation of abolitionist supporters—mostly women—importantly set a foundation for future feminist civil society groups working on the international level, as well as points to certain evolutions in abolitionist positionings to governmental powers. For instance, British suffragette Alison Neilans, head of the Association for Moral and Social Hygiene, echoes many of the early discourses on the double moral standard seen in its predecessor, the Ladies' National Association, and seems to have remained true to Josephine Butler's Moral Liberal ideals which made the safeguarding of prostitutes' rights paramount. For instance, in 1922, Alison Neilans led an assault on the solicitation laws in force in England on a similar basis, noting that while prostitutes were subject to legal intervention, they benefited from no legal safeguards. As she writes:

> The prostitute is the scapegoat for everyone's sins, and few people care whether she is justly treated or not. Good people have spent thousands of points in efforts to reform her; poets have written about her; essayists and orators have made her the subject of some of their most striking rhetoric; perhaps no class of people have been abused, persecuted, hated, or, alternatively, sentimentalized over as prostitutes have been, but one thing they have never had yet, and that is simple legal justice. Ought we not to secure legal justice for the "common prostitute" before we set out to reform her?[148]

Her emphasis on "legal justice" over "reform" is important given the dominant views of women in prostitution as being deviant or degenerate. Such arguments were used to qualify governmental or societal interference as rightful because it prevents harm to others or because an individual is incapable of wielding self-regarding action because of immorality or incompetency. In this light, Josephine Butler's continued influence can be seen, given her own insistence on the moral redeemability[149] of the prostitute as not only referring to her worthiness of compassion but also her worthiness of civil liberties. Alison Neilans' position did not represent the majority, however, as she argued for a framing of the prostitute not as a moral, philanthropic, literary, or medical problem, but instead as an individual defined deviant, controlled, and wronged by the justice system. On the other hand, she wished to end prostitution by changing public opinion through moral leadership and education with the help of state-run medical authorities.[150] This reflects certain influences of imperialist humanitarianism and social hygienism, but also a growing faith in state authorities instead of distrust. She also actively campaigned for the inclusion of women in the police force, not only to advance female employment in public professions but also to improve the treatment of prostitutes.

However, over time, staunch resistance from supporters of regulated prostitution (namely, the French), rising nationalism, and internal rifts among abolitionists over issues such as the forced expulsion of foreign prostitutes and the extension of the Convention of 1921 that made it illegal to transport minor girls for immoral purposes to women over the age of 21 diminished the Advisory Committee's effectiveness. As Alison Neilans bemoaned this shift in concerns in 1930:

> The Anti-Traffic in Women movement is less and less inclined to touch the Regulation system and more and more disposed to protect women as though they were children, with the net result that if they had their way it would be difficult for women under 21 to move about Europe at all.[151]

This shift was, as already discussed in the previous chapter on Purity Crusaders and the passing of the British anti-trafficking law of 1912, fueled by xenophobic and eugenic fears and revulsion at the idea of foreigners corrupting the nation and pure white womanhood which dominated the interwar period. By the time the League's Advisory Committee was re-structured in 1936 to grant governments more control, the feminist abolitionist influence had essentially ended, but not before inspiring a younger generation to continue aspiring for women's rights in other areas and arenas.[152]

4

Global Doldrums and National Vestiges (1940s–1960s)

As described at the end of the previous chapter, the international abolitionist movement—especially its female component—saw a surge and then a loss of its influence within the League of Nations during the interwar era. The League, as a transnational institution for circulating norms and advice, allowed in an unprecedented way for the populations within the sovereign states themselves to be targeted as objects of international discourse and regulation.[1] Granted, the effectiveness of the League's governance in this and other domains was limited; however, its construction of trafficking and prostitution as social problems in these reports and conventions was translated into those of the United Nations, most demonstrably in the Convention for the Suppression of the Traffic in Persons and of the Exploitation of the Prostitution of Others passed by the General Assembly in 1949. Although it brought the issue of trafficking, the protection of the vulnerable trafficking victim, and the criminalization of third-party profiteers under its purview, this resolution was slow to be ratified by sovereign states—such as France, which only did so in 1960—if ratified at all.

The participation of women's organizations in transnational civil society having already been established during the interwar period, their inclusion in the activities of the newly formed United Nations was undisputed. Some international abolitionist actors such as the International Abolitionist Federation and the International Bureau continued to participate in different congresses, reports, and conventions with the United Nations, which called upon them as experts. Yet, as the United Nations' *Study on Traffic in Persons and Prostitution* published in 1959 demonstrates, the rising sexual promiscuity of states' general populations overtook the view of the prostitute as spreader of venereal disease and further undercut the abolitionist cause.[2] As psychological discourses began to supersede hygienic ones on the matter of prostitution, authorities tended to qualify it as more of a domestic matter for the budding welfare sector and social services. Prostitution also did not resonate much as an issue within the contemporary international women's movement which deflated once nations granted women voting rights and socioeconomic transformations—namely, the rise of the service sector—which were conducive to female employment.

Because of this fragmentation of the abolitionist cause at this phase of the movement's history spanning from the postwar period to the 1960s, this chapter looks at the prevailing attitudes and emotional patterns in Western countries when abolitionism fell silent instead of focusing on a single emotional community. This helps to better understand the settings in which the international abolitionist movement waned and then came back to life in the 1970s. This chapter also touches on where the embers of abolitionism continued to burn through the example of France, where it transformed to adapt to local attitudes and preoccupations. Indeed, the aftermath of war impacted the world's concerns and forever changed many of its ways of understanding society—from the very historical and cultural foundations upon which collective identity was based, to the nature and role of the individual therein, as well as the legitimate means and moral duties of societal governance.

The Psychological Turn

The widespread psychological turn in the 1950s was a major driver of many of these changes, influencing and intertwining with institutions of domestic life, public welfare, education, religion, legislature, and even capitalism. The advent of sciences of the mind occurred from the turn of the century to the interwar period, developing somewhat differently in the United States and across Europe due to different local religious and scientific traditions. Yet, their similar objectives and study subjects—for instance, deviance and feeble-mindedness which later yielded to war-mobilizing efforts—resulted in some contact and exchange. This flow of knowledge escalated with proponents of psychoanalysis from the Nazi Germany and Eastern Europe finding refuge in Great Britain and the United States with the outbreak of the Second World War.

After the war, efforts in the reconstruction of Europe and the treatment of those touched by the devastations of war led to a surge in government funding, interdisciplinary collaboration and especially with the social sciences, and expanded research opportunities for the sciences of the mind and society.[3] However, in the immediate postwar era, psychiatry and anthropology in particular became fundamental tools for ensuring international harmony, egalitarianism, compassion, and world peace as scientists aimed at re-defining the prevailing understandings of human diversity and conceptualizations of race.[4] For instance, the United Nations Educational, Scientific and Cultural Organization (UNESCO), established in 1945 to "embody a genuine culture of peace,"[5] issued a "Statement on Race" in 1950 which dismissed any scientific basis or justification for racial bias, challenging not only Nazi racist discourse but also segregation policies in force in the United States. Of course, while such tendencies of scientific, medical, and political discourses towards universalism sought to dismantle hegemonic notions of white Western superiority developed during imperialism and colonialism, these theories and paradigms were difficult to shake off as intellectual frameworks continued to use the same norms of modernity and development, perpetuating the stadial notion of civilization or individual development.[6]

The broader effects of the psychological turn on society and the conceptualization of individual within it were numerous once Freudian ideas entered public consciousness in the 1950s. This established a therapeutic ethos that heightened sensibility while placing a greater emphasis on notions of self-esteem and personal identity, as well as the living of an authentic emotional life. Implying new ways of thinking about the self, its past, its relations to others, and its potentialities, this ethos had come to even define a dominant emotional style in Western societies by the end of the 1960s.[7]

Psychological discourses also permeated contemporary understandings of social issues, including that of prostitution. On the international level, expert authorities began recommending rehabilitating and treating prostitutes in welfare and psychiatric centers for their deviance, and clients as well were increasingly believed to be over-sexualized and suffering from psychological and affective deficiencies. The psychological turn, with its tendency towards universalism which aimed to efface human differences and its therapeutic ethos, inherently entailed a depoliticization of issues, at least during the early postwar period. As James Jasper succinctly put it:

> As we have come to understand the social and structural factors that shape our desires and actions, we are less likely to hold individuals responsible for their destinies. As blame becomes diffused, it is harder to identify credible villains or heroes. No one is strong enough to carry out all her intentions [...] Passivity erodes all the characters, who become the tools of circumstance.[8]

Thus, at its heart, the psychological shift was a cultural one which proffered new understandings of human behavior based not on moral or religious beliefs of guilt or sin, but rather on health and sickness.[9]

Towards Permissiveness

The psychological turn and the rise of therapeutic culture did much to bring the Western world closer to a permissive society, especially once the sexual repression of Victorianism was charged with causing psychological suffering. As Frank Mort argues in his study of postwar London as the capital became central to national and world affairs, the rise of permissiveness did not necessarily represent a new, linear, progressive, emancipatory, or modernizing force that culminated with the sexual liberation of the swinging sixties.[10] Victorianism had even spurred changes in mainstream culture by proffering new notions of romantic love and marital happiness, as seen in the previous chapter with New Woman fiction. Socioeconomic changes leading to the rise of the middle class made companionate marriage possible, with the public love story of Queen Victoria and Prince Albert also feeding the romantic imagination. Contemporary fiction demonstrates the growing emotional complexity of marital unions within the public consciousness, with some local variances such as a more erotic turn in France like the work of Rachilde when compared to the more prudish works in England like those by Jane Austin. To achieve this ideal of romantic love which was the joining of two spiritual halves as well as the mixture of sexual desire and emotional affection, the homosociality which had characterized society started to diminish. New forms and spaces for mixed entertainment, such as nightclubs or dance halls, emerged and the rules of courtship changed, especially in urban culture. This had a significant impact on sexual behaviors and values, such as the greater acceptance of premarital sex, as well as the emergence of new methods of birth control and a rising sexological discourse.

As described in the previous chapters, the initiatives to educate the public in matters of sexual health during the interwar period led not only to a vulgarization of scientific discourse but also contributed to public interest in deviant behaviors. For instance, exploitation cinema produced popular films such as *Damaged Lives* (1933), *Reefer Madness* (1936), or *Mom and Dad* (1945) which avoided censorship laws for being educational in nature. They tackled provocative subjects including premarital sex, venereal disease, and drug use in a sensationalist manner, all the while casting light upon the dark underworld of vice by featuring burlesque shows, wild parties, homosexuality, and promiscuity. This is not to say that guilt surrounding sexual impulses completely disappeared. As Peter Stearns demonstrates in his work on the history of sexuality, it was very much a Victorian watchword, along with fear in more extreme cases.[11] Yet the devastations of the two World Wars saw a certain amount of hedonism emerge, especially in postwar Europe, where the idea that life needed to be enjoyed sooner rather than later included sexual pleasures. Contrary to the focus on, and perhaps even obsession with, morality which prevailed in the Victorian era, the psychological turn thus provided new understandings of deviant sexuality which interrogated the inner emotional self.

Already in the late nineteenth century red-light districts emerged in Western cities, which attracted young middle-class people seeking lurid and exciting forms of entertainment and were tolerated by local authorities.[12] Julia Laite, who has done some amazing work on commercial sex in London both past and present, offers some insight into developments in prostitution and in its treatment by local authorities during this permissive period. While the city saw a sudden concentration of both troops and prostitutes during the World Wars, a moral panic prompted by the visible presence of commercial sex in the streets during the postwar era led to the passing of the Street Offences Act of 1959. As Laite explains, this piece of legislation marked a major shift in prostitution policy toward the criminalization of everything except the act of selling sex itself—which continues to this day—and allowed police powers to clear the streets of prostitutes who faced steep fines or imprisonment. "Virtually overnight," Laite explains, "London went from being a city with one of the most significant street prostitution scenes in the western [sic] world to one in which prostitution occurred almost exclusively behind closed doors."[13] This criminalization of street solicitation was fought by the Association for Moral and Social Hygiene, which set up a working party in 1962 to offer alternatives, maintaining its legal focus standing for social justice and equality of all citizens before the law.[14] Nonetheless, a surge in prostitute arrests and in publicized scandals brought prostitution into the limelight alongside related larger social and ideological issues. Yet this interest still managed to largely bypass any greater visibility of the buyers of sex beyond the stereotypical ideas of "the john" which largely depended on the era and the framer, as seen earlier with Josephine Butler's character work on the immoral aristocratic client. But, as Julia Laite explains, there is convincing evidence that the purchase of sex occurred at all levels of the social spectrum.[15]

Women's Work and Pervasive Dissatisfaction

Women in particular embraced the psychological turn, especially as the contemporary notions of gender developed a women's culture of looking inward and to more complex emotional knowledge. As described in the previous chapters, the growing encroachment of state and medical control over the bodies of "Others"—the female, the poor, the animal, the colonial subject—in the logic of modern science faced resistance and spurred various antagonistic discourses in the late nineteenth century. Feminine moral virtue was, for example, proffered as gender-specific emotional expertise and a source of power emerging from notions attached to Victorian gender roles. The culture of domesticity, or true womanhood[16] in the United States, helped to forge an image of woman as keeper of the moral and emotional interior, so to speak, which, some have argued paradoxically,[17] was used to advocate her role in public life and delineate certain social problems—prostitution, maternity, child-rearing—as "women's issues."

During wartime, this notion of women's work expanded as women were mobilized to fill the labor shortage; however, they were forced to leave positions in "men's work" as the wars ended and soldiers returned home. Job opportunities were easily found elsewhere, as the economic boom—and in Europe, the postwar reconstruction effort—expanded the labor market as new means of production helped produce goods cheaply and in great number, fueling a culture of consumerism and a new lifestyle of the middle-class consumer. Jobs in the emerging service sector and the welfare state were quickly occupied by women, who became nurses, cleaners, secretaries, or assembly workers. "Women's work" was often low paid and was still considered secondary, despite the rising rates of female employment. This was curbed in some countries like Great Britain and Sweden where local policies banning married women from employment emerged.

While some women found a sense of identity and personal fulfillment in waged employment, a number of others returned home and raised children. The postwar period was thus also marked by the rebirth of the culture of domesticity, especially in the United States where anti-communist anxieties molded an American way of life centered around the nuclear family, free enterprise, and consumer culture. Yet women broadly speaking were marrying younger and having children sooner, resulting in a baby boom in the United States and Europe. The new feminine ideal had much in common with the nineteenth-century's domestic angel dedicated to the needs of her family, except with some nuances such as sexualized marriage and civic mothering—an acceptable extension of feminine emotional strengths into the public sphere. However, a woman's duty was first and foremost to her family, and the media, education system, and popular culture did much to propagate this notion, for instance, as seen in the trope of women only going to university to land a husband.[18] The appearance of the modern-day housewife in American television in the 1950s, such as *I Love Lucy* (1951), *Father Knows Best* (1954), and *Leave it to Beaver* (1957), not only cemented this ideal feminine image—white-washed, suburban, and middle-classed—but also depicted clearly defined borders of men's work and women's work, respectively outside the home and within it. Likewise, the commercialization of power couples like Frank Sinatra and Ava Gardner in the emerging Hollywood film industry offered an ideal model demonstrating socially sanctioned ways of falling in love, of courtship, and of marriage.

Opposition to these essentialized gender roles which sparked the second wave of feminism and gave new purpose to the women's rights movement appeared in the form of Betty Friedan's *The Feminine Mystique* in 1963. Highlighting the work of social psychologists such as Abraham Maslow, she spoke of the pervasive dissatisfaction felt by women unable to live up to the feminine ideal. This "problem that has no name" outlined by Betty Friedan was heavily informed by the therapeutic ethos, focusing on women's stunted human potential both personally and professionally based on an individualist model of personal achievement. As this second wave spread from the United States throughout the Western world to mix and inspire local feminisms, new issues came under the movement's purview, such as sexuality and reproductive rights, existing gender roles and norms, and workplace discrimination. The formation of the American National Organization for Women (NOW) in 1966 by Betty Friedan and other feminists marked an important step to achieving sexual equality. Yet imagining women as a universal social category would soon prove problematic to the feminist cause, as various fissures emerged in terms of sexual identity, political orientation, class, and race.

Fragmented Identities and the New Left

The renewed impetus of the feminist cause was but one of many identity-based movements emerging between the late 1950s and the late 1960s worldwide. The geopolitical upset caused by the devastating wars fueled by the nationalism of competing imperialist powers had deep and lasting effects on the hearts and minds of the world's populations. This sometimes led to the questioning of existing structures of power, especially those inhabiting the colonized lands. As the United States and the Soviet Union emerged front and center as superpowers on the postwar stage, the Western European Empires eclipsed. Between 1945 and 1960, dozens of new states in Asia, the Middle East, and Africa achieved autonomy, sometimes under new reinvented forms of colonization—or outright independence. All followed very different paths to decolonization, yet the result was nonetheless often the same: a decentered and fragmented sense of identity. The therapeutic ethos often underpinned projects to form a new postcolonial identity which emerged often during the local nationalist campaigns—primarily centered on culture or language, such as the *Négritude* current aiming to create a Black collective consciousness in 1935—which preceded those for independence. The most emblematic example of postcolonial instrumentalization of sciences of the mind can be found in French-Caribbean Franz Fanon's application of psychoanalysis to the effects of Western practices of imperialism and colonization on Black colonial subjects. He identifies a colonial psychopathology in his book *Black Skin, White Masks* written in 1952 that effectively reduces them to an agonizing and dehumanizing psychological position in which to be black is to be subhuman. In the same vein, nearly a decade later he published *The Wretched of the Earth* which argued that the only way to decolonize the mind was through violence.

This subversive, radical, and revolutionary ethos is to varying degrees palpable in many of the new social movements emerging at this time and culminating in the passionate politics of the 1960s—a decade that has achieved almost mythical status in Western popular culture. Referred to sometimes more broadly as the New Left movement, this ethos swept across the West from the late 1950s and tended to focus on social issues directly related to notions of individual agency, class, and culture. Some frequently cited examples include the American civil rights movement emerging in protest of racial segregation and discrimination, the anti-war movement protesting the American military involvement in Vietnam, or the May 1968 student revolt which escalated into a massive general strike in France and reverberated throughout Europe. The social and intellectual currents emerging at this time and dubbed "New Left" were quite divergent in terms of worldview, objectives, and strategies. For instance, some abided by Marxism, communism, or socialism, while others abhorred them; some were secular, while others were tied to religion; some were intertwined with local youth cultures or working-class cultures, while others were not; some radically called for an upheaval of the structural order, while others had conservative or orthodox undertones.

Demonstrating these nuances well are the radical Catholic Left currents emerging in Western Europe in the postwar period. In fact, it is this Catholic Left ethos that kept the embers of abolitionism burning in France during this global doldrum period. Growing out of the initiative to curb the increasing influence of atheist socialism among the working classes during the interwar period, groups such as the Jeunesse ouvrière chrétienne (JOC, "Christian Labor Youth") and Mouvement populaire des familles (MPF, "Popular Family Movement") led a social reform mission—the Action catholique ouvrière (ACO, "Labor Catholic Action")—in the postwar era which straddled political radicalism and religious orthodoxy by aiming to both humanize and Christianize French and Francophone society.[19]

The French abolitionist campaign was a critical one for the early abolitionist movement due to the state's role in championing their system for regulating prostitution, as described in the previous chapters. The government remained the bulwark for the social hygienic perspective of regulationism and, despite the work of some influential French actors like Avril de Sainte-Croix, the abolitionist campaign failed to find much local traction due to its Protestant, bourgeoisie, and English character. However, the Liberation of France carried new opportunities for abolitionism once brothels were targeted for shut down amid feelings of anger, shame, and anti-German sentiment, the managers seen as having collaborated with the Nazi occupiers by providing them with Frenchwomen.[20] The abolitionist victory surrounding the closure of brothels under the law dubbed the Loi Marthe-Richard in 1946 was short-lived, as new measures to criminalize solicitation and to keep medical and social records on prostitutes emerged shortly thereafter. Created that same year as part of the AOC, Le Nid became active in providing direct social relief to prostitutes. This focus on evangelical outreach work distinguished Le Nid from the Cartel d'action morale et sociale, the successor to the French branch of Josephine Butler's Federation, which focused on public awareness-building and lobbying. The character work apparent in the story of Le Nid's creation by Abbé André-Marie Talvas and the alcoholic prostitute Germaine Campion highlights its moral convictions and the value placed on the former's capacity for compassionate love and the latter's redeemability. As Lilian Mathieu's investigation of their literature has yielded, Le Nid systematically constructed an etiology imbued with a sympathetic passion for moral and physical suffering[21] which pointed to socially derived psychological and affective shortcomings lying at the heart of a woman's "lapse" into prostitution. Modern trends including women in male occupations, unwed motherhood, increased sexual content in popular culture—anything construed as detrimental to the traditional family—were critiqued for prolonging this scourge.[22] Anxieties surrounding a perceived depreciation of traditional family values with the rise of commercialism translates into their defense and enforcement in Le Nid's proposed societal solutions. Turning again the early years of Le Nid, male and female members used the evangelical model of outreach and the paternalist model of care to approach prostitutes "hoping to startle the unhappy woman with an admission of disgust and weariness, to offer her a fraternal hand, to offer her familial shelter."[23] Once given new instruction and example in Catholic heteronormative ideals, the former prostitute was encouraged to find gainful but gender-appropriate employment to fund her trousseau and conform to the role of wife, mother, and homemaker. Such prescriptions, goals, and strategies surrounding Le Nid's social outreach work—which continues to this day albeit with some organizational changes—had lasting effects on how the issue of prostitution would be framed and treated as a social problem in French abolitionism upon the movement's resuscitation locally in the 1990s.

5

Radical Feminists and Raging Wounds (1970s–today)

Unsurprisingly given its feminist history as well as the role played by the women's movement in the very development of civil society and vice versa, feminist groups and associations form the base of the abolitionist movement today, as well as orient and head most of its projects both nationally and internationally. This feminist component of the abolitionist movement owes much of its constitutive ethos to American and Swedish second-wave strains of radical feminism, of which a defining feature is a discourse in which gender justifies a given point of view in such a way that no other could seem possible. This categorical perspective has proven problematic and even derisive at times; however, especially when a given point of view is not shared among feminists. Prostitution is one of these polarizing subjects in the contemporary women's movement.

As discussed earlier, second-wave feminists challenged the essentialized view of women as biologically, culturally, and sexually inferior to men, and aimed at establishing equality between the sexes. However, in elaborating this new vision of women, sexuality emerged as a major subject of contention, especially as more radical currents emerged in the 1970s under the influence of the New Left and radicalized branches of the civil rights movement. The result was a ten-year debate known as the feminist sex wars, a contentious site within which the Radical Feminist abolitionist emotional community would begin to take form. Two different visions of sexuality were set against each other. In one, women could claim sexual pleasure and agency within a patriarchal society. For instance, Call Off Your Old Tired Ethics (COYOTE), an American sex workers' rights organization preceded by the group Whores, Housewives, and Others (Lesbians), was created in 1973. The other one believed that so-called deviant sexualities such as pornography or sadomasochism constituted violence against women and participating in them was to submit to patriarchal ideals.[1] Prostitution emerged as either a means of sexual liberation or of sexual domination; as either chosen or forced; as either sex work or sexual slavery.

The latter qualification—sexual slavery—was and remains to be a crucial and reverberating signifier for the Radical Feminist emotional community, especially on the international level. As seen earlier, the international abolitionist movement had lost its main purpose as prostitution became framed as a domestic issue and its minimal activism only found traction on the subject of trafficking. However, feminist participation in the rights-based claims of new social movements—recognition or identity movements—which rang out from about the 1970s earned them valuable experience in interest-group politics, particularly in civil society. Once state and feminist projects became aligned, the latter's ideas and practices were transposed into the mainstream of state and non-state institutions. In line with the strategies of the international women's movement which aimed to solicit transnational governmental action on issues of domestic violence and rape in the 1980s, Radical Feminists also drew international attention to prostitution as sexual slavery, drawing the same connections abolitionists made during the white slavery moral panic to emphasize the international aspects of the activity, as well a causal link between regulated prostitution regimes and sex trafficking. Led by American Radical Feminists like Janice Raymond, activism centered on the United Nations Working Group on Slavery which had been created in 1974 and sat at the very bottom of the United Nations' human rights hierarchy.[2] Yet this unassuming Working Group proved highly receptive to working with NGOs—including the International Abolitionist Federation which had continued to exist although suffering from various organizational and budgetary problems—and offered a high degree of procedural flexibility. Although this particular mobilization against sexual slavery would fall short, the Working Group on Slavery acted as a major platform upon which a distinctively Radical Feminist framing of the issue of prostitution as sexual slavery could be made and disseminated.[3] Alongside providing feminist NGOs with invaluable experience and creating a precedent for more advocacy work with the United Nations, this mobilization served to breathe new life into abolitionism.

The abolitionist emotional repertoire was thus focused on this Radical Feminist construction of the figure of the prostitute—female, often foreign and trafficked—as a victim of male violence. Yet the scene in which this new abolitionist campaign emerged had changed dramatically since the Josephine Butler's crusade and involved new actors—supporters and opponents alike— new arenas, and new emotional regimes that inevitably shaped abolitionist discourses, emotional communities, and emotional styles. The advent of the international sex workers' rights movement—many advocates of which, such as Carol Leigh (as known as the Scarlet Harlot), appear front and center early in the feminist sex wars—is the most notable of these changes.[4] This mobilization of the supposed victims of prostitution whom abolitionists aim to protect has created a tension never before seen in the early abolitionist campaign, where others spoke for them. The consequences on contemporary abolitionist activism are twofold: first, the use of character work to construct black-and-white representations of victims, villains, and minions becomes absolutely vital and second, their cause hinges on the epistemic worth of the subjects involved. Put simply, the knowing victim must be set against the knowing sex worker which places a new emphasis on the rules defining who can be a knower, what can be known, and what constitutes valid knowledge.

Affective Dissonance and the Erotic

The roots of the Radical Feminist abolitionist emotional community lay in the American anti-pornography movement by Women Against Pornography and Women Against Violence in Porn and the Media, both founded in 1976 under the initiative of Catharine MacKinnon, Andrea Dworkin, Adrienne Rich, Laura Lederer, Kathleen Barry, and Gloria Steinem. Although pornography received great attention among anti-sex feminists, it was but a signifier for the dominance of men over women in society alongside other abhorred subjects like sexual violation, physical violence, and prostitution. The transformation sought by Radical Feminists was in fact normative. As the NOW's Statement of Purpose put it in 1966, the aim was to protest and change "the false image of women now prevalent in the main media, and in the texts, ceremonies, laws, and practices of our major social institutions."[5] At that time, of course, Betty's Friedan's *Feminine Mystique* was shaping the directions of the Second Wave. The pervasive dissatisfaction collectively felt by women for not achieving or finding happiness in the feminine ideal spoke to a broader affective dissonance—a sense that something was amiss or the inability to feel what they were expected to feel—experienced by women in the 1960s. The shift in consciousness that resulted from this affective dissonance fostered a gender-based affective solidarity[6] that drew from a broader range of emotions—rage, frustration, a desire for connection—to inspire collective feminist political action. As legal victories were made, such the American federal civil rights law Title IX which forbade sexual discrimination in education in 1972, more radical views about the domination of women by men emerged and took shape in the sex wars.

Yet one might say that Radical Feminists took this affective dissonance a step further by claiming that even sexuality had been corrupted and seized by patriarchal practices and institutions which American legal scholar Catharine MacKinnon famously analogized as being "to feminism what work is to Marxism: that which is most one's own, yet most taken away."[7] This called for the complete overthrow of the patriarchal system and a new feminist epistemology, as opposed to finding liberation from within which would only reproduce injustices. In this view, it seems that the minions refer to just about everyone—women included—until they made the choice to either break the status quo and become heroes or buttress it and become villains. This can be seen in the anti-sex protest of a conference entitled *The Scholar and the Feminist IX: Towards a Politics of Sexuality* in 1982 at Barnard College fatefully organized by Carol Vance to find a feminist consensus on the issue of sexuality. Instead, this key event in the sex wars debate revealed an insurmountable divide between the two camps, as the accusations leveled against pro-sex feminists in this leaflet:

> No More Nice Girls, Samois, The Lesbian Sex Mafia, and the butch-femme proponents [...] are denying that these values are patriarchal. And even more dangerous, they are actively promoting these values through their public advocacy of pornography, sex roles, and sadomasochism and their insistence that this kind of sexuality means liberation for women.[8]

The eradication of pornography, according to Catharine MacKinnon, was a top priority due to its primordial role in defining and institutionalizing "the sexuality of male supremacy" through eroticizing "the unspeakable abuse: the rape, the battery, the sexual harassment, the prostitution, and the sexual abuse of children" and normalizing it by calling it sex.[9]

Central to her thought was Black feminist Audre Lorde's concept of the erotic, a uniquely feminine resource "firmly rooted in the power of our unexpressed or unrecognized feeling."[10] Looking back to the term's etymology in the Greek word eros—love in all its aspects, born of chaos and force of creation—Audre Lorde called for the erotic—"the lifeforce of women"—to be rehabilitated after its perversion and use against women by the patriarchy as pornography.[11] This concept is reminiscent of early Maternal Feminist discourses championing the immaterialist value of womanhood—deemed contemporaneously as a sort of moral purity—depreciated and set in opposition to the masculine materialist realm of science and reason. For Audre Lorde, this feminine resource is knowledge emitted by the body as feelings or emotion and by using it women may reclaim their language, history, and power, as she writes elsewhere, "our feelings and the honest exploration of them become sanctuaries and spawning grounds for the most radical and daring of ideas."[12] Affective dissonance is arguably a tool for signaling that something is not right, while emotion offers a path to authenticity. Yet Radical Feminists follow the anti-sex structuralist argument according to which any "who have been socialized in patriarchal society [...] have internalized its sexual patterns of dominance and submission."[13] As Pierre Bourdieu has posited in *Méditations pascaliennes*, just as the body exists in the social world, the social world also exists in the body.[14] Emotions, according to the German historian Monique Scheer, are also thoughts of that socially situated and enculturated body whose history has been internalized so as to become second nature; that is, automatic and forgotten.[15] Thus, a true feminist epistemology requires a sort of decolonization of the body. As Radical Feminist Adrienne Rich implored, women have "to think through the body, to connect what has been so cruelly disorganized"[16] to establish a new feminist body politic.

Feminist Anger and Solidarity in Suffering

In the Radical Feminist abolitionist emotional community, the buds of feminist anger seen among the Maternal Feminists—a gendered, self-righteous, just anger felt on behalf of women as a social class and directed at their oppression—blossomed.[17] As was the also case for their predecessors, existing emotional conventions were unfavorable to women's expression of anger and yet second-wave feminists overall were much more willing to directly challenge this. As one feminist scholar, Julia Lesage, wrote:

> Yet as we seek mutually to articulate the oppression that constrains us, we have found few conceptual or social structures through which we might authentically express our rage. Women's anger is pervasive, as pervasive as our oppression, but it frequently lurks underground. If we added up all of woman's depression; all her compulsive smiling, ego-tending, and sacrifice; all herpsychosomatic illness, and all her passivity, we could gauge our rage's unarticulated, negative force.[18]

In fact, feminist works on anger and rage are innumerable between the 1970s and 1980s—from poetry like "Phenomenology of Anger" by Adrienne Rich to literary theory like *Art & Anger: Reading like a Woman* by Jane Marcus. Among Black feminists, works on anger and rage, such as that of Audre Lorde or bell

Hooks who aimed to subvert the "angry black woman" trope, are especially poignant against the backdrop of racial politics.[19] This emphasis on liberating or even decolonizing women's emotional lives was part of a collective project to establish a new feminist epistemology. As such, while Maternal Feminists tended to point their anger indirectly at male sexual license through the metaphor of venereal disease, Radical Feminists were much more direct and made the patriarchy their enemy. Yet rather than appearing as true villains or anti-heroes, men are depicted as a class of ordinary monsters who are inherently misogynist:[20]

> The common erotic project of destroying women makes it possible for men to unite into a brotherhood; this project is the only firm and trustworthy groundwork for cooperation among males and all male bonding is based on it.[21]

Andrea Dworkin, the writer of this quote, arguably set the bar for this emotional style through her forceful, uninhibited, and even melodramatic rhetoric. Her words aimed to mercilessly attack the male patriarchy and all its institutions—such as her most controversial essay *Intercourse* which likened heterosexual sex to rape—as well as to elicit feminist anger for its hatred and oppression of women. Alongside breaking free of gendered emotional conventions, righteous anger such as this has the power to both assign blame and rally support. As she said in one of her speeches given on prostitution:

> I am asking you to make yourselves enemies of male dominance, because it has to be destroyed for the crime of prostitution to end [...] everything else is besides the point, a lie, an excuse, an apology, a justification, and all the abstract words are lies, justice, liberty, equality, they are lies. As long as women are being prostituted they are lies.[22]

Her repeated use of "lie" is significant here. The worldview upon which her arguments are set is black and white, meaning that any compromise with the opposition whatsoever counts as a failure and will become the object of feminist anger.

A miserabilist portrayal is common to the Radical Feminists' emotional style because, alongside its shock value, it invalidates any claim that prostitution could be practiced as a freely made choice. In "Prostitution and Male Supremacy," Andrea Dworkin paints a vile portrait of life as a prostitute:

> She is perceived as, treated as—and I want you to remember this, this is real—vaginal slime. She is dirty; a lot of men have been there. A lot of semen, a lot of vaginal lubricant. This is visceral, this is real, this is what happens. Her anus is often torn from the anal intercourse, it bleeds. Her mouth is a receptacle for semen, that is how she is perceived and treated.[23]

Importantly, Andrea Dworkin spoke from her first-hand experience as a victim of domestic violence and former prostitute, a new facet to the contemporary abolitionist movement treated in a later chapter. Yet several such accounts emerge from Radical Feminists working in the field as academics, social workers, or journalists—in many ways representing an updated and professionalized version of Social Mothers' volunteerism in the nineteenth century—such as Norwegian sociologists Cecilie Høigård and Liv Finstad explaining in their book on commercial sex in Oslo: "no one 'wants' to rent out her vagina as a garbage can for hordes of anonymous men's ejaculations."[24]

Together with feminist anger, Radical Feminists strive to demonstrate the ubiquity of male violence in the figure of the prostitute to foster a sense of solidarity. This necessarily required character work by Radical Feminists in order to not only depict the act of prostitution as abhorrent and the prostitute as a victim of violent sexual exploitation and dehumanization but also as a symbol for women's subservient status in patriarchal society. As American Radical Feminist Dorchen Leidholdt writes:

> Far from being about similarly situated individuals, prostitution is a paradigm of sexual and racial inequality. In fact, prostitution doesn't have much to do with individuals. Individuality is the very attribute that prostituted women are denied—along with that related characteristic, humanity.[25]

The conditions or circumstances leading to this are inconsequential: she is any woman; she is every woman, as Andrea Dworkin writes:

> She is, of course, the ultimate anonymous woman. Men love it. [...] When men use women in prostitution, they are expressing a pure hatred for the female body. It is as pure as anything on this earth ever is or ever has been. It is a contempt so deep, so deep, that a whole human life is reduced to a few sexual orifices, and he can do anything he wants.[26]

The prostitute thus becomes a decontextualized object of suffering—a gendered suffering—that spurs affective solidarity both in feelings of sympathy and anger in her defense.

Through a similar process the victims of prostitution become decontextualized objects of female suffering and thus the Radical Feminists' drive to see the agents of their suffering stopped is framed as an act motivated by solidarity. Solidarity is an empowering emotion; for instance, when asked if she ever intended to pass her feminist torch, Radical Feminist Gloria Steinem responded that she would instead use it to light a thousand other torches.[27] Radical Feminists also evoke solidarity with the objects of suffering originating in other patriarchal structures of oppression, such as racism, classism, or speciesism.[28] Yet inherent to this solidarity with other victims of male oppression is the production and reification of women's victim status which may feed a vicarious form of resentment. Resentment is felt by the victim and directed towards the culprit, but it can become vicarious when experienced by an agent in response to a perceived harm of someone else and/or directed at someone who is like the offender. Radical Feminist anger, and especially in its extreme form of rage, has thus the potential to be socially derisive; not only is it victimizing in itself, but it also ascribes blame to men as a group of oppressors. Christina Hoff Sommers goes as far as to argue that Radical Feminist resentment sets men and women against each other in a gender war, creating a bias.[29] If fueled by a culture of fear, resentment could foster a poisoned worldview in which heightened vigilance and coercive punishment of this guilty group may seem increasingly warranted.

Resentment and Desire for Punishment

Indeed, the identifying and targeting of the clients of prostitutes was a major change seen in contemporary abolitionism compared to the earlier phase in which sex buyers were virtually invisible. Early in the Radical Feminist framing of prostitution as sexual slavery, a desire to punish emerged in response to the dehumanization and objectification of the prostitute by the sex buyer. This a central feature of Kathleen Barry's seminal work *Female Sexual Slavery* in which she exposes the abuses suffered by prostituted women and girls in countries in Latin America and Africa. She argues that their reduction to the status of commodities on the sexual market makes prostitution "the most rudimentary definition of slavery"[30] made possible by the absence of laws to stop it:

> Why do men do these things to women? Because, in part, there is nothing to stop them. Norms and sanctions are rarely applied against female sexual slavery. And so, like the child who tests every limit he or she discovers until there is adult interference, there are men who will trample on every human value, every standard of human decency, every vestige of respect for human life, beyond almost every taboo.[31]

Identifying a structural cause to this violence lying in society's permissive attitude towards the unhinged sexuality of men, Kathleen Barry makes a case for substantive law reform. She would once again echo this law-and-order ethos while applauding feminists' decision at the 1980 World Conference on Women in Copenhagen to lobby the issue of trafficking at the United Nations:

> This international attention to female sexual slavery will now enable channels to be opened which will provide an opportunity for women to report crimes and seek remedies.[32]

This shift towards blaming and wanting to punish sex buyers was translated—and somewhat transformed as "blame" became "burden"—in the Nordic Model treated in the next chapter.

The miserable portrayal of prostitution common to Radical Feminists continues today as an emotional style, as Inna Schevchenko, spokeswoman of FEMEN—whose conspicuous shock campaigns often appear in the international press—similarly affirms:

> Europe must get rid of its romantic vision of prostitution as a choice. These situations exist certainly, but in a tiny percentage, and should not be used as an excuse (easy and cowardly) to ignore the suffering of millions of others.[33]

She also states that:

> FEMEN's position is firm: prostitution is a traffic in human beings, it is the exploitation of one sex by the other by means of force or lies; society must strictly prohibit it.[34]

Of course, to strictly prohibit something is to forbid it by authority or by law—speaking to the law-and-order ethos common to Radical Feminists. Based on the belief that the patriarchal oppression is deeply engrained into social structures and conducts, many view the state's political, judiciary, and police powers as necessary to achieving effective change. Laws which criminalize the traffickers, pimps, and clients aim to punish offenders and—through this punishment—to dissuade others from adopting the same behaviors.

To Radical Feminists, punishment is necessary because men are either inherently violent and abusive or are at least encouraged to be so due to the pervading rape culture. In a FEMEN campaign in 2013 for the penalization of clients and against prostitution, activists stood with *Pas de demande, pas d'offre* ("You don't buy, I don't sell") written on their exposed chests in different locations considered to be red-light districts in Paris, France. In the photos taken by FEMEN during this protest, the ones taken respectively in front of the Moulin Rouge and under the metro at Barbès-Rochechouart on the same stretch of Boulevard du Clichy at night stand out. This area is home to a number of sex shops, bars, and clubs, and the activists attracted a great deal of attention. The photos show the women standing stoically amid crowds of male and female bemused onlookers, as men dance around them or grab them from behind. The words on their chests paired with these images are a powerful indictment of male sexual aggressivity and support the abolitionist truth claim, to use the words of Radical Feminists Melissa Farley and Vanessa Kelly, that "[i]n prostitution, demand creates supply."[35] The primary driver of this activity for male pleasure is men, not women. As depicted here, male sexuality is aggressive whether it is active, as shown by those touching or dancing around the activists, or passive, as shown by the objectifying male gaze of leering spectators affixed on their bare breasts.[36] Through such fetishized constructions of male sexuality as deviant and dominating, prostitution emerges as a system of oppression against which the government must take action.

The beforementioned campaign undertaken by Radical Feminists Catharine MacKinnon and Andrea Dworkin for the adoption of their anti-pornography civil rights ordinance in 1983 did much for shaping emotional styles in regards to how calls for legal action and punishment would be made, as well as set the foundation for the development of this law-and-order ethos.[37] Their ordinance aimed to re-frame pornography as both the subordination of women and a form of sexual discrimination so as

> [...] to make available an effective remedy [for] the systematic discrimination, the condoned brutality, and the glorified debasement that defines the condition of an entire group of people.[38]

Like with other anti-discriminatory laws, the ordinance provided a cause of action on the basis of an injury committed against one party (e.g., coerced into posing, faced with a hostile work environment where pornography is hung up) by another (e.g., pornographer, employer, bookseller) through the administrative apparatus of the Human Rights Commission and in the courts.[39] Although ultimately declared unconstitutional due to its violation of the First Amendment which guarantees freedom of speech, the ordinance is significant for two reasons: first, by arguably creating a precedent for the anti-sex feminists finding an ally in the New Right due to their similarly inflexible distain for non-traditional sex practices,[40] and second, by adopting a civil rights discourse as a means of redress. Both these aspects will be seen in the anti-trafficking movement which came to dominate anti-sex feminist preoccupations and internationalize the abolitionist cause once more.

While the ordinance ultimately suffered defeat, it serves to demonstrate how radical feminism has contributed to what Wendy Brown[41] has contended is the recasting of "woman" into an identity which is discursively entrenched in injury—leading to what has been since derogatorily called victim feminism. This construction and proliferation of essentialized accounts of victims (and perpetrators) is even more evident in other anti-sex movements like anti-rape and domestic violence, where Catharine MacKinnon and other Radical Feminists were influential. Violence against women was targeted as the key instrument for oppressing women. This attachment to a perceived injury and social-material exclusion found at the center of Radical Feminists' rage, solidarity, and resentment sees the suffering body become a symbol of women's identity and experience.[42]

The radically social and anti-liberal discourses and Radical Feminist emotional styles emerging in American feminism in the 1980s and 1990s served more and more as a "call to legal arms"[43] for the criminalization of sexual violence, a trend which has been since dubbed carceral feminism.[44] Yet this inscribes itself within a larger sociopolitical context. Ronald Reagan's election to the presidency in 1980 on an anti-crime platform marked the pinnacle of the American war on crime, drastically changing conceptualizations of values like freedom and equality.[45] The result was the development of the United States into one of the most punitive and carceral states in the world. As Roger Lancaster points out, when fear becomes the normative condition, it inaugurates a broken social order based on mistrust, resentment, and ill will which feeds a sort of poisoned solidarity and worldview in which heightened vigilance and coercive punishment are obligatory.[46] Discussed in greater detail in a later chapter, the anti-rape, domestic violence, and crime victims' rights movements played a vital role, unwittingly or not, in this project. Movement actors—many the same Radical Feminists involved in the sex wars—had to work within local contexts of this culture of fear and of a weak welfare state and thus made strategic moves and concessions to secure funding to see their goals met.[47] The legal mobilization to reform medical and legal responses to sexual violence saw a major rapprochement with the law-and-order ethos of conservative actors like the Women's Crusade Against Crime.[48] This alliance may have been an implication of Catharine MacKinnon's anti-liberal dominance feminism—as Wendy Brown has suggested—in which the legal protection and political equality of women are more critical than her freedom.[49] Whether co-opted by neoliberalism or demobilized by its legal focus,[50] the shift of Radical Feminists towards this desire to punish did much to align movement strategies to the state's desire to increase penal enforcement and saw the national and international success of movements against sexual violence—including sex trafficking which brought abolitionism back to the international scene.

While American Radical Feminists and their emotional styles were increasingly influencing feminist and abolitionist currents abroad, they actually shifted their attention away from sexual slavery and towards sex trafficking with the creation of the Coalition Against Trafficking in Women (CATW) in 1988. Prostitution being mostly illegal in the United States, there was room for traction in the anti-trafficking field amid heightened international concerns over border security and transnational organized crime.[51] Much like the early abolitionist movement under Josephine Butler which connected the state's regulation of prostitution to the continuance of the white slave trade, the CATW portrayed sex trafficking as an overwhelming phenomenon that required a hard-hitting international response. The Third World prostitute was put forward to advance the cause which seemingly saw white women joining forces with key sites of institutional power in order to save brown women from brown men.[52] Yet this also did much to dismiss and silence migrant sex workers who in such a discourse became indiscernible from trafficking victims, having lasting local and international consequences and motivating sex workers' rights activism, as seen in the creation of the Global Alliance Against Traffic in Women established in Thailand in 1994. This injection of the sex wars debate into the international field of anti-trafficking as fierce and emotional clashes ensued as both sides fought to have their normative position laid out in what would be the first internationally accepted definition of trafficking, including who are its victims, for what exploitative purpose, and—broadly speaking—whether commercial sex can be consensual.[53] The resulting Convention and its Protocols represented a hard-fought compromise in 2000, but the United States importantly emerged as a "global sheriff"[54] of trafficking. It established its own domestic policy—the Trafficking Victims Protection Act of 2000—which began providing the indicators used by the State Department to produce an annual *Trafficking in Persons* report, ranking each country for its actions taken against human trafficking. George W. Bush's presidency ushered in a nearly exclusive focus on sex trafficking which, as related by Elizabeth Bernstein, saw Radical Feminists making "strange bedfellows" with the evangelical religious Right through a "shared commitment to carceral paradigms of social, and in particular gender, justice [...] and to militarized humanitarianism."[55]

6

Social Regulators: Shifting the Burden (1980s–today)

From the mid-1980s, the contemporary abolitionist movement began to take shape as its diverse actors—old and new; feminist and non-feminist—tried to find common ground, particularly within the beforementioned United Nations Working Group on Slavery. In so doing, a new emotional community of Social Regulators emerged which blended the emotional styles of abolitionist actors with their own local heterogeneous emotional regimes. Communications and meeting minutes from the International Abolitionist Federation dating from the 1980s and early 1990s demonstrate a diversification of their interests—such as pornography, mail-order brides, sex tourism, and child prostitution in Asia and Latin America—attesting to both the changing scope of the sex industry and the spread of the Radical Feminist influence. For instance, when UNESCO's Division of Human Rights and Peace organized a Group of Experts on the social and cultural causes of prostitution and strategies for the struggle against procuring and sexual exploitation of women in 1986, Kathleen Barry was among those to participate along with Denise Pouillon-Falco, French president of the *Union contre la traite des Êtres Humains* and active member of the International Abolitionist Federation. In the final report, the experts outline the "new approach to the study of prostitution as an extreme form of sexism"[1] which at first glance blends Josephine Butler's abolitionism—seen with a reference to the "double moral standard"[2]—and Radical Feminist ethos by refusing any distinction between forced and voluntary prostitution by calling it "a form of sex discrimination, sexual violence and a violation of human dignity."[3] Yet the report also reveals some familiar points of contention among the experts seen in the interwar and early postwar period:

> Some participants expressed reservations as to whether the client was engaging in a criminal act, arguing that although the laws of many countries and the [1949] Convention itself made provision for his sentencing, their application

was in fact determined by the morals of our societies, in which it was widely felt that prostitution was an inevitable and necessary evil. The refusal to treat the client as a criminal revealed a certain ambiguity with respect to prostitution, which was extremely widespread even among those who acknowledged that prostitution was a violation of human rights.[4]

It must be kept in mind that the sexual liberalization seen in the West during the postwar period blended with local cultures and historical practices to establish various conceptualizations of prostitution. For instance, in the Netherlands a policy of tolerance and local sex worker activism led to commercial sex becoming a legal profession in 1988. While those at this meeting agreed that normalizing prostitution in this way was not an option, some were reluctant to challenge well-entrenched fatalist views of prostitution and to extend punishment to the client.

Regardless of these differences, Federation members like Denise Pouillon-Falco supported Radical Feminists Kathleen Barry and Dorchen Leidholdt's foundation of the CATW while others still would jump ship to join them. This is likely due as much to the power struggles occurring particularly among its French evangelical and feminist constituents[5] as to the International Abolitionist Federation's inability to keep up with the changing times. For example, contentions between the General Secretariat Hélène Sackstein in Geneva and the President of the International Committee Brigitte Polonovski culminated in the latter holding a Crisis Committee held in Paris in 1996 to force the former to relocate to Paris. As influential Federation member and French historian Malka Marcovich explains in her resignation letter in 1998:

> I joined the IAF in 1993 [...] I had already realized that there were internal conflicts [...] Gradually, there were systematic blockages at different levels, which weakened dramatically the Federation, discredited our fight, finding themselves today with an ensanguined IAF. I will cite as an example the loss of the consultative status we had at UNESCO. [...] I would like to emphasize here that these conflicts have in fact encouraged profound political differences between France and the International, the religious and the secular, and a growing opposition to feminist currents.[6]

Joining the Radical Feminist ranks, Malka Marcovich would create the *Mouvement pour l'Abolition de la Prostitution et de la Pornographie et toutes formes de violence sexuelles et discriminations sexistes* that same year and then come to lead the European branch of the CATW in 2005.

What would help bridge the differences between these actors was a sort of resurgence of the moral panic on white slavery seen at the end of the nineteenth century. Beginning with the beforementioned alliance between Radical

Feminists and the American Right in the anti-trafficking movement in the 1990s that led up to the United Nations Convention and Protocols in 2000, a global moral panic ensued which rendered trafficking into a decontextualized hyper-reality inherently connected to prostitution thereby distilling the issue to create a simple moral imperative. Vague, unverified, and grossly exaggerated figures were used by activists and governments alike and repeated by the media to create a frenzy, as Ronald Weitzer puts it, with the poor, young naïve woman from the Third World or Eastern Europe cast as the trafficking victim in the place of the nineteenth-century's white slave.[7] By 2003, over 900 entities worldwide were involved in combating the traffic, with the United States leading the way. This resulted in the Radical Feminist's law-and-order ethos being exported and translated into numerous national and international neoliberal governance feminist projects dealing with sex trafficking and prostitution.

In Europe, the expansion of the European Union eastward in 2004 sparked various local moral panics and crusades against sex trafficking, for instance, in Great Britain and in Sweden[8]—the latter emerging as another heavyweight in the anti-trafficking field. Coinciding with state agendas and international efforts to regulate borders, the Swedish government has been its regular partner in funding initiatives such as a joint Coalition Against Trafficking in Women and European Women's Lobby project in 2006 entitled *Promoting Preventative Measures to Combat Trafficking in Human Beings for Sexual Exploitation.*[9] Yet the Swedish model offers a different anti-trafficking paradigm which targets its perceived structural causes, namely the system of legalized prostitution which caters to male demand for commercial sex. This approach centered on the Sex Purchase Act passed in 1999 as part of a larger Swedish feminist agenda to treat issues related to gender equality and gender-based violence. The discourses employed were consistent with that of Radical Feminists: prostitution was considered an extreme form of violence used by men to subordinate women and thus its existence undermined gender equality. While displaying similar rhetorical tendencies, the Swedish ethos differs from the American one by emphasizing a more restorative justice model—a sort of Radical Feminist and Social Regulator hybrid. Prostituted women being the victims of social circumstances and coercion, it made little sense to view prostitutes and clients as equally culpable and subject to the same treatment by law. As such, sex buyers alone faced a fine and maximum incarceration of one year. The woman or child victim was given social assistance to escape prostitution.[10]

The initial reaction to what is now referred to as the Nordic Model was that it was preposterous. Yet after building momentum through a series of events together with the European Women's Lobby—a key one being Swedish Member of European Parliament Marianne Eriksson's press conference, public hearing and report on the *Consequences of the Sex Industry in the European Union* in 2004—the resulting attention helped bring the framing of prostitution as a public problem within the purview of the European Union and the Nordic Model as the best solution to the scene. Here, European governance structures present itself as a site for fashioning a new European ethos on an issue which had historically been carefully avoided by policymakers. This has been largely made possible through advocates making the disputed link between legalized prostitution and trafficking. Another key element in seeing the Nordic Model's success in Europe is the early support it found in the European Women's Lobby, the largest umbrella organization of women's associations in the European Union. During their annual general meeting in September 2001, it passed a Resolution that their member organizations lobby both nationally and regionally at the European Parliament for adopting a law that would criminalize the purchase and use of women for sex by men, and would assist the prostituted woman.[11] Compared to the carceral paradigm promoted by American Radical Feminists, the Nordic Model's focus on restorative justice offers a more mainstream solution that is more readily amendable to the diverse pre-existing local cultures and systems of prostitution. Despite the use of the Radical Feminist vocabularies to lobby global governance structures, it demonstrates a more conciliatory middle-ground feminism[12] which attempts to tread an ambiguous path by supporting the rights of prostitutes without supporting the right to prostitution.[13]

Clearly Radical Feminists did much to rejuvenate and bring unity to the fractured and somewhat antiquated abolitionist cause in the 1980s and 1990s through their initiatives on the transnational level to advance women's rights and to combat sex trafficking through substantive law reform. However, the consequences of this on the women's movement and its related campaigns have varied, from facilitating its spread and influence on the international level to narrowing its participants due to its operation within existing power imbalances—for instance, by favoring feminist organizations and structures most able to professionalize and adapt their administrative practice. This also encouraged the creation of a sort of governance feminism[14] arising from the mobilization of the women's cause in multiple social spheres under the initiative of gender mainstreaming since 1995, but also the activation of non-feminist state-centered forms of power on women's questions. On the one hand, the result has been the production of feminist expert discourse and legal norms. On the other hand, governments selectively engage with feminist ideas depending on political agendas and tend to understand gender discrimination as a single and ubiquitous phenomenon, ignoring women's economic, social, and racial differences.[15] As Wendy Brown has suggested, emancipatory politics when "pursued within largely repressive, depoliticizing, and regulating environments" run the risk of coming "to resemble the arena they intend to subvert."[16] By entering the mainstream, feminist practices—as well as emotional styles—from various original sites of feminist production have not been left unmarked from their travels. Instead, they have been subject to translation and modification in accordance with the valuation deemed by the economies of the arenas in which they take place.

In Defense of Society

In many ways, the emotional repertoire of Social Regulators appears to contain moderate versions of Radical Feminist emotional styles: anger and rage became moral outrage and the desire to punish became a desire to reform and educate. However, the origins of the Social Regulator emotional community date back to the early postwar period as a more socially oriented outgrowth of the Purity Crusaders. The developments seen in French abolitionism discussed earlier demonstrate this emotional style well, as a Social Catholic ethos emerged in the work of Le Nid—predecessor to today's Mouvement du Nid and l'Amicale du Nid once the organization split to respectively tackle more advocacy-based projects and serve a social function through direct intervention in the field. The Social Regulators abhor bad conduct, but not necessarily bad people. Much like the religious adage "Love the Sinner; Hate the Sin," their objective is to use rules to hold wrongdoers responsible, to teach them about their moral obligations, and then to see that they are reintegrated into society. Before their reframing as victims of gender-based violence in the 1990s, prostitutes were predominantly framed as wayward or deviant women in need of re-education and re-orientation onto the correct path. Such prescriptions of society and prostitution persisted well into the 1980s, as demonstrated by the Belgian branch of Le Mouvement du Nid's newsletter *Les Nouvelles du Nid*:

> Children who have not found their place in familial affection do not find their place in society. Children who have not been loved, will not be able to love in turn, and there is a lot of chance that the 'homeless' can never settle.[17]

This focus on the spiritual worked in tandem with a denunciation of the material, prostitution being an "open wound on the flank of society" revealing "the breakdown of a civilization where MONEY has become the MAIN engine. No matter what you sell, the key is to 'earn'. Money, always more money!"[18] Indeed, the Moral Regulators' belief in the errant person's desire for rehabilitation appears self-evident; she is simply not yet aware of it herself—as one newsletter explained, prostitutes all carry deep down the hope to one day leave prostitution.[19] Once re-educated in the ways of family life, marital happiness, and stability, it seemed sure that she would never go back. Such success stories were proudly recounted in newsletters to inspire and encourage fellow Social Regulators in their work, as testified by one issue celebrating the Belgian Mouvement du Nid members' attendance to a former prostitute's wedding in Paris.[20] Therefore, rather than zealously targeting sin out of a fear of divine rebuke or degeneration, Social Regulators view wrongdoers with compassion and look at their correction as being to the benefit of society as a whole.

Social Regulators also share certain features with Moral Liberals, notably an attitude of self-righteousness based on a belief system which triggers not only moral indignation or outrage when something or someone runs contrary to this system but also a strong sense of duty to correct it. Looking at another example of abolitionism in France, it is clear how this also applies in contemporary political settings. When the Nordic Model was being considered by French lawmakers before its enactment in 2016, various Social Regulator emotional styles appeared in defense of different conceptualizations of society, of citizen rights therein, and of state duty. For instance, the socialist deputy Catherine Coutelle evoked feelings of injustice and of duty to penalize sex buyers as part of France's larger commitment to the defense of human rights. She reasoned:

> It is also the last violence against women that the law does not recognize; our job is to put the fight against this violence into law. Gradually, our societies have forbidden the *droit du seigneur*, harassment, rape. There can be no male sexual right over women.[21]

Note that "societies" is used to extend the issue beyond the borders of France to include those of developed countries bound by their belief in democratic principles acting together in solidarity. UMP deputy Guy Geoffroy also reflects this sentiment by speaking about the responsibilities of a "true democracy" to combat violence of which prostitution—"God knows"—is a part:

> There is no true democracy that consents to violence; there is no true democracy except that which fights with all its might against violence in all its forms. And God knows that prostitution—no one, including among those, as there remains some, who are hostile to our text, denies it—is one of the most unsustainable, the oldest, the most rooted violence, and that the time has come to fight it.[22]

Much as seen earlier with Moral Liberals denouncing the state and its actions in regulating prostitution and promoting vice, this Social Regulator challenged France's longstanding indifference or even reluctance to deal directly with the issue of prostitution by drumming up a feeling of duty, of state obligation, and this from their authority as elected officials.

Of course, although many of their arguments repeat the basic tenets of contemporary abolitionism since the emergence of the Nordic Model, these French policymakers' emotional styles are performed in negotiation with socioculturally contingent structural elements which thereby shape their discourses. This is most pointedly seen in a general avoidance of overly feminist discourses, attesting to the appearance of depoliticized governance feminist projects resulting from feminist initiatives being undertaken by non-feminist officials. As deputy and abolitionist advocate Marie-Louise Fort puts it: "The issue [of penalizing clients] deserves better than to please a solitary feminist club."[23] Buzzwords like feminism or gender equality carry little weight in France, especially on the level of government. By way of example, following Laure Bereni, the institution of political parity in France was negotiated to conform with the dominant discourse of Republican universalism and technocratic discourse rather than that of gender so that by the time quotas were instituted in 1995 under the initiative of the Socialist Party, it had become less a feminist issue than a response to a public problem of political representation.[24] Thus, while the Swedish law was developed based on a view that the purchase of sexual services refutes society's overall goal of gender equality, it was French Republican values and norms which were deployed by abolitionist policymakers in this debate to communicate their moral outrage towards sex buyers. Central to this is the conceptualization of freedom not as an individualist notion, but as a social one, as attested to in Article 4 of the French declaration of rights: "Freedom is to be able to do anything that does not harm others."[25] Working together with the abolitionist claim that prostitution is a form of violence, the harms suffered if only by a few warrants legislative action against sex buyers:

> In the name of what should we accept to sacrifice the rights, the lives of women and men? To satisfy the sexual desires of a few? This is not the society we want![26]

In fact, as the Rousseau-inspired social contract upon which French law is based holds that it is an expression of the general will[27] and not one of individual interests, the conceptualization of prostitutes as victims of violence—note that both male and female prostitutes are included in the quote above—legitimately places prostitution under the legislative purview. As Senator Laurence Rossignol argues:

> The consent of some or a few is not an irrefutable argument. Not to resort to prostitution is a matter of ethics; it is a social and not a private matter.[28]

It is worth noting that despite taking inspiration from the Swedish law, the *Loi visant à renforcer la lutte contre le système prostitutionnel et à accompagner les personnes prostituées* ("Law aiming to reinforce the fight against the prostitution system and to support prostituted persons") passed in 2016 in the French National Assembly reflected many local specificities, notably the framing of prostitution as above all a social issue. For instance, funds were allocated to associations and programs providing social assistance to help transition victims—no matter the gender or nationality—out of prostitution and back into normal society.

While many detractors do challenge the legitimacy of legislating over citizens' sexuality, clients and prostitutes alike, the focus on the body, notably respect for the body as seen above, brings us to another way in which the French Republican ethos is employed by policymakers to better communicate abolitionist knowledge. Under French law, an individual's own body is jurisdictionally distinct from his or her person which places a limit on personal bodily exercise in a nod to the natural rights granted to an individual upon birth. The guaranteed respect of one's body, indivisible from one's mind, places it outside the realm of commerce, as upheld notably in France's ban on surrogacy and the sale of organs in 1994.[29] Laurence Rossignol draws a parallel between the commercialization of sex and the commercialization of the body here:

> Our country for instance prohibits the sale of organs from the human body. Yet I am sure that some of our fellow citizens would agree to sell their blood, or even their kidney, for a few thousand euros. Only, we have collectively decided that this practice is contrary to human dignity.[30]

This qualification of prostitution as an affront to human dignity and body integrity not only reinforces its connection to the human rights paradigm dominant these last two decades but also to contemporary protests surrounding the commodification of the body initiated by the predominantly Christian conservative *La Manif pour tous* from 2012 to 2016. While also focused on opposing gay marriage rights and the teaching of gender theory in schools, the movement's platform against adoption, assisted reproductive technology, and surrogacy in defense of the traditional—that is, heterosexual—family model was arguably its most resonant. This framing of their argument based on ethical stances against the commodification of the human body—understood here as creating a market both for women's wombs and for babies—was taken up by

National Assembly members Philippe Gosselin and Valérie Boyer who proposed a draft for constitutionally recognizing the inviolability of the human body.[31] Importantly, deliberations on this draft were held in the months following the passage of the Nordic Model, making prostitution a cultural resource to be instrumentalized by its advocates to evoke indignation, as testified to by Valérie Boyer:

> Mrs. Bechtel, like you, I was shocked by Parliament's differential treatment of prostitution and surrogacy. Like you, I have made the analogy between the two subjects, and that's why I used the expression 'procreative pimping' in my explanation of the motives behind my law proposal. I also think that these women who are in great distress must be protected from themselves, and that in any case it is our duty to not condone these practices. They shock us in the same way that we are shocked when an individual in financial distress sells one of his or her organs.[32]

This draft was ultimately rejected by the National Assembly and today's government under President Emmanuel Macron seems more favorable towards the recognition of parentage in the case of surrogate births abroad.[33] Europe has arguably played a part in this, applying pressure from its governance structures which has undermined local authorities' regulation of international surrogacy.[34] For instance, in 2014 the European Court of Human Rights had found France's refusal to recognize parentage between a French father and his biological children born abroad via a surrogate as contrary to the European Convention on Human Rights—a reprobation which had indeed fueled the *Manif pour tous* actions to maintain the local stance on the issue.

While animated, the French policymakers' discourses on sex buyers demonstrate feelings of moral outrage, but without seeking revenge or even necessarily punishment—instead its scolding. Very much in line with the Swedish law which launched the Nordic Model in 1999, the fine and awareness course encapsulate shaming tactics for a moral condemnation which aims for normative change, not the incarceration of sex buyers. As such, the supporters of the law want it to be pedagogic, but which at times seems infantilizing and paternalistic towards clients who are framed as misbehaving children:

> We raise our children telling them that we do not steal candy from the bakery and that we do not settle our conflicts with fists on the playground. We also teach them respect for the body, the desire and the consent of the other. We do not want the body of our daughters to be sold, nor that our sons use the power of money to buy consent.[35]

Seeking Male Shame

Both Purity Crusaders and Social Regulators hold a high regard for rules which they see as protecting society; however, they instrumentalize them differently. Because Social Regulators see individual conduct and moral behavior as amenable in the social, rules serve pedagogic aims. Thus, rather than seeking simply to create rules and punish those who do not follow them, Social Regulators use rules to inculcate moral norms whose regulatory effects will lead to positive change on all levels of society. As Lev Vygotsky's work has suggested, moral norms operate like policemen[36] by orienting individuals away from moral degradation for fear of humiliation or punishment and towards moral heroism through arousing a thirst for veracity and honor. Indeed, the propensity of humankind towards both requires a strong moral education which Lev Vygotsky, echoing William James and Baruch Spinoza, argues is best when based on the notion of what is good and not on the fearful avoidance of what is evil. To a certain degree, this is the common view of Social Regulators who appeal to positively evaluated notions related to a salient ideology, such as religion, cosmopolitanism, communitarianism, humanitarianism, gender equality, or human rights. For instance, the European Women's Lobby debunks one of *18 Myths on Prostitution* in which "Prostitution is about sexual freedom, abolition is anti-sex" by calling on a health rights frame to define what "good" sexuality is:

> Everyone agrees that sexual freedom consists of enjoying sexual health and rights, based on equality and free from any discrimination, coercion or violence [...] Abolitionists are pro-sex: they want genuine sexual freedom and equality between women and men, and this cannot be achieved as long as sexuality is placed within the scope of the market.[37]

Aiming to inculcate a regulatory norm in which prostitution is a deviant sexuality, Social Regulators rely on its opposition to a constitutive norm of healthy sexuality understood through the prism of human rights: the purchase of sex denies that person's right to sexual desire, which is the very goal of good sex.

This desire to educate the wrongdoer is evident in a video spot produced by the European Women's Lobby in which a man is portrayed orally pleasuring women one after the other in a hotel room.[38] This transformation of the prostitute from an object of desire to an object of pity is forced through perspective-taking. The women—clearly playing the role of male clients by seeming blinded by their own selfish desires for pleasure—push the man's head down between their legs and moan. This is especially resonant as cunnilingus, a sex act aimed at providing female sexual pleasure, is viewed by some as an abhorrent, unclean, or sinful practice despite its normalization in Western cultures. Between each client, the man fervently brushes his teeth out of disgust for himself and for what he is doing. He appears more and more disconnected, dehumanized until a voiceover asks: "'If I had to have sex ten times a day with strangers for a living, at what point would I start to feel sick?" "From the beginning surely," he answers, "yet this is the daily reality for prostituted persons." Called *For A Change of Perspective*, this clear inversion of roles—sexually aggressive women and a victimized man— aims to evoke feelings of repulsion and self-deprecation within male viewers whose capacity to empathize is evoked by seeing another member of their sex take the role of the prostituted Other, shattering any glamorous or sexy notions they may have had regarding transacted sex. "Prostitution is a form of violence and oppression," concludes the man's voiceover, "I refuse to be a party to it. What about you?" With these words, the roles revert back to the male as the exploiter and the female as the exploited. With this new perspective reinforced by the disgust evoked by the clip, the abolitionist claim that prostitution is always exploitation of one party by another is thus defended. Confronted with the miserable reality in which the prostituted other lives, this perspective-taking exercise incenses male viewers to feel responsible and thus guilty for this exploitative situation, regardless of whether they have ever solicited a prostitute. They feel collective shame for their gender; as men, they are responsible for prostitution which is the result of society-approved male sexual license.

Social Regulators employing emotional tactics to construct and impress social morals depend on the regulative effects of feelings of guilt and shame, as well as the overall exaltation of good conduct and abhorrence of bad conduct. As demonstrated, the Nordic Model's focus on sex buyers demonstrates this very well: the penalties for first offense are relatively low and include a mandatory awareness-building course because the law's main objective is to teach men that women and girls are not for sale through institutionalized moralization. This pedagogy relies on shaming techniques, as Simon Häggström from Stockholm police's Prostitution Unit explains:

> You have to understand the Swedish culture and context, and the normative impact of this legislation. [...] Buying sex is now one of the most shameful crimes you can be arrested for. If it becomes public, you risk losing everything: your job, your family, your whole social network. The buyers know they have to behave, not because they care about the women, but because it's in their own interest, because they care about themselves.[39]

This approach is arguably utilitarian in that the individual's desires are secondary to society's overall benefit and solidarity. The Swedish Sex Purchase Act is at the very least pedagogic and at the very most proselytizing, going by the way its advocates describe it. For instance, Gunilla Ekberg, a feminist lawyer who was instrumental in its passing, writes that not only is it the "concrete and tangible expression of the belief that in Sweden women and children are not for sale,"[40] but also "effectively dispels men's self-assumed right to buy women and children for prostitution purposes and questions the idea that men should be able to express their sexuality in any form and at any time."[41] This treatment of prostitution through emphasizing social controls and substantive legislation points to the continuity of the country's approach encouraging normative social citizenship through coercive social control which encumbers individual rights. For instance, this underlies Swedish drug policy, as the 1982 Misuser Act allows the authorities to place serious drug users in mandatory treatment—a policy already in effect for serious alcoholics.[42]

Turning once more to the example of Social Regulators' shock campaigns, a video spot produced by Le Mouvement du Nid and the press agency McCann Paris called *Girls of Paradise*[43] chronicled the launch of a fake website by abolitionists in 2016 aiming to trigger shame and build awareness amongst sex solicitors by confronting them with the violence of prostitution and their direct role in it. Demonstrating well what Lilian Mathieu has called an awareness-building tactic of using approximate quantitative terms to qualify the activity of prostitution as immense,[44] a caption pops up explaining how the website received over six hundred calls during the first week, with extracts between male callers and female actresses provided as evidence.[45] These men contact and chat with the fake prostitutes, only to discover that they have been murdered or have committed suicide through a dramatic reveal—they cannot meet because they are "victims of pimping, like thousands of others."[46] As a rhetorical strategy, the use of figures such as this—although often aggrandized, approximated, uncontextualized, lacking specification, or source—utilizes an objective scientific register to render the problem of prostitution real and tangible, but also to gain legitimacy for their endeavor to stop it. Yet, as Lilian Mathieu argues, the aim here is less to appeal to the public's reason but more to mobilize their emotions.[47]

Working together with this solicitation of male shame for bad behavior, this campaign also seeks moral outrage not only that prostitution and its related violence continue to exist, but that it does so on such a massive scale. A sense of urgency to do something about it is provoked. Indeed, this clip also aims to raise funds from viewers, casting Mouvement du Nid's work as heroic, courageous, important, but heavily under-financed: "We are giving it our all to expose the reality of prostitution, but our means are a thousand times lower than those of the sex industry."[48] The character work done to portray clear notions of who is good and who is bad also instrumentalizes more positive feelings of nationalist pride, ending with a laudatory sequence on their role in shifting public opinion by awakening the moral sensibilities of the French and inspiring the historical decision of French legislators to penalize the clients of prostitutes. The viewer is left with a renewed sense of hope for justice and a better future. The fight is being waged on multiple levels of society because prostitution is not a fatality, an abolitionist tenet which runs counter to popular understandings of it as the world's oldest occupation. Ending on a positive note is also strategic since studies have shown that most people tend to resign themselves to a negative situation rather than engage themselves in protest politics or advocacy.[49] Here, the message is that something is being done and the viewer can—and should as a moral imperative—contribute to these efforts.

Yet *Girls of Paradise* is a shock campaign, the clip and the project itself, intended both for those inside, and those likely to be supportive of, the abolitionist movement, as well as those acting in direct opposition to it. As one of many recent initiatives directed at men to communicate the abolitionist claim that prostitution is a form of violence, the project used ten true tragic stories of deaths involving prostitutes and while only few details are provided, these are of brutal violence: being stabbed fifty-three times, thrown off a bridge, hacked and slaughtered with brass knuckles, burnt and beaten to death. Graphic images of these and other women—bruised, bloody, disheveled, accusatory, barely conscious—are shown or described to generate feelings of empathy or pity amongst the clients, presumably driving them to feel guilty for their actions and to change their behavior. A common motif of campaigns against domestic violence, sex trafficking, and other forms of gender-based violence since the 1990s, shocking representations of the victimized female body reify the abolitionist truth claims of prostitution as inherently and inevitably violent all the while rendering that victim body into a pure eternal signifier of violence in prostitution absent of any context or agency.[50] For despite these women having truly existed, their names, faces, bodies, and deaths have been curated and staged into fetishized objects of suffering ready for deployment in emotional practices of pity, outrage, guilt, and so on, to produce moral shock.

It is important to note the highly reflexive aspect of character work necessary in protest movements. A keen awareness of the collective "us" is needed to foster solidarity: our history, our values, our achievements, our goals. But equally important is a "them" against which "us" is set apart and reinforced in difference. In other words, "them" helps to define the boundaries of "us." Painting a vilifying or demeaning portrait of "them" is another strategy in the Social Regulators' aim to solicit male shame. From sex profiteers to states, organizations, or persons defending an alternative view, Social Regulators frame their opinions and actions as threatening or damaging behaviors. As suggested by the sociology of moral panics, this serves to create what Stanley Cohen has famously dubbed folk devils,[51] or enemy agents completely void of any favorable attributes. For example, in another video spot called *Les Bourreaux*[52] ("The Executioners") produced by Le Mouvement du Nid, a montage of different actors who profit from prostitution—from pimps to clients. Each is shown behaving like brutish animals, grunting and breathing heavily as they distort their faces and gyrate their bodies grotesquely. Such suasive images[53] can be sensibly grasped by the viewer in whom negative emotions like revulsion, shame, or dread are aroused, strengthening the qualification of these actors and their behaviors as deviant, as uncivilized, as inhuman. Such advocacy serves the double purpose of not only communicating the abolitionist worldview but also buttressing a feeling of belonging through an economy of difference in which "they" are immutably deviant and detrimental to society whereas "we" are heroic and just. Thus, the creation of a seemingly diabolical enemy strengthens the abolitionist resolve that hope and courage be maintained during this fight for the betterment of society.

It is worth noting that while traffickers, pimps, and clients seem like the obvious targets of abolitionists' identity-affirming self-righteous anger, enemies also take the form of oppositional lobbies and associations who challenge abolitionist measures. Taking another example from the contemporary movement, Amnesty International ranks high amongst abolitionist opponents since it came out in support of the full decriminalization of sex work in February 2014. As their *Policy Background Document on Decriminalization of Sex Work* states:

> Amnesty International does not take a position on the morality of sex work. Our focus is on how to ensure that all human beings, including those who engage in sex work, are most empowered to claim their rights and live free from fear, violence and discrimination.[54]

In response, the European Women's Lobby issued a statement that they were "deeply concerned"[55] by the stance of this organization with which they have done joint work. They accuse them of not taking a strong enough "women's human rights perspective."[56]

> Let us not be naïve about the reality of the sex industry; let us be courageous enough to have a critical eye on its power dynamics, functioning and benefits, and how it fosters trafficking.[57]

Alongside this questioning Amnesty International's competence to see the real issue right before them, these words subtly suggest that it folded under some external pressure. The feelings of betrayal and deception expressed here are also found in the online petition for Amnesty International to change their pro-sex stance initiated by the CATW and signed by the French chapter of the European Women's Lobby which depicts a woman shackled with the words "Amnesty International: Don't Turn Your Back On Me."[58] Other abolitionists had more scathingly accusatory reactions, like the British Nordic Model Now, altering Amnesty International's logo to discredit this institution renowned for protecting human rights. The most derogatory of all was a series of memes appearing on various blogs and websites depicting an ejaculating phallus instead of the iconic candle. To date, Amnesty International has not retracted their position—even publishing a report in 2016, *The Human Cost of 'Crushing' the Market*, calling for the repeal of the Nordic Model in Norway.[59] Its divergent opinion led to it being qualified as "them," both for being blind to the abolitionist interpretation of reality and being deluded by the corrupting force of the pro-sex lobby. Clearly, emotional styles of Social Regulators have the potential to bind together a group of people, all the while excluding others.

Shaping State Subjectivities

Considering the importance of French abolitionism to the movement today, it is notable that the Nordic Model was slow to take hold in France—even among local feminist abolitionist actors like Malka Marcovich and Christine Legardinier.[60] Responsible for this change was the Swedish government who not only actively sought to export its model of anti-trafficking and prostitution policy abroad but also waged war against the normalization of sex work in debates in the European Parliament from 1997. It has in many ways become a Social Regulator of states, demonstrating a transparent desire to be the moral guiding light in Europe and the world. This ambition can be seen as twofold: to safeguard their own gender equality policies[61] and to actively export them abroad under the banner of the Swedish Model, an image of Sweden as a kind of socially engineered moral superpower to help weak individuals and small countries which persists to this day. This may have had various motivations, but it most definitely stems from a willingness "to create and uphold a national identity of being the moral consciousness in the world."[62] For instance, during debates over Sweden's joining the European Union, Social Democrats argued their membership would make the European Union a "living democracy."[63] With Sweden's ascendancy to European Union's presidency in 2001, the notion that their gender equality policy was to be emulated by other member nations became official policy.[64]

Yet is also essential to point out that entry into the European Union presented Swedish feminists with an enormous opportunity to raise issues on the regional level that were difficult to approach on the national one. In fact, Swedish feminism has been described as feminism without feminists.[65] Like elsewhere in the world, American second-wave feminism reached Sweden in the 1960s and 1970s, drumming up heightened interest in women's issues such as domestic violence, rape, and prostitution.[66] However, these mobilizations ran into difficulties due to the universalistic framing of citizenship which glossed over more intersectional dimensions of issues in relation to gender, ethnicity, or race.[67] Even when economic crisis struck in the early 1990s and a more neoliberal vision of the welfare state emerged, the enculturation and institutionalization of the moral obligation and responsibility to maintain solidarity remained. Furthermore, early gender mainstreaming that occurred resulted in a highly institutionalized form of feminism that reflected little diversity in actors and claims, leaving little room for grassroots initiatives and leaving hegemonic representations of women unchallenged.[68] As such, it has been in the transnational arenas that Swedish feminists have been most active, especially in Europe where they are seen setting agendas from platforms like the European Women's Lobby to promote gender equality.[69] The Swedish Women's Lobby was created in 1997 to facilitate its work "together and through"[70] the latter for this very purpose.

Social Regulators in Sweden played a large role in shaping European subjectivity to regulate not only collective emotional experience but also culturally bound dispositions for institutional political action. Occurring in a context in which the European collective identity is continuously being constructed and negotiated, abolitionist regional-level lobbying efforts—notably the *For a Europe Free From Prostitution* campaign launched in 2012 by the European Women's Lobby—have aimed to establish their own emotional norms amongst Member States, especially through the promotion of the Nordic Model. An important aspect of this is the extension of existing emotional norms. However, the proliferation of group emotional norms across this collective by abolitionists has not gone unchallenged: actors have had to negotiate with existing conventions—including those upholding normative societal orders—and contend with rival groups. In the English preface to his book *Shadow's Law: The True Story of a Swedish Detective Inspector Fighting Prostitution*, Simon Häggström of the Stockholm Prostitution Unit proudly refers to Sweden's success in this project to win states over: "Today, the world is no longer laughing at us."[71] Indeed, what is most impressive about today's abolitionist movement is how quickly and completely it has come to dominate how prostitution is framed as a public problem in the European Union.[72] The best evidence of this was the key abolitionist victory in 2014, when the European Parliament passed a non-binding resolution recommending that Member States adopt policies to attack the demand for prostitution by punishing the clients, not the prostitutes.[73]

Like all public policy, the Nordic Model is a normative device; therefore, its primarily pedagogic aims are based on a very exacting worldview. Thus, by advocating for the Nordic Model on the European level, where prostitution has been left to the discretion of Member States, the abolitionist lobby—and now the European Parliament itself—is cultivating a set of emotional norms regarding prostitution which states are pressured to incorporate to be aligned to the salient collective European identity and corresponding ethos. To gain insight into the mechanisms behind this, Eilis Ward and Gillian Wylie[74] apply Martha Finnemore and Kathryn Sikkink's oft-cited study of norm life cycles to the transnational spread of the penalization of clients through international (such as the United Nations) and regional (such as the European Union) structures. Using a vocabulary of "norm entrepreneurs" and "norm battles," they suggest that the norm of penalizing clients is close to reaching "critical mass"—a tipping point from which, if more countries follow suit by adopting it, it will "cascade" into the international system in such a way that a government will rapidly adopt it because of being aware that this "has become an expected aspect of legitimate behavior."[75] The end of this life cycle is achieved when the norm becomes part of what is understood as commonsense or obvious. Just as seen in the shaping of individual subjectivity through social interaction, states are socially embedded and subject to the same processes of socialization and enculturation as an individual in the constitution of its sense of self, and this in anticipation of others' reactions—that is, praise or punishment—to its behavior.

From the 1990s with the institution of European Civil Society's participation in the European Union decision-making process to the 2007 Treaty of Lisbon's laying out of "the [citizens'] right to participate in the democratic life of the

Union,"⁷⁶ the European project of a blended participatory and representative democracy based on the notion of active citizenship—"the glue that keeps society together"⁷⁷—was reified. Thus, while European governance structures and institutions are understood as a space of cooperation, it is also one of competition and debate in which the performative and subjectivizing dimensions of emotion can be seen. As Swedish Social Regulators endeavored to exert their influence on social issues upon its entry into the European Union, debates on prostitution contrasting the Swedish and the Dutch models emerged in the European Parliament between 1997 and 2014. After building momentum through a series of hearings together with the European Women's Lobby in 2002,⁷⁸ in 2004 Marianne Eriksson auditioned both abolitionist supporters like the Coalition Against Trafficking in Women's Janice Raymond and pro-sex work experts like Marjan Wijers to speak to the connection between the sex industry and trafficking. However, the result was an attack of the porn industry, as well as various NGOs—particularly HIV/AIDS groups—being funded by the European Union's initiatives.⁷⁹ Accusations were angrily leveled against Member States of having "capitulated to the sex industry" instead of fighting sexual exploitation, thereby becoming "yet another profiteer on the market."⁸⁰ Such biased and calculated insults made by abolitionists against Member States which had legalized prostitution, as Greggor Mattson argues,⁸¹ were blatantly constructed so as to make any sort of consensus with their opposition on, for instance, key issues such distinguishing between forced and voluntary prostitution, impossible.

The reaction this demonstrably abolitionist-biased event fueled amongst the sex work lobby was similarly uncompromising. In 2005, sex workers mobilized as the International Committee on the Rights of Sex Workers in Europe gathered for a three-day event in Brussels combining participation as members of civil society—participating in a conference and European Parliament session—with public protest, carrying red umbrellas through the city streets. They additionally drafted two documents, *The Declaration on the Rights of Sex Workers in Europe* and *Sex Workers in Europe Manifesto*⁸² which outlined various policy recommendations, but also set out their rights to exercise their bodies as they see fit and to receive equal protection under the law. They lashed out against those wishing to sacrifice them "for religious or sexual morals"⁸³ and the abolitionist framing of prostitution:

> Any discourse that defines sex work as violence is a simplistic approach that denies our diversity and experience and reduces us to helpless victims.⁸⁴

Looking at this mobilization, Rutvica Andrijasevic has put forward that sex workers' advocacy work raises various challenges to the conception of active European Union citizenship on the basis of it questioning its territorially and culturally bounded practices, but also of it wielding a marginal account of knowledge as those who are usually considered objects rather than subjects of politics.[85] While such "acts of citizenship"[86] hold radical potential, the dominant tendency to view prostitutes as essentialized victims—just as were the slaves in the historical antislavery movement—hampers their efforts to be reimagined as political subjects, for these acts are borne of a socially embedded actor of "prostitute" whose subordinate and passive status contradicts any free exercise of their capacity for speech and action in the political realm and thus of full personhood.

In contrast, the abolitionist camp includes actors with tremendous cultural authority and lobbying experience, especially in promoting gender equality and combating violence against women: the European Women's Lobby and the government of Sweden. European Civil Society being a space highly institutionalized and professionalized by the culture of expertise,[87] it is also worth mentioning that the former's Observatory on Violence Against Women set up in 1997 in the context of the Beijing Conference and Platform for Action of 1995 is a major referent for European policymakers. The latter's successful marketing strategy of its policies promoting gender equality has built it a solid international reputation, as evidenced by governments considering similar reforms visiting the country to learn from its example or by them calling upon its representatives to weigh in locally as experts. Furthermore, relations between these two were facilitated by the beforementioned foundation of the Swedish Women's Lobby as a European mouthpiece for Swedish women's associations. Hence, the successful appropriation of the ownership of the prostitute and trafficking problem by the European Women's Lobby and its Swedish allies has relied on its power and status, as well as their ability to define it using a well-honed critical expert discourse. For instance, in the aftermath of Swedish Member of European Parliament Marianne Eriksson's hearing and report, a number of reports and studies were commissioned by various parties, including governmental bodies on all levels, NGOs representing various interests, and academics. The Swedish government in particular appointed the Committee of Inquiry to Evaluate the Ban against the Purchase of Sexual Services in 2008. In 2010 it published the so-called *Skarhed report*, named after its chairwoman, on its findings which presented the law as a success: a decrease in street prostitution and "a change of attitude with regard to the purchase of sexual services, which coincides with the criminalization of the purchase of such services."[88] Such modes of action blending feminist protest with technocratic discourse[89] has helped bring the framing of prostitution as a public problem within the purview of the European Union and the Nordic Model as the best solution to the scene.

The Nordic Model as public policy proposed to govern the social is a socializing device with a normative function which actively constitutes what citizens call reality. This reality reflects the worldview of Radical Feminists—especially from the American anti-trafficking movement—in which the sex-profiteer (client, pimp, or trafficker) represents the sexually dangerous potential of men if left to their own devices, but also an ethos of humanitarianism found among Social Regulators in which the suffering of the prostitute as a victim of violent sexual exploitation warrants urgent attention and intervention. Extending the emotional norms surrounding what has become a mainstream understanding of the ubiquitous nature of gender-based violence to include the practice of prostitution is strategic as it challenges the indifference caused by society's permissive stance towards male aggressive sexuality. By eliciting compassion for an innocent victim and outrage for a violent agent, the action tendencies to protect the object of violence and punish the author of violence are triggered as part of Social Regulators' emotional styles. The Nordic Model represents a moral condemnation of prostitution which, like domestic violence before it, moves its violence from the private to the public sphere. The status of the prostitute herself, as Lilian Mathieu remarks, shifts from a socially inept to a victim of violence which makes the economic and social context of her selling of sexual services pale in comparison to its (largely) moral condemnation.[90] In such a view, prostitution, he continues, is no longer the result of structural inequalities, but rather a personalized, individualized violent assault (and thus punitive action) involving a victim and a culprit. Thus, emotional norms are constructed around each of these by Social Regulators: for the prostitute, compassion as a victim requiring a protective response; for the sex-profiteer, scorn as a perpetrator requiring punishment. For instance, in a 2015 press release from the European Women's Lobby:

> As long as we don't transform our societies and mentalities (including through legislation), we will continue to see the most vulnerable ones being used by a system driven by profit. Decriminalising a whole system which benefits from inequalities will not strengthen the human rights of the persons in that system. On the contrary, it will strengthen the impunity of those benefiting from inequalities and injustice.[91]

Encouraging a worldview depicting the exchange between prostitute and client in such a way by Social Regulators is an emotional practice to regulate the emotions surrounding these subjects, inculcate their own emotional styles, and normalize the action tendencies of protection and punishment with the ultimate aim of eradicating this practice which is offensive to an accepted set of collective European values.

From Swedish Member of European Parliament Marianne Eriksson's 2004 report taking a hostile stance towards Member States attempting to normalize prostitution to the European Women's Lobby's critically disappointed reaction to Amnesty International's support of full decriminalization of the sex trade, the Social Regulator's definition of legitimate behavior is to put measures in place to abolish prostitution because it is not compatible with a gender equal and democratic society. Thus, deviation from this is qualified as illegitimate or aberrant behavior. The best demonstration of this in the case of the European Women's Lobby's emotional norm entrepreneuring may be the Brussels' Call *Together For A Europe Free From Prostitution*[92] planned from 2010 and launched in December 2012 in concertation with French abolitionist groups Le Mouvement du Nid and Fondation Scelles. The project coordinated by Pierrette Pape, policy officer of the European Women's Lobby Secretariat in Brussels, consisted in the production of various lobbying resources ranging from affective to cognitive, such as the beforementioned shock campaign *For A Change In Perspective* and a leaflet *18 Myths On Prostitution* aiming to cut through misconceptions by providing "human rights evidence based answers to the reality of prostitution and trafficking in women in Europe and in the world."[93] Alongside this willingness to put forward their issue framing and remedy is the aspiration to link the abolitionist worldview to larger feelings of European identity and unity. This is apparent not only through the quotes from Social Regulator supporters they wish to highlight—like this one from Swedish Member of European Parliament Mikael Gustafsson:

> With the Brussels' Call, we clearly see that the abolition of prostitution is a value shared by many across Europe [...][94]

But also, the decision to preface nearly all campaign materials with this famous quote from *Les Misérables* by French novelist and politician Victor Hugo:

> They say that slavery has disappeared from European civilization. That is incorrect. It still exists, but now it weighs only on women, and it is called prostitution.[95]

Adding "He would have signed. What about you?"[96] this evocation of this figure known across Europe for supporting social values—despite being somewhat political erratic—is meant to create an important symbolic connection between the abolitionist cause and the European identity. The message is clear: the prostitute, the lowest among us (a slave), should be protected and to neglect to do so is to be misaligned with European social values. Further, as demonstrated in Brussels' Call lobbying material, the European Union risks being globally culpable of rejecting the prescriptions inherent to its moral system since the persistence of full decriminalization in Member States indicates "the failure at the European level to reach gender equality and promote women's rights."[97]

The Brussels' Call included an extensive lobbying of European Parliament, for instance, in October 2013 the European Women's Lobby arranged a day-seminar for European parliamentarians on the reality of prostitution with the participation of the Swedish and German police, as well as abolitionist activists.[98] The European Women's Lobby's efforts were facilitated by finding an important ally and Social Regulator in British Member of European Parliament Mary Honeyball of the Women's Rights and Gender Equality Committee, who was an early and staunch advocate for the abolitionist cause as demonstrated by her blog *The Honeyball Buzz*.[99] Her report on sexual exploitation and prostitution and motion for a European Parliament resolution demonstrates a clear alignment with the abolitionist views—she cites Fondation Scelles, the European Women's Lobby, and American Radical Feminist abolitionist Melissa Farley—which she connected effectively to the convictions and obligations of the European Parliament:

> Prostitution is a very obvious and utterly appalling violation of human dignity. Given that human dignity is specifically mentioned in the Charter of Fundamental Rights, the European Parliament has a duty to report on prostitution in the EU and examine ways in which gender equality and human rights can be strengthened in this regard.[100]

The non-binding resolution passed by the European Parliament—with dissenting opinions from MEPs from Germany, the Netherlands, Spain, Luxembourg, and Austria—recommending the adoption of the Nordic Model by Member States marked a major step towards seeing the abolitionist worldview become normative in Europe.

The debates for and against the Nordic Model by Social Regulators see European Civil Society present itself as a site for fashioning a new European ethos on an issue which, until recently, was carefully avoided by policymakers.

The abolitionist campaign in Europe has made it impossible for the European Union to remain silent on the matter due to their directive to combat traffic.[101] Given that public policy is wielded to control the social, the Nordic Model promotes very specific emotional norms regarding prostitution which Social Regulators aim to see in Europe, and which European authorities must decide to authenticate or not. The patterned meanings invested in these symbols of prostitute and client are tied up in those of gender and sexuality which will have an overarching impact on the construction of a European collective subjectivity.

7

Survivors: Suffering as Expertise (1980s–today)

One of the largest differences between the historical and contemporary abolitionist movement is the rise of a new actor and thus of a new emotional community: Survivors. Survivors are an abolitionist emotional community whose convergence is necessarily the result of a shared and yet individually lived injury caused by an experience in prostitution. In the historical campaign, it was Josephine Butler and other abolitionists who gave their voice to these victims. Today, the victims speak for themselves and actively engage in prostitute prevention, conversion, or outreach initiatives. Their political activism has tended to be more personal and individualistic, with their own experiential knowledge of prostitution serving to both provide visibility and creditability to the overall abolitionist movement.

However, recently Survivors have been increasingly forming their own professionalized advocacy groups such as Space International which was created in Dublin in 2012. The direct adversary of this emotional community is the sex workers' rights movement and any supporter of the industry of commercial sex. This has inevitably shaped emotional styles on both sides, as they share the agentic practice of testimony and yet their lived experiences, as well as the worldviews they support, run counter to one another. For each, the epistemic value of their testimony relies on discrediting the other. This has become even more evident since the explosion of #MeToo in 2017 uncovered the ubiquity of sexual harm caused by male predation and the failure of the law-and-order ethos to protect women. Yet, while responsible for consciousness-raising and for injecting testimonial practices with new power, #MeToo has also given new impetus to the feminist sex wars, dubbed "Sex Wars 2.0" by Brenda Cossman.[1]

It is notable that the Survivor emotional community emerged at the same time as the Radical Feminists—originating from the anti-pornography movement—with whom they overlap a great deal in terms of emotional styles. Yet a key difference lies in the solidarity emerging, on the one hand, from an often essentialized experience of shared suffering as women living in a patriarchal society among Radical Feminists and, on the other hand, from a personal experience of shared suffering—specific, irreducible, and incommensurable—among Survivors.[2] This convergence based on private experiences of suffering—feelings such as pain, sorrow, shame, and loss—has been heavily impacted by AIDS activism, which is most apparent in the Survivor emotional style of transforming these negative emotions into anger and action. Much like ACT UP's likening of silence to death in their iconic Silence=Death poster from the late 1980s, Survivors feel a distinct sense of urgency to speak, to render visible the horrors of prostitution, and to gain recognition—publicly, politically, legally, socially—for the harm it causes. Yet the politicization of sexual violence by feminists and the anti-victim backlash of the 1990s had lasting effects on Survivors and their emotional praxis, especially as new fetishized representations of the victim as an object of suffering and the perpetrator as an object of anger emerged along gendered and racialized lines.

Emotional Economies of Injury

The anti-pornography campaign was given momentum through the testimony of coercion, torture, and abuse by her husband at the time given by well-known porn actress Linda Lovelace published in her autobiography *Ordeal* (1980). Revealing the dark truth behind the film *Deep Throat* (1972) which had drawn attention beyond the sex industry and established a lasting cultural legacy, she shocked the public by stating: "Virtually every time someone watches that film, they are watching me being raped."[3] Such revelations attest to the rise of storytelling of injuries as a social practice and the forging of the victim as a sociopolitical identity within concurrent movements against rape, domestic violence, child abuse, and for victims' rights occurring from the late 1960s and 1970s. While international in scope, the different local contexts shaped various features and interpretations of these movements—each of which had its singularities. For instance, the crime victims' movement had a very diverse base, including both the civil rights' movement and the women's movement, making its roots irreducible to one actor. Nevertheless, as discussed earlier, America's war on crime, its amplification of a culture of fear which continues to shape citizens' everyday lives and construct different bodily subjectivities, and the Radical Feminists' shift towards increasingly carceral politics influenced conceptualizations of justice and of the role of the state for legal protection abroad.

Personal testimonies of injury also increased public awareness by rendering various forms of violence visible which in turn triggered public action. NOW, for instance, formed a task force on rape in 1974 and another on domestic violence a year later. Approaching sexual violence was framed by dominance feminists like Catherine MacKinnon not as related to sexual desire, but as a violent tool par excellence of male oppression. Their findings along with the *Rape and Its Victims* report published that same year by the Law Enforcement Assistance Administration revealed not only high rates of violence occurring between intimate parties—thereby challenging the popular assumption of "stranger danger"—but also shed light on the phenomenon of double victimhood suffered by women in the judicial and medical systems.[4] Combined with the escalating culture of fear, this new awareness and seeming impending threat of crime facilitated the public's embrace of new forms of neoliberal power.

This also resulted in the rise of a market for victims' stories. A commodification of victimhood was made most obvious by the plethora of sensationalizing talk shows like *The Sally Jessy Raphael Show* (syndicated 1983 to 2002 by USA Networks Inc.) or *Gerald Rivera* where victims were invited to tell their story and were even sometimes put into challenging positions, for instance, by presenting a surprise guest who contended the victim's version.[5] Additionally, the victim must command enough power to establish herself as an ideal victim, but not enough to become a threat to other important interests.[6] This had a reverberating influence on the political and cultural framing of victims and perpetrators of gender-based violence both locally and abroad in the decades to come.

A major consequence of the aligning of Radical Feminists and the state has been the adoption of a neoliberal approach to resolving gender-related problems which places the responsibility of the individual—not the social welfare state—at the forefront. Instead of enacting systemic change, this entails penal systems punishing psychotically disturbed male reprobates and state infrastructures offering individualized curative therapies to female victims. Furthermore, a distinction was made between the "good victim" who assumes responsibility and the "bad victim" who blames others.[7] For instance, in *Framing the Victim: Domestic Violence, Media, and Social Problems,* Nancy Berns opens her analysis of the media's construction of victims with an example of an episode of *Oprah*, one of the most popular and influential American talk shows in which the host opened the episode with the following speech:

> For years, I have done shows on battered women and domestic violence, and for decades, it has been believed that family violence was a social problem with one

solution: Men who are violent should be punished, and the women they hurt are victims and helpless and should leave. But now there are some new voices [...] that we are underestimating the role that women play in an abusive relationship.[8]

The backlash against "victim feminism" mentioned earlier as well as the rising self-help movement in the 1990s made it the job of the victim to assume responsibility for minimizing the debilitating effects of victimhood. The rise of the notion of survivor to denote empowerment demonstrates the internationalization of such a concept by victims themselves. This evolution of an increasingly neoliberal brand of feminism from the 1990s and onward saw the displacement of the "true victim" label from the Western white woman to the non-Western non-white one,[9] reinforcing racial and colonial stereotypes of the Other—especially visible in violence against women actions undertaken in a human rights frame on the transnational level.

Overlying this development of the victim as a sociopolitical identity, advocacy for the international recognition of women's human rights placed a strategic focus on violence against women which would set the dominant frames for subsequent feminist mobilizations—including those against sex trafficking and prostitution—both nationally and internationally. In fact, the use of violence—particularly sexual violence—as the entry point for advancing women's human rights, as the scholar and activist Alice Miller explains, was due to the "deeply ironic"[10] failure of equality and anti-discrimination to do so. Yet casting violence against women as a violation of women's human rights so as to place it under international law and jurisprudence proved difficult. One of the central aims behind the creation of the United Nations in the aftermath of the Second World War was to protect against international human rights violations, as outlined in Articles 1(3), and 55(c) of its Charter[11] and later reaffirmed in 1948 by its adoption of the Universal Declaration of Human Rights.[12] Yet the early rationale behind international human rights law was to prevent abuse by the state or its agents—not by non-state actors. The result was thus a dichotomy of private and public crimes falling respectively under domestic and international scopes.[13]

Violence already finding itself a major preoccupation of Radical Feminists with their dominance structuralist perspective focusing on women as a group made it possible to frame gender-based violence as a form of discrimination. As Catharine MacKinnon argues, rape and sexual assault constitute sex discrimination on the basis of women being target "on the basis of sex, because of their membership in a group defined by gender."[14] The threat of violence thus arguably diminishes the autonomy of women by effecting their exercise of agency in deciding their lifestyles and choices.[15] Such arguments were used to try and draw violence against women out from the private sphere and into the public one. The United Nations' Convention on the Elimination of All Forms of Discrimination against Women passed in 1979 marked a major turning point for placing women's issues prominently on the international agenda and ushered in the Decade for Women.[16] However, it continued to be marginalized even at the World Conference to Review and Appraise the Achievements of the United Nations Decade for Women in Nairobi in 1985.

Human rights being a "chameleon-like practice, despite its rhetoric of political purity,"[17] the contemporary mainstream paradigm saw torture as the ultimate rights violation. Advocacy such as Amnesty International's 1977 campaign that earned them the Nobel Peace Prize promoted a frame of torture focused on bodily suffering, individualized harm resulting from acts committed or condoned by the state.[18] Feminist activists thus focused on reframing wartime rape—which is seen as a harm against a woman's honor or community rather than her person—according to the torture paradigm in the area of international humanitarian law, particularly once accounts of sexual assault during armed conflicts in Yugoslavia and Rwanda began attracting global attention.[19] The notion of breaking the silence through storytelling was an essential advocacy tool. By presenting brutal rape stories told by victims whose experiences "embodied a horror that could not be ignored,"[20] activists would eventually bring the issue of wartime rape and other issues relating to the visibility and mainstream success of gender-based violence at the 1993 World Conference on Human Rights in Vienna and then again at the 1995 Fourth World Conference on Women in Beijing.

Yet activists against gender-based violence also had to work against the dominate view which saw human rights as dividable between negative and positive rights. This meant, for instance, that a state would meet its obligations by simply not engaging in torture and thus did little to break down the public/private dichotomy in violence against women.[21] The rise of a health and human rights discourse was accompanied by a language of positive obligations, which emphasized the harm caused by the state's inaction. A better understanding of the psychological as well as physical harms of trauma[22] helped legitimize claims of the state's obligation to act by providing services to treat the suffering caused by sexual harm as well as to protect women against it in the first place. Thus, a rather abrupt shift occurred in international law towards reduced national sovereignty and an expanded international crime enforcement system holding private individuals accountable for severe infringements of international human rights and humanitarian law—including sexual harm.[23]

Paid Rape: Female Suffering in Prostitution

Since the abolitionist cause's shift from seeking the end of the state's regulation of prostitution to the end of prostitution itself, "paid rape" has become an oft-repeated term for the act of commercial sex in the contemporary abolitionist movement among Radical Feminists, Social Regulators, and Survivors alike.[24] To understand its affective value as an object of female suffering, it is necessary to look more closely at the signifier of rape. Its current form is the by-product of the feminist initiative to see women's human rights included within international human rights, a field dominated by "torture" and "health rights" paradigms. Strategically focusing on "violence against women"—a concept borne of the anti-rape and domestic violence movements which accompanied second-wave feminism—rape emerged as an object of specifically female suffering to spearhead the drive to bring private forms of violence into the public sphere through a focus on its harm to an individual's physical and psychological health. This project led to the inclusion of wartime rape in international humanitarian law, itself becoming a fetish object in the political economy of security.[25] To date, it remains the only form of gender-based violence that has made it into international law, a lacuna which remains a top priority on the political agenda of feminists. In fact, that violence against women tends to be approached from the perspective of international security has drawn some criticism, including that it constructs women as victims inherently vulnerable to violence and in need of male protectors (e.g., United Nations' peacekeepers).[26] This aspect can be traced back to the law-and-order ethos of Radical Feminists which helped draw sexual and gender-based violence issues into the field of national and then international security in the first place by seeking the criminalization of male offenders by the state.

Yet, in this case, the designation of the client or the pimp as an offender depends on the committing of a crime. To be viewed as such, paid rape hinges on the inexistence of voluntary prostitution and thus on a disempowered victim. This is rooted in the notions of structural and symbolic violence which underpinned the remobilization of the abolitionist cause in the feminist sex wars of the 1970s and 1980s. Here, the prostitute was shaped into the ultimate female victim of patriarchal oppression, for what could be more exploitative than being coerced through payment for sex which is, as Radical Feminist Catharine MacKinnon has argued, already in all its forms intrinsically violent?

Compare victims' reports of rape with women's reports of sex. They look a lot alike. [...] In this light, the major distinction between intercourse (normal) and rape (abnormal) is that the normal happens so often that one cannot get anyone to see anything wrong with it.[27]

Granted, the anti-sex sentiment expressed in the Radical Feminist origins of contemporary abolitionism—which departed from Josephine Butler's tenets in many ways, but primarily by viewing marriage itself as rape—now represents an extreme position; it has since been transformed by more mainstream abolitionist actors like the European Women's League into the qualification of anything falling outside the lines of consensual—that is, made via informed decision by an empowered agent—sex as rape. The issue of the prostitute's consent in the case of transacted sex, however, has been subject to much debate[28] which centers around the ethical/religious question of whether the body can and should be sold—also relevant to the subjects of surrogacy and the selling of organs. It is notable that abolitionist actors are also engaged in efforts to abolish all forms of surrogacy; for instance, the European Women's Lobby launched a campaign in 2017 called Stop Surrogacy Now. Groups in Sweden, Spain, Italy, and France have been most influential in bringing the anti-surrogacy lobby to the European Parliament on the basis of it being "a global trade of women's bodies."[29] Evoking the structural and symbolic violence they believe inherent to the overall system of prostitution, abolitionists liken transacted sex to slave labor with Kathleen Barry's *Female Sexual Slavery*, alongside the works of Andrea Dworkin and Catharine MacKinnon, re-popularizing this historical connection between abolitionisms. When incorporated into the market economy, as Swedish Radical Feminist Kajsa Ekis Ekman argues, the patriarchal phenomenon of prostitution becomes a capitalist one in which the relationship between men and women—a power struggle exemplified in sex—commodifies a depersonalized form of sex in the form of rape.[30] The transacted sex act is thereby a violation of bodily integrity, an element of human dignity which is a key concept in the field of international human rights. The prostitute's ability to consent is thus invalid and illusory: a person's decision to engage in an activity which is contrary to her health, her dignity, and her self-interest is proof of her not being truly master of her own existence due to her vulnerability or psychosocial ineptitude.[31] As Maltese abolitionist Lorraine Spiteri explains:

[A prostitute] consented because she doesn't have a choice. She might not have the money, might not have the options, is a drug addict, has no home to go to, has no money, was abused and pushed into prostitution.[32]

Due to the beforementioned causal connection established by activists in both phases of the abolitionist movement between trafficking and (regulated) prostitution, the construction of prostitute-as-victim has also been heavily informed by the appropriation of the already-fetishized trafficking victim of white slavery by the anti-trafficking movement launched by radical feminists in the United States and made global in the late 1990s. Homogenized and decontextualized into an "ideal victim"—a young, innocent, naïve, vulnerable foreign woman[33]—its circulation and accumulation of affective value as an object of compassion has contributed to the—oft-criticized as paternalist—definition of a person trafficked for the purpose of exploitation as "victim" irrespective of his or her consent in the 2000 United Nations' Palermo Protocol.

The perpetrator of paid rape, the client, appears as an object of anger which is typically construed as a sort of ordinary monster,[34] embodying simultaneously a sexual sadist and an average joe. For instance, the opening page of a 2011 publication by the Swedish Institute entitled *Targeting the Sex Buyer. The Swedish Example: Stopping Prostitution and Trafficking Where It All Begins* describes the client in the following way:

> He could be your neighbor, even your best friend. Or perhaps he is a colleague at work or someone you talked to at a party last weekend. He appears to live a normal life – he is married, has children, a good job – in other words, he is a regular guy. But he also buys sexual services and thereby supports the market for sexual exploitation, prostitution and trafficking. And under Swedish law he is a criminal.[35]

Like other forms of gender-based violence, paid rape is ultimately interpersonal, but because it derives from unequal power relationships between the sexes and is condoned by patriarchal society, it seems common and ubiquitous. To Survivors of prostitution, however, paid rape is more personal; as Rachel Moran charges, "[t]hese men know perfectly well the evil they're committing"[36] but they either prefer to allude themselves, are indifferent to it, or derive sexual pleasure from knowing it is rape. What emerges in both these cases is the certitude that clients will not stop buying sex until the government forces them to stop. Here, the fetishization of the injury of paid rape makes it so that, in an emotional economy of feminist anger, its offender is generalized to the point where men appear as a class of sexually selfish dominants, a class of male perpetrator of violence against women, to echo Wendy Brown's work on feminist identity politics by which "the condition of subordination of women […] is both bodied in femaleness and enacted in sexual experience."[37] Such Radical Feminist constructions placing the system of prostitution on the same plane as that of marriage is a far-cry from Josephine Butler and other Maternal Feminists' view of marriage as the saving grace for their fallen sisters whose moral status would be consequently rehabilitated. This stems from a notable shift in conceptualizations of womanhood from one rooted in motherhood to one victimized by male viciousness pervading all levels of patriarchal society.

Converting Shame and Loss to Anger

As Survivors have typically exited prostitution years before, the injury caused by their experience in prostitution tends to be expressed in abolitionist literature psychologically as a sense of loss; for instance, Rachel Moran in her memoir *Paid For: My Journey Through Prostitution* writes:

> The overriding feeling when reflecting on the experience of prostitution is simply this: loss. Loss of innocence, loss of time, of opportunity, credibility, respectability, and the spiritually ruinous loss of connectedness to the self. I could go on and on, but the primary element is always loss.[38]

This feeling goes hand-in-hand with her qualification of prostitution as abuse based on its dehumanizing and degrading aspect made inherent by the prostitute and her clients knowing that she is "there for one reason and one reason only—so that [her] body would be used as a receptacle for their sperm."[39] To this routine effacement of self-respect, as Rachel Moran explains, "shame is simply an inevitable response."[40] As a moral emotion, that which causes shame is judged as violating socially determined norms. Yet importantly—like guilt or pride—the object of shame is the self, hence this feeling of loss which Rachel Moran speaks of. She explains elsewhere:

> Because shame is such an ever-present and abiding feeling among prostitutes and the former prostitutes alike, the process of letting go of it is of paramount importance [...] how we react to the feeling [...] dictates whether it will improve or corrode our lives.[41]

Shame has been shown to promote defensiveness, interpersonal separation, and distance—an action tendency to hide. By coming forward and exposing their stories to public scrutiny, Survivors can aim to face their shame, using their desire to transform it as a motivational force:

> I imagine shame to wear a mask [...] I have decided not to wear a mask here, not even one I like in some ways, because to take my mask off is my way of confronting shame and daring it to do the same thing. That is why I've decided to tell the world my name is Rachel Moran.[42]

Of course, blaming emotions are not restricted to the Survivor herself, but also felt towards the actors involved in their experience of prostitution. Transacted sex acts in particular are understood as incidences of interpersonal violence whose offenders may have a face, a name, a body, a smell, a taste, a voice. Survivors may therefore direct the other-blaming emotion of anger at specific persons against whom they hold resentment. They may wish to seek justice—if righteous anger resulting from a perceived injustice—or revenge—if traumatic anger. While the lived experience of prostitution is personal, it can become shared amongst Survivors. This can perhaps lead to developing proactive ways to channel negative feelings which reduce individual suffering—such as through political activism—but also may result in their collective magnification. For instance, Survivor Rebecca Mott writes in her prose poem *To All Punters*:

> Know in every cell of your mind and body—that we the prostituted hate you. We know who you are, and that should terrify you. Our strength is growing—we refuse to be control [*sic*] or owned any more. The silent screaming of the whore becomes a yell of war with exited prostituted women.[43]

She addresses the plural subject "you" to speak on behalf of the plural subject "we," employing violent and hostile words of "hate" and "war." The empowering shift from "silent screaming" to "yell of war" echoes the metaphor of breaking the silence popularized by victim movements in the United States during the 1990s.

Voicing Emotion: From Silence to Speech

Survivor testimony is a valuable tool for bringing legitimacy to the abolitionist cause, as sex trafficking Survivor Rebecca Bender writes:

> Every organization wants and needs a survivor. Not only does it help in showing the reality of the facts that can often get regurgitated, but ONLY survivors can truly understand what is happening in the dark world of human trafficking.[44]

Survivors are thus significant both for their situated knowledge of prostitution and for their ability to give it a face and a voice. Their stories of violence and degradation elicit moral outrage and compassion—key emotions for gaining public interest and support. As one particularly abject testimony given by Survivor Bridget Perrier exemplifies:

> The scariest thing that happened to me was being held captive for a period of 43 hours and raped and tortured repeatedly at 14 years of age by a sexual predator who preyed on exploited girls.[45]

However, Survivor testimony occurs within the social field and thus their discourses must be translated and negotiated within hegemonic structures. In this regard, it is important to bear in mind that not all Survivors are "professionalized" in the same ways as the activists of institutionalized abolitionist groups with which they often collaborate or join. For example, in 2017 Rosen Hicher spoke before a group of students at the initiative of l'Amicale du Nid, and Osez le Féminisme 38 at the Université Grenoble Alpes in Saint-Martin-d'Hères, and Space International together with la Fondation Scelles and the CATW hosted a conference Strategies to Address Prostitution and Sex Trafficking at the French Consulate in New York during which Rachel Moran was one of the guest speakers.

Survivors' activities are necessarily shaped by their potential as an advocacy resource. For instance, the Nordic Model Now explained in a recent article posted on their website began by explaining that "people often berate us for not 'listening to sex workers'" and yet "our group includes survivors of the sex trade" before going on to expose the testimonies of these said survivors which necessarily earns the group and its cause credibility.[46] Yet this may explain why some like Rachel Moran and Rosen Hicher would create organizations specifically for former prostitutes—respectively, Space International and le Mouvement des Survivantes de la Prostitution—or why articles like *7 Ways Your Organization Could be Re-exploiting Survivors* would be published by Survivors. Rebecca Bender explains how this is common but often unintentional on the part of organizations, which do not always treat the survivor as a professional both in terms of monetary compensation and esteem:

> Do not discredit what they have to say, or demean their input based on a possible lack of a degree. My education came from the game, and if that's what the organization is trying to break into, I would have a Masters, okay??[47]

When dealing with audiences who are external to the movement, the stakes for Survivors are arguably high considering not only the stark opposition of the sex work lobby but also the transgressive character of their testimonies which presume objects which are antithetical to the dominant discourse—such as paid rape. From the historical precedent set by psychiatrists like Sigmund Freud and Alfred Fournier to reject stories of sexual abuse as fantastical to the phenomenon of victim-blaming which reverberates on all levels of society today, the very designation of a victim as such is politically charged and subject to controversy. Survivor testimony must adopt different discursive strategies, such as alignment with what their audiences already know to be true for credibility and resonance, and exercise emotional intelligence to gauge whether the emotional content is appropriate to the given context. For instance, in their study of childhood sexual abuse, Linda Alcoff and Laura Gray explain how survivors must navigate between settings in which their credibility relies upon intense and explicit emotional displays, and others in which too much emotion casts it into doubt.[48]

The empowered notion of Survivor which emerged in the wake of backlash following the rise of the victim as a social category champions this shift from powerlessness to agency. Viewed in juxtaposition to the loss Survivors experience as expressed earlier, political activism provides a means to resuscitate, re-appropriate, and vindicate one's sense of self. The institutional recognition of suffering as expertise makes Survivors knowledgeable victims with valuable resources to provide, necessarily providing them with a sense of purpose and of duty. For instance, Survivor Fiona Broadfoot, a representative of Space International explains:

> I exited prostitution almost 22 years ago, and I have campaigned for the abolition of the sex trade ever since. Not just because of the damage I experienced and still experience due to my involvement in this brutal trade, but also for the hundreds of women I have supported over the years, the women who are so damaged they self-medicate with alcohol and other substances, the many women who suffer with chronic health problems that are both mental and physical. Mostly I continue to campaign for the individuals who have been murdered, of which there are many.[49]

Finding validation and valuing of their experience in prostitution, demonstrated by others through feelings of caring, compassion, and respect, is a significant aspect of Survivor empowerment. In many ways, a Survivor can be understood as a "whistleblower"—a term designating an employee who steps forward and accuses an organization of wrongdoing—who is denouncing "sex work" as a legitimate form of employment. For instance, Survivor Sabrinna Valisce recalls:

> When New Zealand passed full decriminalisation, things changed in unexpected ways and I came to understand that the myths of legal protection, autonomy, increased choice and greater community acceptance were unfounded. We didn't have the legal protections we expected because we sat in a grey area between employee and independent contractor. […] I had no choice but to fight against this model ever spreading to another country.[50]

As is typical in the case of whistleblowers, there are often as many who will applaud their bravery and courage for stepping forward as there are others who will aim to discredit them as inauthentic on the basis of being crazy or disgruntled, especially those who defend the complete legalization and normalization of the sex trade. Speaking about the "relentlessly abusive treatment" she has received from sex work lobbyists from the very start of her campaign to criminalize sex buyers, Rachel Moran explains:

> I had no way of protecting myself against the lies that were told online about me [...] But to know that your character is being taken daily, that you cannot protect yourself against it, and that the best you can do is trust to the judgment of strangers places a person in an extraordinarily vulnerable position.[51]

Opposition is not limited to the internet; sex worker advocates also protest at various abolitionist events. For instance, Elena Jeffreys from the Scarlet Alliance and others allegedly bullied and intimidated Survivors during an event organized in Australia around the launch of a book *Prostitution Narratives* recounting their sex industry abuse. The "booing, hissing, calling out" grew to the point that they were forced to change venues, "jammed into a corner of a bar, with a live band right next door, where people could barely hear us."[52] In response to hostile opposition and gaslighting tactics, some Survivors may be silenced, whistleblowers being found more susceptible to increased anxiety, interpersonal sensitivity, and distrust.[53] Others speak of it as incentivizing, as one Survivor puts it: "It just fuels my fire and my passion to speak out more."[54]

Conclusion

The emotional histories of abolitionism traced in this book through the investigation of six different emotional communities—Moral Liberals, Purity Crusaders, Maternal Feminists, Radical Feminists, Social Regulators, and Survivors—and their emotional styles began with Josephine Butler's crusade to end the laws regulating prostitution in Great Britain and its colonies. Emerging and evolving at the turn of the twentieth century amid "great and sudden change," to borrow the words of Mary Shelley, the period during which this mobilization took place also marked the rise of new sociopolitical actors parallel to—if not because of—the imperialist projects of the State and the wave of rapid industrialization with its accompanying laissez-faire capitalism. While not exclusively, the newly empowered middle class mobilized most of all to solve society's troubles, often forming local and international voluntary associations of which women were often active participants. Antecedent movements against slavery and for animal welfare emerged out of providentialist concerns for public morality in a time of great socioeconomic change following the industrial revolution. Anxieties surrounding foreign influences infiltrating the homeland and destabilizing its foundations found expression in these nationalistic and moralizing campaigns against the barbaric treatment of animals and the encouragement of violence seen as inherent to political radicalism. Positivist science bringing credence to the notion that civilized man was only a few steps away from his beastly ancestor, a moral-medical paradigm emerged which informed most domestic public welfare and health initiatives. In terms of attitudes directed abroad, imaginaries of empire—the imperialist project necessitating the mobilization of all levels of society—reflected paternalist and liberalist ethos which employed vocabularies of alternatively moral, cultural, or racial superiority and inferiority to outline the respective roles and duties of the benefactor and the benefiter in a system of interdependence. This laid the foundations for international humanitarianism which would later inform the new forms of transnational governance emerging in the wake of the World Wars.

It is within this context that the abolitionist campaign and its first emotional communities—Moral Liberals and Maternal Feminists—emerged. Spurred by a religiously inspired feminism and granted opportunity by a voluntarist philanthropy cultivated decades before, Josephine Butler and other female campaigners joined forces with like-minded male peers and members of the working class, whose fears of the encroaching powers of the state, medicine, and police were piqued by mounting legislation—for instance, making smallpox vaccination obligatory—targeting their bodies. In this and concurrent campaigns against vivisection, against slavery, or for women's suffrage, the discourses employed by female campaigners were feminist and yet tended to mirror the dominant discursive frames of nationalism, imperialism, and liberalism. Carving out a feminine space within societal governance by evoking the either naturally or divinely ordained maternal duty to the spiritual and moral well-being of man, female campaigners wielded gender-based anger and compassion that both constituted and were constituted by uniquely feminine knowledge. Such notions of sexual difference were to a certain extent bolstered by Darwinism and other scientific discourses which tended to reinforce dualisms of masculine–feminine, sexually active–sexually passive, material–immaterial, and so on. With the emergence of scientific medicine, some eugenic currents of feminism sought to emancipate women via in their role in regenerating the race. However, feminist abolitionist campaigns tended to focus on pitting feminine sentimentality and innate sense of morality against masculine scientific rationality. The police doctors' internal inspections of suspected prostitutes for venereal disease were likened to medical rapes which—much like the act of vivisection—debased all parties involved: the doctor who performed it, the prostitute whose bodily sanctity was violated, the state which ordained it, the public which ignored it.

Yet another important—and to a certain extent overlapping—component of the international abolitionist movement which, while not exclusively, mobilized more conservative male actors was that of social purity. The beforementioned anxieties related to moral contamination and deviance found clear expression in a moral panic on white slavery. Here, Purity Crusaders' view of men as inherently evil and thus in need of rules and punishment aligned with states' desires to better police their borders and the behaviors of those within them. The depictions present in the contemporary accounts of purity crusaders' vigilante escapades employ a sensationalist register of life and death to detail the omnipotence of evil and the powerlessness of its victims. While demonstrating much of the xenophobia witnessed in stories of Arab slave-traders in the antislavery movement—for instance, with tales of Jewish procurers of local naïve young girls—the influence of scientism saw a shift from the production and instrumentalization of knowledge on moral deviance by purity crusaders to one of racial degeneration. New sciences like psychology or psychiatry gave new weight to arguments to regulate female bodies and sexuality which increasingly shifted attention away from the original abolitionist goal of abolishing the state's regulation of prostitution to establishing even more repressive laws to tackle sexual deviancy overall. Although Josephine Butler was herself against repressive measures to forcibly moralize the population, her call for a single moral standard between the sexes in which both man and woman were to be held equally responsible for their transgressions did echo this purity crusader discourse. An important difference seen in Butlerian abolitionism is the belief in an innately superior moral and spiritual authority of women compared to men—the latter often portrayed as more susceptible to vice both due to cultural factors, such as the permissive stance taken by society to male wanton sexuality, as well as a natural predisposition.

While early abolitionism in its various forms waned in the aftermath of the Second World War, this feminine immaterialism found expression in American radical feminism, first amongst ecofeminists and second, in a translation of Audre Lorde's notion of the erotic by Catharine MacKinnon in her crusade against pornography into American dominance feminism. This—paired with other local ethos such as Swedish moral feminism or French social Catholicism—helped breathe new life into the abolitionist movement and gave rise to Radical Feminists. They joined other abolitionist activists which had all but disappeared on the international level where its minimal activism focused on slavery and trafficking and had been transformed locally to demonstrate various socio-cultural specificities influenced by various structural settings and contexts. In line with the strategies of the contemporary women's movement which aimed to solicit state action on issues of domestic violence and rape on the level of an emergent transnational civil society, the revitalization of abolitionism was spurred by feminists aiming to bring international attention to prostitution as sexual slavery. Taking shape within the United Nations Working Group on Slavery in particular, this discourse likening prostitution and sex trafficking to slavery developed alongside feminist initiatives to see women's rights included, like human rights, in the developing field of international law.

When geopolitical changes and economic crises of the 1990s shifted national and international concerns to that of state security, sex trafficking rather than prostitution regimes emerged as a key issue with traction. Actors like the Coalition Against Trafficking in Women emerged and diffused what had become a carceral or law-and-order feminist ethos. Fitting within what had become a kind of militarized humanitarianism, sex trafficking morphed into a decontextualized hyper-reality of unquantifiable proportions inherently connected to prostitution—much like the white slavery moral panic seen in at the turn of the twentieth century. However, an important difference from the earlier moral panic was a focus on its victims—an outgrowth of the contemporaneous crime victim's movement which had spread internationally to form not only a kind of social currency of victimhood—split in a neoliberalism logic between the "good victim" who assumes responsibility and the "bad victim" who blames others—but also an epistemic one. This is indeed something Survivors continue to grapple with today.

It is thus within this context that the impetus to treat the sex buyer—largely absent from early abolitionist rhetoric—as a criminal emerged along with Social Regulators. By employing the dominance feminist ethos to refuse any distinction between forced and voluntary prostitution, the criminalization of clients outlined first in Swedish prostitution law in 1999 was presented by abolitionists as morally justifiable and legally sound. The testimonies of prostitution survivors aided in this, especially when they emphasized the visible and invisible harms of trauma which had become dominant in gender-based violence rhetoric in line with the discursive paradigms of human rights practice to oblige state attention. Of course, on the European level, the more American tendency to incarcerate was translated into a more pedagogic punitive treatment of the sex buyer/criminal. Despite some adaptations on the local policy level, the Nordic Model debated in European Parliament between 1997 and 2014 remains more a measure to enculturate and institutionalize gender equality—which is impossible within a society in which prostitution exists—as a matter of moral obligation and responsibility. Abolitionists today thus wield this device as a socializing one: through punishing sex buyers using emotional practices of shame or guilt, it holds a normative function which operates predominantly in the symbolic field. This is indeed what makes the Nordic Model an adaptable legal device to tackle prostitution in a geopolitical space like Europe where local regimes and cultures are so diverse and speaks to its growing popularity and dominance.

An Emotional Legacy

The debate which opened this book was that of Laura Agustin's to Julie Bindel's claim that the abolitionist's current aim to eradicate prostitution rather than normalizing it is the continuation of the work of Josephine Butler. In fact, as

Laura Agustin touches on, Josephine Butler did not condemn prostitution. Instead, she aimed to defend the legal rights and the overall moral consideration of the women—her poor sisters—in prostitution. Her indignation was leveled at the technocracy of government, state doctors, and police which did not hold men and women up to the same moral standard, forcing prostituted women alone to carry the burden—physical, social, and psychological—of mandatory registration and regular internal medical exams for venereal disease. Her abolitionism was born of a larger feminist project imbued with liberal and Christian egalitarian ideals, but also subject to various influences both external and internal to the causes to which she committed her attention, to name but a few: the empathy of humanitarianism, the civilizing mission of imperialism, the anti-scientific materialism of the anti-vivisection and anti-vaccination movements, the fears of degeneracy and demoralization of moral and social hygienism, the moral panic of white slavery, and feminism in its various manifestations.

More to the point, as Josephine Butler and her fellow campaigners enlarged and internationalized their advocacy, the heterogeneity of involved actors grew and the movement fragmented. This resulted in the existence of multiple forms of abolitionism, diversified in terms of approach, strategy, and aim, being pursued by actors on the national and transnational levels before largely waning from the 1950s. Of course, as its founder and most active participant, Josephine Butler's involvement left many lasting marks on the abolitionist movement. Firstly, it set a precedent for an emotionally charged and expansively accommodating discourse calling for the public—particularly women—to act out of a sense of gender-based, anti-aristocratic, religious, nationalist, liberal indignation and moral duty to those less fortunate. It is crucial to bear in mind that the abolitionist cause addressed unpopular subjects, namely sex, poverty, venereal disease, prostitution, and gynecology, and thus movement entrepreneurs like Josephine Butler were quick to adapt their discourse to achieve greater resonance amongst the public. As such, another mark left by her involvement was a viewpoint that the issues of prostitution and trafficking are inherently intertwined. This position was strategically encouraged in the wake of the international white slavery moral panic initiated by a series of sensationalized news stories appearing at the time.

And yet, like Laura Agustin, I remain dubious of the static genealogical link drawn between the abolitionists of the past and the abolitionists of today. Studying the overall movement from the perspective of its emotional communities and emotional styles, I argue that it would be reductive to view the feminist anger which spurred Josephine Butler and other Maternal Feminists to action to end the state's regulation of prostitution as the same as the feminist anger which has driven Radical Feminist abolitionists like Julie Bindel today since the remobilization of the abolitionist cause against prostitution itself in the 2000s. It is worth noting that the Josephine Butler Society—successor to the Ladies' National Association and the Association of Moral and Social Hygiene—signed an open letter in April 2021 opposing the introduction of the Nordic Model in the United Kingdom.[1] The organization today seems to have maintained its Moral Liberal focus on reducing the stigma placed on commercial sex in order to reduce the vulnerability faced by its participants, but also reflects numerous Social Regulator characteristics by pointing to the duty of government to ensure this and by their prioritizing of community-led approaches to issues surrounding prostitution.

Abolitionist Emotional Histories

The emotion work of protest movements like the abolitionist campaigns can both challenge and defend existing social conventions for they are generated and performed by socially situated agents. As tools of social practice, emotions reflect sociocultural structures, arrangements, and understandings—a central theoretical premise of this book. Firstly, these are perceivable through their construction of objects of concern which resulted in a group-contingent emotional style characteristic of a given emotional community while also contributing to the history of these said objects. Secondly, these sociocultural structures, arrangements, and understandings can be grasped through the heterogeneous and even unequal distributions of emotion amongst agents. Indeed, emotion is carried out by an enculturated body embedded in the social field and thus necessarily requiring not only its negotiation with structuring elements of the given emotional arena but also with those resulting from the historicity of that very body, producing what Adrienne Rich has put forward as a sort of "locatedness" and what Donna Haraway has called situated knowledges.[2] The situated emotional knowledge of abolitionists can be looked at as a spectrum polarized by hostility (fueled by anger, contempt and disgust) and esteem (respect, consideration, and admiration—indicates positive worth or approval)—the emotions of both directed towards things both material and immaterial. This contributed to the construction of specific abolitionist emotional styles.

For Maternal Feminists, feminist solidarity was born of compassionate love for their fellow sisters, silent and passive victims of suffering and bolstered by antislavery as well as the contemporary civilizing mission. For Radical Feminists and Survivors, this rose from shared victimhood status or feelings of vulnerability. It fueled outrage against the violence committed by men and the patriarchy, represented either generally as structural violence or individually as personalized violence. To protect themselves, they look to the state for both recognition of their need for protection and also for vindication. For Social Regulators, the "feminist" signifier shifts towards "gender equality" and in close connection to human rights discourse—historically rooted in the emotional community of Moral Liberals characterized by an esteem for justice and an intolerance of injustice, but for which a sort of sensationalism is inherent in drumming up sympathy for the suffering other. However, contrary to Moral Liberals, for Social Regulators the creation of transnational civil society opened terrain for participative governance structures and their contempt for aristocracy and fear of government and police powers were reduced if not lost. The focus has thus shifted to changing the perspectives of states and use them to change the behavior of men. Failure of states to do so has led to yet another abolitionist political emotion: righteous outrage. For Social Regulators, directed against state inaction and sex profiteers, this manifests in emotional practices of guilt and shame to foster knowledge and reform.

This, of course, differs greatly from Purity Crusaders of the past and from Radical Feminists and Survivors of the present given a differing view of man—respectively as inherently evil and as innately sexually predatory. In the case of the former, this was born of the contempt and disgust directed at sin and the sinner, leading to a desire for law and order to punish and correct behavior which fed Radical Feminists' thirst for retributive justice. This necessarily translated into narratives of violence as justification for righteous outrage and an expertise on suffering. Yet this suffering described in abolitionist narratives both past and present of physical violence and abuse highlight most especially the violation of a specifically feminine immaterial worth—first seen in Maternal Feminists' anger directed at men of science for their instrumental rapes.

Toward an Emotional Feminist Future

The feminist debate surrounding prostitution continues to rage on, finding a new home in the #MeToo movement, or Sex Wars 2.0, as referred to earlier. But what is the emancipatory potential of politics based on the women's diverse lived experiences of gender-based violence—and the situated knowledges of fear, anxiety, humiliation, or anger they generate—when the extent to which they are relatable or even commutable to others (and vice versa) remains so limited by the current (largely patriarchal and capitalist) rules defining who can be a knower, what can be known, and what constitutes valid knowledge? Despite having entered the "post-truth" era, it is painfully obvious that rather than generating long-lasting and widespread indignation, the rendering public of a private experience of gender-based violence necessarily shapes, structures, and mediates it in accordance with the dominant discourses and codified norms of a society in which the subordination of women—as well as of their lived experiences, their knowledges—remains endemic. The controversies which continue to be raised by *#MeToo* strike as clear proof of this, for while celebrity testimonies of sexual assault have served to reveal that the rape culture permeates all levels of society, the disclosure of less clear-cut narratives highlighting the ambiguity surrounding our society's notion of consent has drummed up skepticism. Of course, it is nothing new for women to be dismissed either as profiteers of society's voyeuristic thirst for others' suffering or, more frequently, as reactionary hysterics—rooted in the longstanding notion that subordinate groups such as women possess greater emotionality whereas rationality is monopolized by the dominant ones.

However, some scholars have noticed that the feminist focus on gender-specific trauma and pain may hinder transformative politics in other ways. For instance, Wendy Brown has famously argued that in their effort to achieve governmental (both local and transnational level) protection for women, the radical feminists of the anti-pornography and anti-rape movements created a fetishized attachment to the "wound" which, by universalizing the harms inflicted upon women and erasing the complex differences between their lived experiences, maintained the patriarchal norms they were aiming to subvert. In fact, as this study into the emotional histories of abolitionism attests, feminist politics tend to be based on knowledge claims sprung from rather essentialized gender-specific lived experiences. These have predominantly highlighted that of maternity, endowing women with the skill of intuitively understanding others' material and immaterial needs, or that of subordination, endowing women with special capacities to identify diverse and multidimensional forms of suffering and injustice. The latter through the efforts of feminist actors of the women's rights movement in particular has been legitimized and institutionalized within transnational governance structures like the European Union, the World Health Organization, or the United Nations as a professional gender-specific expertise. Given this arguably extensive reach and influence of feminist politics today, the capacity to translate "the personal"—including the diversity my own and others' lived experiences—of the famous feminist slogan "the personal is political" into its knowledge claims (visible in its values, strategies, goals) becomes all the more important. This has indeed been the project of Kimberlé Crenshaw's intersectionality which by taking differences in cultural patterns of oppression beyond gender into account has since helped grant feminism this abovementioned legitimacy and esteem. And yet that there remains more work to be done is exemplified by the heated debate raging amongst feminists today between those supporting sex work and those combating prostitution which itself largely hinges on the epistemic worth of the subjects involved, that is to say, the knowing sex worker versus the knowing victim.

Inspired by her work in affect studies, Sara Ahmed has made a case for *sensational* feminism, not simply in terms of *provocation* but also of *sense-making*, so as to make feminism into a movement *of* and *to* consciousness. When on the busy daylit streets of Paris an oncoming male pedestrian cuts me off and whispers into my face at just a few centimeters' distance that I am "*très charmante*," it is not a warm feeling of pleasure that I feel—as one "should" when receiving a compliment—but a searing hot mixture of fear and revulsion. My emotional dissonance signals to me that something is wrong, that this is not how I should feel when receiving a "compliment" when I am moving within public space. Pointing to the example of the *Everyday Sexism* project—an online platform on which women testify to their encounters with sexism—Sara Ahmed explains how through sharing, repeating, understanding, recognizing, and making connections, women can *make sense* of their lived experiences and transform their individual harm into a collective one. By giving up one's own object of anger, for instance, in favor of a collective feminist one, she sees the potential to sort of sublimate feminism's wounded attachments, as identified by Wendy Brown, and achieve truly emancipatory politics. Similarly, Teresa Langle de Paz draws from a phenomenological approach to gendered affect to propose emotionality, namely through the pervasive primary agency found in the affective unconscious component of feminist emotion, as an epistemic site for resituating narratives of women's subordination and passive victimization, especially in the transnational context where such discourses dominate along racial, classist, and economical lines.[3]

I find great inspiration in such feminist projects to instrumentalize emotion in an epistemological and materialized way. Demonstrating clear epistemological functions, emotions are sense-making; most—like anger or compassion—are intentionally directed towards objects which they appraise, interpret, define, shape, and even subjectivize. In this sense, emotions are also socioculturally constructed on multiple levels: my culture determines whether the sight of someone spitting on the sidewalk disgusts me or not; whether or not I show my disgust and, if so, how I would go about doing it; and, finally, what my knowledge of disgust is in terms of how frequently I experience it, which additionally depends on my situatedness—namely my proximity to objects likely to trigger such an evaluation in me. Consequently, emotions are inequitably experienced and distributed across different levels of the same society. By way of example, being part of a socially subordinate group affects members' lived experience of shame so that it becomes less a precise episodic feeling or emotion, as Sandra Lee Bartky has argued, but a "pervasive affective attunement to the social environment"[4] resulting in large part from an internalized low evaluation of one's own self as a member of that said group. This makes emotion an important site for perceiving of, understanding, and acting against these inequalities. However, as Sara Ahmed rightly warns, it is essential to maintain a critical relationship with emotion:

> [I]t is important that we do not make feminist emotion into a site of truth: as if it is always clear or self-evident that our anger is right. When anger becomes righteous it can be oppressive; to assume anger makes us right can be a wrong. [...] Feminist emotions are mediated and opaque; they are sites of struggle, and we must persist in struggling with them.[5]

Indeed, the great mobilizing capacity of emotions—as the moral panics of the past and the populist politics of the present have surely demonstrated—transforms them into vital tools for not just constructing meaning but also prescribing goals and directing actions on the collective level. They should, however, be used responsibly and thus with an understanding of the histories from whence they have come as well as of where we want them to take us.

Notes

Introduction

1. Survivors' Agenda. "The Survivors' Agenda." https://survivorsagenda.org/agenda/full-agenda/.
2. Lucia Graves, "The Strange Alliance between #MeToo and the Anti-porn Movement," *The Guardian* (2018). Melissa Farley, "#MeToo Must Include Prostitution," *Dignity: A Journal on Sexual Exploitation and Violence* 3, no. 1, art. 9 (2018): 1–5.
3. Anne Summers, "Which Women? What Europe? Josephine Butler and the International Abolitionist Federation," *History Workshop Journal* 62, no. 1 (2006): 214–31. Judith Walkowitz, *Prostitution and Victorian Society: Women, Class, and the State* (Cambridge: Cambridge University Press, 1980). Lilian Mathieu, *La fin du tapin. Sociologie de la croisade pour l'abolition de la Prostitution* (Paris: François Bourin, 2014).
4. Julie Bindel, *The Pimping of Prostitution: Abolishing the Sex Work Myth* (London: Palgrave Macmillan, 2017), 2.
5. Laura Maria Agustin, "The New Abolitionist Model," *Jacobinmag*, 2017. https://www.jacobinmag.com/2017/12/sex-work-the-pimping-of-prostitution-review.
6. Respectively from reader reviews accessed at https://www.goodreads.com/book/show/34428143-the-pimping-of-prostitution and https://www.bookdepository.com/Pimping-Prostitution-Julie-Bindel/9781137558893.
7. Mathieu, *La fin du tapin*, chapter 3.
8. Barbara H. Rosenwein, *Emotional Communities in the Early Middle Ages* (Cornell: Cornell University Press, 2006), 2.
9. Benno Gammerl, "Emotional Styles: Concepts and Challenges," *Rethinking History* 16, no. 2 (2012): 163.
10. It is worth mentioning that the abolitionist campaigns investigated here have built their understanding of prostitution around a cis-gendered female prostitute. For instance, Nordic Model Now explicitly calls for separate social services provisions between cis-gendered females and males and transgender people in prostitution because "punters are almost entirely men," Nordic Model Now, "What is the Nordic Model?" https://nordicmodelnow.org/what-is-the-nordic-model/.
11. Monique Scheer, "Are Emotions a Kind of Practice and Is That What Makes Them Have a History? A Bourdieuian Approach to Understanding Emotion," *History and Theory* 51, no. 2 (2012): 193–220.

12 Sara Ahmed, *The Cultural Politics of Emotion* (Edinburgh and London: Edinburgh University Press and Routledge, 2013), 93.

13 Anna Durnová, "Lost in Translation: Expressing Emotions in Policy Deliberation" in *Handbook of Critical Policy Studies* eds. Frank Fischer, Douglas Torgerson, Anna Durnová, and Michael Orsini (Cheltenham: Edward Elgar Publishing, 2015), 222–40.

14 Pierre Bourdieu, "Décrire et prescrire," *Actes de la Recherche en Sciences Sociales* 38, no. 2 (1981): 69–73.

15 Ibid.

16 Michel Foucault, *L'archéologie du savoir* (Paris: Gallimard, 1969).

17 James M. Jasper, Michael P. Young, and Elke Zuern, *Public Characters: The Politics of Reputation and Blame* (Oxford: Oxford University Press, 2020), 2.

18 Ibid., 3.

19 IAF, *The New Abolitionists: A Narrative of a Year's Work: Being an Account of The Mission Undertaken to The Continent of Europe by Mrs. Josephine Butler, and of The Events Subsequent Thereupon / Published under the Direction of the British, Continental, and General Federation for the Abolition of Government Regulation of Prostitution* (London: Dyer Brothers, 1876), 26.

20 L. Hay-Cooper, *Josephine Butler and Her Work for Social Purity* (London: Society for Promoting Christian Knowledge, 1922), 15.

21 Anna Fisher, "Josephine Butler: Pioneering Feminist Activist," Nordic Model Now, June 1, 2020. https://nordicmodelnow.org/2020/06/01/josephine-butler-pioneering-feminist-activist/

22 It is worth mentioning that Josephine Butler penned two biographies herself: *Life of St Catherine of Siena* (1898) and *Life of Pastor Oberlin* (1882).

23 In an article appearing in the short-lived journal *Review of Internationalism*, cited in Madeleine Herren, "Governmental Internationalism and the Beginning of a New World Order in the Late Nineteenth Century" in *The Mechanics of Internationalism: Culture, Society, and Politics From the 1840s to the First World War*, eds. Martin H. Geyer and Johannes Paulmann (Oxford: Oxford University Press, 2001), 121.

Chapter 1

1 Alexandre Parent-Duchâtelet, *De la prostitution dans la ville de Paris considérée sous le rapport de l'hygiène publique, de la morale et de l'administration* (Paris: J.-B. Baillière et Fils, 1836).

2 Alain Corbin, *Les filles de noces: Misère sexuelle et prostitution au XIXe et XXe siècles* (Paris: Aubier Montaigne, 1978), 17.

3 See Auguste Comte, *Cours de philosophie positive par M. Auguste Comte*, 1 (Paris: Rouen Frères, Bachelier, 1830).

4 William Acton, *Prostitution, Considered in Its Moral, Social, and Sanitary Aspects, in London and Other Large Cities and Garrison Towns, with Proposals for the Mitigation and Prevention of Its Attendant Evils* (London: J. Churchill, 1857), 34.

5 See notably David Arnold, *Colonizing the Body: State Medicine and Epidemic Disease in Nineteenth-Century India* (Berkeley: University of California Press, 1993).

6 Philippe Ricord, *Traité pratique des maladies vénériennes* (Paris: Librairie des Sciences Médicales de Just Rouvier et E. le Bouvier, 1838).

7 Parliament, *Vagrancy Act of 1824*, Section 3. http://www.legislation.gov.uk/ukpga/Geo4/5/83/contents/enacted. For more, see Julia A. Laite, "The Association for Moral and Social Hygiene: Abolitionism and Prostitution Law in Britain 1915–1959," *Women's History Review* 17, no. 2 (2008), 207–23; Julia A. Laite, *Common Prostitutes and Ordinary Citizens: Commercial Sex in London, 1885–1960* (London: Palgrave, 2012).

8 William Acton, *Prostitution, Considered in Its Moral, Social, and Sanitary Aspects, in London and Other Large Cities and Garrison Towns, with Proposals for the Mitigation and Prevention of Its Attendant Evils*, 2nd edition (London: J. Churchill, 1870), 99.

9 Acton, *Prostitution*, 2nd ed., 208.

10 Ibid., 205.

11 Walkowitz, *Prostitution and Victorian Society*, 90–1.

12 Peter N. Stearns, *Global Outrage: The Impact of World Opinion on Contemporary History* (Oxford: Oneworld Publications Limited, 2005), 78.

13 Barbara H. Rosenwein, *Anger: The Conflicted History of an Emotion* (New Haven: Yale University Press, 2020), 122–8.

14 Chauncy A. Goodrich, et al. *Webster's Complete Dictionary of the English Language* (London: George Bell & Sons, 1886), 682.

15 Josephine Elizabeth Grey Butler, "Letter to her Niece Edith Leupold, 8 March 1867," in *Josephine Butler and the Prostitution Campaigns: The Moral Reclaimability of Prostitutes*, ed. Jane Jordan and Ingrid Sharp (London: Taylor & Francis, 2003), 82.

16 Ibid.

17 Ibid., 83.

18 Josephine Elizabeth Grey Butler, *An Autobiographical Memoir*, ed. George W. and Lucy A. Johnson (Bristol: J. W. Arrowsmith Press, 1909), 88.

19 Society of Friends, *Petition from London Yearly Meeting of the Society of Friends, Presented to Parliament On 16 June 1783*, 1783. http://abolition.e2bn.org/source_34.html.

20 Michael Barnett, *Empire of Humanity: A History of Humanitarianism* (Ithaca: Cornell University Press, 2011), 57.

21 James A. H. Murray, ed. *A New English Dictionary of Historical Principles* (Oxford: Clarendon Press, 1901), vol. 5, 214–15.
22 Righteous indignation arguably became a longstanding feature of English emotional culture during this time. Anthropologist Kate Fox noted in her ethnography *Watching the English: The Hidden Rules of English Behaviour* that experiencing feelings of shock, outrage, and righteous indignation constitutes one of the most beloved of English pastimes.
23 William T. Stead, "The Steamy Side of Empire," *Pall Mall Budget*, February 3, 1887, 6.
24 Brycchan Carey, *British Abolitionism and the Rhetoric of Sensibility: Writing, Sentiment and Slavery, 1760–1807* (New York: Palgrave, 2005), 1.
25 Ibid., 5, 37–8.
26 Josephine Elizabeth Grey Butler, "The Modern Slave Trade. Letter to the Editor of the Shield. 1 May 1880," in *Josephine Butler and the Prostitution Campaigns: Child Prostitution and the Age of Consent*, ed. Jane Jordan and Ingrid Sharp (London: Taylor & Francis, 2003), 22.
27 Walkowitz, *Prostitution and Victorian Society*, 110.
28 Christopher Leslie Brown, *Moral Capital: Foundations of British Abolitionism* (Chapel Hill: UNC Press Books, 2006), 57.
29 Ibid., 25–6.
30 Joseph R. Gusfield, *Symbolic Crusade: Status Politics and the American Temperance Movement* (Chicago: University of Illinois Press, 1986).
31 Sara Ahmed, *The Promise of Happiness* (Durham, NC: Duke University Press, 2010), 124.
32 Ibid., 124–5.
33 Ibid., 125.
34 Barnett, *Empire of Humanity*, 49.
35 See also Chapter 5 of Carey, *British Abolitionism and the Rhetoric of Sensibility*, for more on this speech's authenticity, its historical context, and its impact.
36 "Debate on Mr. Wilberforce's Resolutions Respecting the Slave Trade" in William Cobbett, *Cobbett's Parliamentary History of England: From the Norman Conquest, in 1066, to the Year, 1803*, 28, ed. William Cobbett (London: T. C. Hansard, 1816), 41.
37 Ibid.
38 Brown, *Moral Capital*, 57.
39 Barnett, *Empire of Humanity*, 60.
40 Walkowitz, *Prostitution and Victorian Society*, 1.
41 Josephine Elizabeth Grey Butler, *Personal Reminiscences of a Great Crusade* (London: H. Marshall and Son, 1910), 59.
42 Thomas Clarkson, *The History of the Rise, Progress, and Accomplishment of the Abolition of the African Slave Trade by the British Parliament* (Farnham: John W. Parker, 1839).

43 Goodrich et al., *Webster's Complete Dictionary*, 682.
44 Butler, *Personal Reminiscences of a Great Crusade*, 166.
45 Ibid.
46 Josephine Elizabeth Grey Butler, *The Constitution Violated: An Essay* (Edinburgh: Edmonston and Douglas, 1871), 5.
47 Ladies' National Association, "The Ladies' Appeal and Protest," *Daily News*, London, January 1, 1870.
48 Ibid.
49 Letter 1513 to an unidentified correspondent, John Stuart Mill, *The Collected Works of John Stuart Mill, Volume XVII – The Later Letters of John Stuart Mill 1849-1873 Part IV [1869]*, ed. Francis E. Mineka and Dwight N. Lindley (Toronto: University of Toronto Press, London: Routledge & Kegan Paul, 1972), 1681. http://oll.libertyfund.org/titles/254.
50 National Association for the Repeal of the CD Acts, *Summary of the Evil Principles and Revolting Practices of the Immoral Laws known as the Contagious Diseases Acts*, Leaflet D, The Women's Library, 3AMS/B/01/02, 1877.
51 John Stuart Mill testified before the Royal Commission in 1870 against the Acts on the basis of the forced internment of women but not men, thereby calling them unjustifiable as they "intentionally" violated the personal liberty of prostitutes and "incidentally" those of all women. Royal Commission on the Contagious Diseases Acts, *Report of Royal Commission upon the Administration and Operation of the Contagious Diseases* (London, Printed by George Edward Eyre and William Spottiswoode, for Her Majesty's Stationery Office, 1871), 99.
52 National Association, "An Address to Working Men and Women, Relative to a Recent Distressing Case of Suicide, at Aldershot, under Cruel, Oppressive, and Immoral Acts of Parliament," *Josephine Butler and the Prostitution Campaigns: The Constitution Violated: The Parliamentary Campaign* 3, ed. Jane Jordan and Ingrid Sharp (London: Taylor & Francis, 2003), 30–7.
53 John Stuart Mill, *On Liberty* (London: Longmans, Green, Reader, and Dyer, 1869), 22.
54 Josephine Elizabeth Grey Butler, "Address Delivered at Croydon [1871]," in *Josephine Butler and the Prostitution Campaigns: The Ladies' Appeal and Protest* 3, ed. Jane Jordan and Ingrid Sharp (London: Taylor & Francis, 2003), 163.
55 Ibid.
56 Josephine Elizabeth Grey Butler, *Social Purity, An Address Given to Students at Cambridge, Social Purity Alliance [1879]* (London: Dyer Bros, 1881). This address was given in Cambridge in May 1879, at a meeting of the Committee of the Social Purity Alliance, created in 1873. Butler would later break with the social purity movement in the 1880s.
57 See for instance Victor Flanchon, "L'affaire Forissier," *La Lanterne*), July 13, 1903.

58 Corbin, *Les filles de noces.*
59 Bernard Porter, *The Origins of the Vigilant State: The London Metropolitan Police Special Branch before the First World War* (Woodbridge: Boydell and Brewer, 1987), 2. He connects Josephine Butler's campaign against the *police des mœurs* and the Fenian bombings to the founding of the London Metropolitan Police Special Branch in 1883, marking an end to Britain's liberal police tradition and indicating a growing feeling of vulnerability by government in the years leading up to the First World War. The Special Branch are political police, handling matters of national security and intelligence.
60 Butler, *The Constitution Violated: An Essay*, 82.
61 Ibid., 91.
62 Josephine Elizabeth Grey Butler, *Government by Police* (London: T. Fisher Unwin, 1888), 80.
63 Ibid., 77.
64 IAF, *The New Abolitionists: A Narrative of a Year's Work.*
65 Butler, *Personal Reminiscences of a Great Crusade*, 62–3.
66 Ibid., 41.
67 Josephine Elizabeth Grey Butler, *Letter to Frederic Harrison*, Women's Library, GB 106 3JBL/02/20, 9 May 1868.
68 Jordan, "Prostitution and the Contagious Diseases Acts."
69 For more on this, see Ruth G. Hodgkinson, *The Origins of the National Health Service: The Medical Services of the New Poor Law, 1837–1871* (Berkeley: University of California Press, 1967).
70 For a discussion of the populist current in the anti-vaccination movement, see Nadja Durbach, *Bodily Matters: The Anti-Vaccination Movement in England, 1853–1907* (Durham, NC: Duke University Press, 2004), 70.
71 In Great Britain, legislation in 1898 and 1907 ended compulsory vaccination by allowing parents to attain exemption certificates.
72 Durbach, *Bodily Matters*, 124.
73 Acton, *Prostitution*, second ed., 219.
74 Adrian Desmond, *The Politics of Evolution: Morphology, Medicine, and Reform in Radical London* (Chicago: University of Chicago Press, 1992).
75 Elizabeth M. Knowles and Angela Partington, *The Oxford Dictionary of Quotations* (Oxford: Oxford University Press, 1999), 3.
76 Jonathan Smith, "The Huxley-Wilberforce 'Debate' on Evolution, 30 June 1860," in *Extension of Romanticism and Victorianism on the Net, BRANCH: Britain, Representation and Nineteenth-Century History*, ed. Dino Franco Felluga, February 2013. http://www.branchcollective.org/?ps_articles=jonathan-smith-the-huxley-wilberforce-debate-on-evolution-30-june-1860.
77 Tzvetan Todorov, *Imperfect Garden: The Legacy of Humanism*, trans. C. Cosman (Princeton: Princeton University Press: 2002), 23.

78 Durbach, *Bodily Matters*, 98.
79 Goodrich et al., *Webster's Complete Dictionary*, 3.
80 Jennifer Worth, *Farewell to the East End* (London: Hachette UK, 2009).
81 Josephine Elizabeth Grey Butler, "Letter to Dr. James John Garth Wilkinson," cited in James John Garth Wilkinson, *The Forcible Introspection of Women for the Army and Navy by the Oligarchy, Considered Physically* (London: J. Pitman, 1870), 23.
82 Wendy McElroy, "The Contagious Disease Acts," *Freedom Daily*, March 2000. https://www.fff.org/explore-freedom/article/contagious-disease-acts/.
83 Josephine Elizabeth Grey Butler, "Letter from Josephine E. Butler to Dr. William Carter. 'Private' 1 April 1880," in *Josephine Butler and the Prostitution Campaigns: Child Prostitution and the Age of Consent*, ed. Jane Jordan and Ingrid Sharp (London: Taylor & Francis, 2003), 17–18. Emphasis appears in the original.
84 Ibid., 18. Emphasis appears in the original.
85 Karen Halttunen, "Humanitarianism and the Pornography of Pain in Anglo-American Culture," *The American Historical Review* 100, no. 2 (1995): 303–34. For a discussion of how melodramatic theater and literature influenced political expression through the example of Josephine Butler and W. T. Stead, see Judith Walkowitz, *City of Dreadful Delight: Narratives of Sexual Danger in Late-Victorian London* (Chicago: University of Chicago Press, 1992).
86 Jenny Sharpe, *Allegories of Empire: The Figure of Woman in the Colonial Text* (Minneapolis: University of Minnesota Press, 1993), 4.
87 Walkowitz, *Prostitution and Victorian Society*, 146.
88 Ornella Moscucci, *The Science of Woman: Gynaecology and Gender in England, 1800–1929* (Cambridge: Cambridge University Press, 1993).
89 Ibid.
90 For instance, abolitionist Dr. Revd. Hooppell described and demonstrated the use of the speculum to working-class audiences only to be stopped by Josephine Butler who called it "needlessly and grossly indecent." Cited in Jane Jordan, *Josephine Butler* (London: John Murray, 2001), 132–3.
91 Josephine Elizabeth Gray Butler, *A Few Words Addressed to True-Hearted Women*, The Women's Library, 3JBL/04/09, March 13, 1872.
92 Émilie de Morsier, "Discours du 7 Dec 1883," in her *La mission de la femme: discours et fragments* (Paris: Fischbacher, 1897), 58. Author's translation.
93 Jack the Ripper's mutilation and murder of prostitutes in London's East End in 1888 was in many ways the very manifestation of such a diabolical nightmare. Contemporary charges that he was a demented surgeon and vivisector were frequent amongst other rumors and speculative stories circulating in the press. For more, see Colin Milburn, "Science from Hell: Jack the Ripper and Victorian Vivisection," in *Science Images and Popular Images of The Sciences*, ed. Hüppauf Bernd-Rüdiger and Peter Weingart (New York: Routledge, 2008), 125–58.

94 Elizabeth Blackwell, *Essays in Medical Sociology*, 2 (London: Ernest Bell, 1902), 42–3.
95 Butler, "Letter to Dr. James John Garth Wilkinson," 22.
96 Georges Vigarello, *Histoire du viol: XVIe–XXe siècle* (Paris: Éditions du Seuil, 1998).
97 James John Garth Wilkinson, *The Forcible Introspection of Women for the Army and Navy by the Oligarchy, Considered Physically* (London: J. Pitman, 1870), 5.
98 Michel Foucault, *Naissance de la clinique une archéologie du regard médical* (Paris: Presses universitaires de France, 1963).
99 For more on Descartes's metaphor of the body as machine and its place in modern medicine, see Donna Haraway, "Situated Knowledges: The Science Question in Feminism and the Privilege of Partial Perspective," in *Turning Points in Qualitative Research: Tying Knots in a Handkerchief*, ed. Yvonna S. Lincoln and Norman K. Denzin (Lanham: Rowman Altamira, 2003), 21–46.
100 Butler, *On the Moral Reclaimability of Prostitutes*.
101 In the case of animals, this implied to various extents a sort of anthropomorphism. For more on the parallels between these two movements, see Moscucci, *The Science of Woman*; Mary Ann Elston, "Women and Anti-Vivisection in Victorian England, 1870–1900," in *Vivisection in Historical Perspective*, ed. Nicolaas A. Rupke (London: Routledge & Kegan Paul, 1987), 259–94.
102 Butler, "Letter to Dr. James John Garth Wilkinson," 24.

Chapter 2

1 Stephanie Limoncelli, *The Politics of Trafficking: The First International Movement to Combat the Sexual Exploitation of Women* (Stanford: Stanford University Press, 2010), 19.
2 IAF, *The New Abolitionists: A Narrative of a Year's Work*, 3.
3 Ibid., 10.
4 For more on the different receptions of and engagements in Butler's crusade by feminists in Switzerland, Belgium, and France, see Christine Machiels, *Les féminismes et la prostitution 1860–1960* (Rennes: Presses universitaires de Rennes, 2016). For a comparative study of abolitionism in France, the Netherlands, Germany and Italy, see Limoncelli, *The Politics of Trafficking*.
5 Josephine Elizabeth Grey Butler, *The Revival and Extension of the Abolitionist Cause, A Letter to the Members of the Ladies' National Association* (Winchester: John T. Doswell, The Women's Library, 3HJW/A/6/03, 1887).
6 Cited in Alan Hunt, *Governing Morals: A Social History of Moral Regulation* (Cambridge: Cambridge University Press, 1999), 162.
7 Alfred Dyer, *The European Slave Trade in English Girls* (London: Dyer Brothers, Paternoster Row, 1882).

8   Butler, "The Modern Slave Trade," 21.
9   Opening address of A. S. Dyer, *The European Slave Trade in English Girls*.
10 See Jo Doezema, "Loose Women or Lost Women? The Re-emergence of the Myth of White Slavery in Contemporary Discourses of Trafficking in Women," *Gender Issues* 18, no. 1 (1999): 23–50.
11 Butler, "The Modern Slave Trade," 24.
12 Mary Ann Irwin, "'White Slavery' as Metaphor Anatomy of a Moral Panic," *Ex Post Facto: The History Journal* 5 (1996). https://www.walnet.org/csis/papers/irwin-wslavery.html.
13 Chieko Ichikawa, "A Body Politic of Women's Own: Josephine Butler, Social Purity, and National Identity," *Victorian Review* 41, no. 1 (2015): 116.
14 Josephine Elizabeth Grey Butler, "A Letter to the Mothers of England: Commended also to the Attention of Fathers, Ministers of Religion, and Legislators [1881]," in *Josephine Butler and the Prostitution Campaigns: Child Prostitution and the Age of Consent*, ed. Jane Jordan and Ingrid Sharp (London: Taylor & Francis, 2003), 80–94.
15 Josephine Elizabeth Grey Butler, "'Laws for the Protection of Youth', Letter Addressed to the Editor of the *Sentinel* [1882]," in *Josephine Butler and the Prostitution Campaigns: Child Prostitution and the Age of Consent*, ed. Jane Jordan and Ingrid Sharp (London: Taylor & Francis, 2003), 103.
16 National Vigilance Association, *The White Slave Trade: Transactions of the International Congress on the White Slave Trade, 21–23 June 1899* (London: Office of the National Vigilance Association, 1899), 6.
17 Other notable anti-trafficking organizations included the Jewish Association for the Protection of Girls and Women, International Catholic Association for the Protection of Girls, the Federation of National Unions for the Protection of Girls, and *les Amies de la jeune fille*.
18 For instance, the International Conventions for the Suppression of the White Slave Traffic passed in 1902 and 1910 committed states to appointing specially trained officials for monitoring borders and employment agencies, and for obtaining information on recruitment strategies from foreign prostitutes under interrogation. For more on this, see Jean Allain, "White Slave Traffic in International Law," *Journal of Trafficking and Human Exploitation* 11 (2017): 1–40.
19 This is Thomas Aquinas's conceptualization of divine providence, which he saw as the very essence of God, Thomas Aquinas, *Summa theologica*, 1702, http://www.documentacatholicaomnia.eu/03d/1225-1274,_Thomas_Aquinas,_Summa_Theologiae-Supplementum,_FR.pdf.
20 Roberts, *Paternalism in Early Victorian England*.
21 Claudius Buchanan, "The Star in the East," in his *The Works of the Rev. Claudius Buchanan* (New York: Whiting and Watson, 1812), 312–13.

22 Stephen H. Gregg, "'A Truly Christian Hero': Religion, Effeminacy, and Nation in the Writings of the Societies for Reformation of Manners," *Eighteenth-Century Life* 25, no. 1 (2001): 17.
23 For more on how these anxieties surrounding effeminates and homosexuality developed across the twentieth century, see Alain Corbin, Courtine Jean-Jacques and Vigarello Georges, eds., *Histoire de la virilité, le triomphe de la virilité, le XIXe siècle* 2. Paris: Le Seuil, 2011., especially Part 6: Le fardeau de la virilité.
24 See Margaret Hunt, "The De-Eroticization of Women's Liberation: Social Purity Movements and the Revolutionary Feminism of Sheila Jeffreys," *Feminist Review* 34, no. 1 (1990): 23–46.
25 Cited in Gregg, "'A Truly Christian Hero,'" 18.
26 Hunt, "The De-Eroticization of Women's Liberation," 27.
27 Cited in Hunt, "The De-Eroticization of Women's Liberation," 26–7.
28 Hunt, "The De-Eroticization of Women's Liberation," 26.
29 See Hunt, *Governing Morals*, particularly chapter 1.
30 Ibid., 67.
31 Christophe Traïni, *The Animal Rights Struggle* (Amsterdam: Amsterdam University Press, 2016) 10–14. French historical sociologist Christophe Traïni reports that this was the case for animal protection and anti-vivisection societies in Germany, Switzerland, and France.
32 Parliament, *The Parliamentary Debates: Official Reports, 36, comprising the period from 29 October 1801 to 12 August 1803* (London: T. C. Hansard, 1820), 845.
33 Ibid.
34 Ibid., 844.
35 Ibid., 840.
36 Ibid., 844.
37 Rob Boddice, *The Science of Sympathy: Morality, Evolution, and Victorian Civilization* (Champaign: University of Illinois Press, 2016).
38 For a comprehensive study, see David J. Cox, Kim Stevenson, Candida Harris, and Judith Rowbotham, *Public Indecency in England 1857–1960: 'A Serious and Growing Evil'* (London and New York: Routledge, 2015).
39 Hunt, *Governing Morals*, 170.
40 Cited in Lucy Bland, *Banishing the Beast: Feminism, Sex and Morality* (London: Tauris Parke Paperbacks, 2001), 104.
41 Lucy Bland, "'Purifying' the Public World: Feminist Vigilantes in Late Victorian England," *Women's History Review* 1, no. 3 (1992): 403.
42 Cited in Hunt, *Governing Morals*, 170.
43 Editor, "The National Vigilance Association," *The Echo*, October 13, 1888, London, No. 6174, 1.
44 A girl aged 10 could commonly be employed as a domestic servant until the Education Act of 1870 which still saw most girls over age 14 engaged in some

form of regular employment. However, this trope of "aristocratic seduction" is not represented in the contemporary rape or sexual abuse cases: most complainants and defenders were of similar rank and social status. Louise A. Jackson, *Child Sexual Abuse in Victorian England* (London and New York: Routledge, 2013), 29.

45 Carol Harrington, *Politicization of Sexual Violence: From Abolitionism to Peacekeeping* (Farnham: Ashgate Publishing, Ltd., 2010), 168.

46 Paula Bartley, *Prostitution: Prevention and Reform in England, 1860–1914* (London and New York: Routledge, 2012), 119–36.

47 Lady Francis Balfour, "The Travellers' Aid Society," *The Sentinel* 8, no. 5 (1886): 56–7.

48 Cited and discussed in Stephen Legg, *Prostitution and the Ends of Empire* (Durham, NC: Duke University Press, 2014), 177.

49 Laura Lammasniemi, "Anti-White Slavery Legislation and its Legacies in England," *Anti-Trafficking Review*, no. 9 (2017): 64–76.

50 Parliament, *Report of the Royal Commission on Alien Immigration*, 1 (London, Royal Commission on Alien Immigration, H. M. Stationery Office, 1903), 426.

51 Lammasniemi, "Anti-White Slavery Legislation and its Legacies in England," 73.

52 In this case, the immigration of Jews fleeing Russia was a target, as well as the reportedly strong presence of Jewish prostitutes in London's East End.

53 Anti-Semitism was rife in white slavery rhetoric, even Adolf Hitler's *Mein Kampf* describes the Jewish traffickers in Vienna. For how this was translated and effectively depoliticized to become a cultural trope in contemporary literature, see Claire Solomon, "Reconsidering Anti-Semitism and White Slavery in Contemporary Historical Fiction about Argentina," *Comparative Literature* 63, no. 3 (2011): 307–27.

54 One of the few challenges to such hyperbolic propaganda came from feminist suffragette Teresa Billington-Greig. See Christine Machiels, "The 'Truth about White Slavery.' Présentation d'une enquête réalisée par Teresa Billington-Greig pour *The English Review* (juin 1913)," *Recherches sociologiques et anthropologiques* 39, no. 1 (2008): 27–40.

55 For an example of convictions happening in the weeks following the act's passing: Constance Backhouse, "The White Women's Labor Laws: Anti-Chinese Racism in Early Twentieth-Century Canada," *Law and History Review* 14, no. 2 (1996): 315–68.

56 Alex Smolak, "White Slavery, Whorehouse Riots, Venereal Disease, and Saving Women: Historical Context of Prostitution Interventions and Harm Reduction in New York City during the Progressive Era," *Social Work in Public Health* 28, no. 5 (2013): 496–508.

57 Jessica R. Pliley, "Any Other Immoral Purpose: The Mann Act, Policing Women, and the American State, 1900–1941" (PhD dissertation, The Ohio State University, 2010).

58 Tommy Fallot, *Communication sur l'organisation de la lutte contre la pornographie: faite au congrès de l'Association protestante pour l'étude pratique des questions sociales. Marseille, 28 et 29 Octobre* (Nice: V.-E. Gauthier 1891), 10.
59 Cited in Susan Kingsley Kent, *Sex and Suffrage in Britain 1860–1914* (London: Routledge, 2005), 154.
60 Elizabeth Blackwell, *Medicine and Morality* (London: W. Speaight and Sons, 1881), 17.
61 Elizabeth Blackwell, *Wrong and Right Methods of Dealing with Social Evil, as shewn by lately-published parliamentary evidence* (New York: A. Brentano and Co., 1883), 43.
62 See Walkowitz, *Prostitution and Victorian Society*; Barry J. Faulk, *Music Hall and Modernity: The Late-Victorian Discovery of Popular Culture* (Athens: Ohio University Press, 2004); Frank Mort, *Dangerous Sexualities: Medico-Moral Politics in England Since 1830* (New York: Routledge, 2002).
63 For instance, the relationship between the NVA and the London Metropolitan Police suffered from the appointment of Commissioner Sir Charles Warren who dismayed Purity Crusaders by ending the active surveillance and suppression of brothels for fear of driving them from the slums to the respectable neighborhoods. Bartley, *Prostitution: Prevention and Reform in England*, 161–6.
64 Wyndham Anstis Bewes, *Manual of Vigilance Law* (London: Office of the National Vigilance Association, 1888). Its opening page refers to article VI of the Vagrants Act (5 Geo. 4 c. 83) allowing for private citizens to make arrests which states: "And be it further enacted, That it shall be lawful for any Person whatsoever to apprehend any Person who shall be found offending against this Act, and forthwith to take and convey him or her before some Justice of the Peace, to be dealt with in such Manner as is herein-before directed, or to deliver him or her to any Constable or other Peace Officer of the Place where he or she shall have been apprehended, to be so taken and conveyed as aforesaid […]"
65 See Edward J. Bristow, *Vice and Vigilance: Purity Movements in Britain since 1700* (Dublin: Gill and Macmillan, 1977), 45. He affirms that the police principally saw such vigilantism as assisting their efforts against vice, particularly given the unpopularity of such arrests and the enormity of the task.
66 Cited in Faulk, *Music Hall and Modernity,* 82.
67 Faulk, *Music Hall and Modernity,* The author argues that the public's lack of support for the crusade of against the Empire is in large part down to the qualification of Laura Ormiston Chant's philanthropic expertise as "amateur" when set against the divergent opinion of male professionals, believing that prostitution was best managed under visual surveillance.
68 Laura Ormiston Chant, *Why We Attacked the Empire* (London: Horace Marshall and Son, 1895), 5–6.

69 Such a notion was buttressed by key advances in scientific research which had immediate revolutionizing effects in scientific medicine, such as Louis Pasteur and Robert Koch's germ theory which led to advanced studies in microbiology or the rise of more effective sanitary practices like Joseph Lister's aseptic techniques which, together with the invention of anesthesia, transformed surgery and clinical research. See Marius Turda, *Modernism and Eugenics* (Berlin: Springer, 2010).

70 Kate Krug, "Women Ovulate, Men Spermate: Elizabeth Blackwell as a Feminist Physiologist," *Journal of the History of Sexuality* 7, no. 1 (1996): 61.

71 Cesare Lombroso and Guglielmo Ferrero, *The Female Offender* (New York, D. Appleton, 1895). http://brittlebooks.library.illinois.edu/brittlebooks_open/Books2009-08/lombce0001femoff/lombce0001femoff.pdf.

72 Phrase borrowed from Heidi Rimke and Alan Hunt, "From Sinners to Degenerates: The Medicalization of Morality in the 19th Century," *History of the Human Sciences* 15, no. 1 (2002): 59–88.

73 Elizabeth Blackwell, *The Human Element in Sex: Being a Medical Enquiry into the Relation of Sexual Physiology to Christian Morality*, Enlarged (London: J. and A. Churchill, 1884), 41.

74 William Booth, *In Darkest England and the Way Out,* Salvation Army (New York: Funk and Wagnalls, 1890), 205.

75 Howard S. Becker, *Outsiders: Studies in the Sociology of Deviance* (New York: The Free Press, 1963), 147.

76 Bureau International, *La Traite des Blanches*, Bulletin du Bureau International, December 1901, no. 4, The Women's Library, 4IBS/4/1, p. 3. Author's translation.

77 Cited in A. Hunt, *Governing Morals*, 162.

78 Editor, "The National Vigilance Association," 1.

79 It is worth noting that a relatively weak number of NVA-involved prosecutions actually ended in conviction or heavy sentences, see Bartley, *Prostitution: Prevention and Reform in England,* 81–3.

80 Parliament, *Vagrancy Act of 1824 Amendment Bill,* revised 1898. https://api.parliament.uk/historic-hansard/bills/vagrancy-act-amendment-bill.

81 Joseph R. Gusfield, *Contested Meanings: The Construction of Alcohol Problems* (Madison: University of Wisconsin Press, 1996), 28.

82 For instance, to close brothels, the NVA encouraged community groups to write letters of complaint to solicit police intervention and aid in prosecutions.

83 Remarks from the *Daily Telegraph* cited in Chant, *Why We Attacked the Empire*, 26.

84 Charles Darwin, *The Descent of Man, and Selection in Relation to Sex*, Reprinted from The Second English Edition, Revised, and Augmented (New York: Clarke, Given and Hooper, 1874), 83.

85 This does not mean that all Purity Crusaders accepted all scientific discourses; a pamphlet from the Gospel Purity Association warns its readers of "the serious

amount of moral and physical harm that is being done to large numbers of young people of both sexes by quacks, semi-quacks, and phrenologists, in the name of Social Purity." Gospel Purity Association, *Licensed Plague Spots: India's Curse and Britain's Shame*, The Women's Library, 3AMS/C/02/01, 1888.

Chapter 3

1 Josephine Elizabeth Grey Butler, *Une voix dans le désert* (Neuchâtel: Bureau du Bulletin Continental, 1876), 5.
2 "Feminism/feminist" is used here despite some arguments that these terms should not characterize movements or campaigns before 1910, for instance, Nancy Cott, *The Grounding of Modern Feminism* (New Haven: Yale University Press, 1987), 3.
3 For instance, see Kat Gupta, *Representation of the British Suffrage Movement* (London: Bloomsbury Publishing, 2017) or Corrine M. McConnaughy, *The Woman Suffrage Movement in America: A Reassessment* (Cambridge: Cambridge University Press, 2013).
4 Cott, *The Grounding of Modern Feminism*, 5.
5 Elizabeth Cady Stanton, *A History of Woman Suffrage* 1 (Rochester, NY: Fowler and Wells, 1889), 70–1.
6 Petition of the women of Spilsby in Lincolnshire to the House of Lords, March 28, 1833, cited in Claire Midgley, "Anti-Slavery and Feminism in Nineteenth-Century Britain," *Gender and History* 5, no. 3 (1993): 351.
7 Similar splits between male and female abolitionists occurred elsewhere, such as in the Netherlands, see Petra de Vries, "Josephine Butler and the Making of Feminism: International Abolitionism in the Netherlands 1870–1914," *Women's History Review* 17, no. 2 (2008): 257–77.
8 Summers, "Which Women? What Europe? Josephine Butler and the International Abolitionist Federation."
9 Jill Suzanne Smith, *Berlin Coquette: Prostitution and the New German Woman* (Cornell: Cornell University Press, 2014), 71–3.
10 In Italy, local abolitionist feminists managed only to repeal a law allowing brothels to operate in Lombardy in 1888; regulationism was formally instituted in 1891 and lasted until 1958. For more on abolitionism's failure in Italy, see Bruno Wanrooij, "Josephine Butler and Regulated Prostitution in Italy," *Women's History Review* 17, no. 2 (2008): 153–71.
11 Summers, "Which Women? What Europe? Josephine Butler and the International Abolitionist Federation," 220.
12 Michael Pearson, *The Age of Consent: Victorian Prostitution and its Enemies* (Newton Abbot: David and Charles, 1972), 173.

13 For instance, Michel Foucault, *Surveiller et punir. Naissance de la prison* (Paris: Éditions Gallimard, 2014). Georges Vigarello, *Le propre et le sale, L'hygiène du corps depuis le Moyen Age* (Paris, Éditions du Seuil, 1985). Deborah Lupton, *Medicine as Culture: Illness, Disease and the Body* (Thousand Oaks: SAGE, 2012).
14 Edwin Hodder, *The Life and Work of the Seventh Earl of Shaftesbury, K.G.* (London: Cassell, 1892), 78.
15 Cited in Edwin Chadwick, *Report on the Sanitary Condition of the Labouring Population of Great Britain: Supplementary Report on the Results of Special Inquiry into the Practice of Interment in Towns*, 1 (London: HM Stationery Office, 1842).
16 For more on different contagion theories during this period, see Michael Worboys, *Spreading Germs: Disease Theories and Medical Practice in Britain, 1865–1900* (Cambridge: Cambridge University Press, 2000).
17 Mort, *Dangerous Sexualities: Medico-Moral Politics in England Since 1830*, 41.
18 Ibid.
19 F. David Roberts, *Paternalism in Early Victorian England* (New York: Routledge, 1979), 8.
20 For instance, Sir Robert Filmer's work was criticized by Enlightenment philosopher and forefather of liberalism in John Locke, *Two Treatises of Government* (London: Whitmore and Fenn and C. Brown, 1821).
21 C. H. D. Saint-Simon, *Oeuvres de Saint-Simon* (Paris: E. Dentu. IV, 1868), 13.
22 Donald Reid, "In the Name of the Father: A Language of Labour Relations in Nineteenth-Century France," *History Workshop Journal* 38, no. 1 (1994): 3. This would be further cemented by French industrialist Eugène Schneider in Le Creusot, along with others influenced by Saint-Simon and his contemporary Frédéric Le Play, establishing what would become a quintessentially French mode of paternalist management.
23 One significant exposition of Britain's social problems was the 1832 report published by Tory politician Michael Sadler on the conditions of factory work which shocked the public.
24 Jeremy Bentham, *The Collected Works of Jeremy Bentham: An Introduction to the Principles of Morals and Legislation* (Oxford: Oxford University Press, 1996).
25 Stewart J. Brown, *Providence and Empire: Religion, Politics and Society in the United Kingdom, 1815–1914* (London: Routledge, 2008).
26 Cited in ibid., 161.
27 Roberts, *Paternalism in Early Victorian England*, 4.
28 Laurence Brockliss and David Eastwood, eds., *A Union of Multiple Identities: The British Isles, c. 1750–c. 1850* (Manchester: Manchester University Press, 1997), 49.
29 Roberts, *Paternalism in Early Victorian England*, 4–7.
30 F. David Roberts, *The Social Conscience of the Early Victorians* (Stanford: Stanford University Press, 2002).

31 Eileen Janes Yeo, "Social Motherhood and the Sexual Communion of Labour in British Social Science, 1850–1950," *Women's History Review* 1, no. 1 (1992): 63–87.
32 Carey Lodge, "10 Inspirational Quotes from William Wilberforce," *Christian Today*, July 30, 2015. https://www.christiantoday.com/article/10-inspirational-quotes-from-william-wilberforce/60570.htm.
33 Coventry Patmore, *The Angel in the House*, 1854. https://www.bl.uk/collection-items/coventry-patmores-poem-the-angel-in-the-house.
34 Lodge, "10 Inspirational Quotes from William Wilberforce."
35 Susan Thorne, *Congregational Missions and the Making of an Imperial Culture in Nineteenth-Century England* (Stanford: Stanford University Press, 1999), 107.
36 See Dror Wahrman, "'Middle-Class' Domesticity Goes Public: Gender, Class, and Politics from Queen Caroline to Queen Victoria," *Journal of British Studies* 32, no. 4 (1993): 396–432.
37 Brenda Mothersole, "Female Philanthropy and Women Novelists of 1840–1870" (PhD thesis, Brunel University School of Sport and Education, 1989).
38 For more on the elaboration of a new model of empire once this one failed, see Karuna Mantena, *Alibis of Empire: Henry Maine and the Ends of Liberal Imperialism* (Princeton: Princeton University Press, 2010) or Jennifer Pitts, *A Turn to Empire: The Rise of Imperial Liberalism in Britain and France* (Princeton: Princeton University Press, 2009), especially 59–96.
39 Mantena, *Alibis of Empire*, 23.
40 George John Romanes, "Mental Differences between Men and Women," *The Nineteenth Century* 13, January/June (1887).
41 James Allen McGrigor, "On the Real Differences in the Minds of Men and Women," *Journal of the Anthropological Society* 7 (1869): 199.
42 Rob Boddice, "The Manly Mind? Revisiting the Victorian 'Sex in Brain' Debate," *Gender and History* 23, no. 2 (2011): 322.
43 George Louis Leclerc Buffon, *Natural History: Containing a Theory of the Earth, a General History of Man, of the Brute Creation, and of Vegetables, Minerals* 7 (London, H.D. Symonds, 1807), 40.
44 Ibid.
45 Corbin et al., *Histoire de la virilité*, 27.
46 William Edward Hartpole Lecky, *History of European Morals, from Augustus to Charlemagne* 2 (Boston, D. Appleton and Company, 1897), 283.
47 Philippa Levine, *Prostitution, Race and Politics: Policing Venereal Disease in the British Empire* (New York: Routledge, 2003).
48 Butler, *Social Purity, An Address Given to Students at Cambridge*.
49 Ichikawa, "A Body Politic of Women's Own," 110.
50 Ibid.
51 Butler, *Une voix dans le désert*, 14. Author's translation.

52 This is the literal translation of the title, however, it later appeared in English as "The voice of one crying in the Wilderness."
53 Butler, *Une voix dans le désert*, 16. Author's translation.
54 Ibid., 7. Author's translation.
55 Butler, *An Autobiographical Memoir*, 148–9.
56 Ibid.
57 Ernest Legouvé, *Histoire morale des femmes* (Paris: J. Hetzel, 1897), 407.
58 For an overview, see Karen M. Offen, *European Feminisms, 1700–1950: A Political History* (Stanford: Stanford University Press, 2000).
59 Josephine Elizabeth Grey Butler, *The Education and Employment of Women* (London: Macmillan, 1868).
60 Ghénia Avril de Sainte-Croix, *Le Féminisme* (Paris: V. Giard and E. Brière, 1907), 161. Author's translation.
61 For instance, Dr. Elizabeth Blackwell believed that both men and women experienced sexual passions and were equally responsible for controlling them. Blackwell, *The Human Element in Sex*.
62 Jenny Daggers, "Josephine Butler and Christian Women's Identity," in *Sex, Gender, and Religion: Josephine Butler Revisited*, eds. Jenny Daggers and Diana Neal, American University Studies Series 242 (New York and Oxford: Peter Lang, 2006), 98.
63 Maria Georgina Grey, *Address to Women of All Classes*, Rome, The Women's Library, GB 106 1BWE/B/2, January 1886.
64 She had already penned *A Vindication of the Rights of Men* (1790) as a scathing response to Edmund Burke's *Reflections on the Revolution in France* (1790) which upheld the Old Regime status quo, called for the end of the landed aristocracy and defended republicanism against "the clogged wheels of corruption continually oiled by the sweat of the laborious poor, squeezed out of them by unceasing taxation" which reigned in the House of Commons where "the majority […] was often purchased by the crown, and that the people were oppressed by the influence of their own money, extorted by the venal voice of a packed representation." Mary Wollstonecraft, *A Vindication of the Rights of Men, in a Letter to the Right Honourable Edmund Burke: Occasioned by His Reflections on the Revolution in France* (Cambridge: Cambridge University Press, 1790). Public reception to her work was, of course, affected by contemporary sexist attitudes; novelist Horace Walpole famously called her writing the illogical passion of a "hyena in petticoats" which could not stand up against manly reason.
65 Barbara Taylor, *Mary Wollstonecraft and the Feminist Imagination* (Cambridge: Cambridge University Press, 2003), 220.
66 Butler, *The Education and Employment of Women*.
67 Ichikawa, "A Body Politic of Women's Own," 109.

68 Josephine Elizabeth Grey Butler, *Address delivered in Craigie Hall, Edinburgh* (Manchester: Ireland and Co, printers, 1871), 13.
69 Cited in Kelly Lynn Trumble, "'Her Body is Her Own': Victorian Feminists, Sexual Violence, and Political Subjectivity" (PhD Dissertation, English Department, The Florida State University, 2004), 1.
70 Butler, *Personal Reminiscences of a Great Crusade*, 320.
71 Blackwell, *The Human Element in Sex*, 6.
72 See for example Frances Power Cobbe, *The Duties of Women, A Course of Lectures* (Boston: Geo. H. Ellis; London: Williams & Norgate, 1881).
73 London Anti-Vivisection Society, "The Growth of the Vivisection Evil," Speech delivered April 26, 1899 by Mrs. Charles Mallet (London: London Anti-Vivisection Society, 1899).
74 Cited in Leah Leneman, "The Awakened Instinct: Vegetarianism and the Women's Suffrage Movement in Britain," *Women's History Review* 6, no. 2 (1997): 272.
75 Ibid.
76 Cited in Leneman, "The Awakened Instinct: Vegetarianism and the Women's Suffrage Movement in Britain," 280.
77 Constance Lytton, *Prisons and Prisoners: Some Personal Experiences* (Peterborough: Broadview Press, 2008), 59.
78 Ibid.
79 Ian Miller, "Necessary Torture? Vivisection, Suffragette Force-Feeding, and Responses to Scientific Medicine in Britain c. 1870–1920," *Journal of the History of Medicine and Allied Sciences* 64, no. 3 (2009): 333–72.
80 Djuna Barnes, "How It Feels to Be Forcibly Fed," *New York World Magazine*, September 6, 1914. http://hdl.handle.net/1903.1/14687.
81 Derived from the Latin "*raptus*" or "*rapere*," to rape was to steal or violate the resources of a land or country. Estelle B. Freedman, *Redefining Rape: Sexual Violence in the Era of Suffrage and Segregation* (Cambridge, MA: Harvard University Press, 2013), 3.
82 See for instance Vigarello, *Histoire du viol*; Bruce A. Macfarlane, *Historical Development of the Offence of Rape*, Canadian Bar Association, 1992, https://archive.org/stream/413655-hist-devel-of-offence-of-rape/413655-hist-devel-of-offence-of-rape_djvu.txt; Freedman, *Redefining Rape*.
83 Lawson Tait, *Diseases of Women and Abdominal Surgery* 1 (Philadelphia: Lea, 1889), 56.
84 Thomas Laqueur, *Making Sex: Body and Sex from the Greeks to Freud* (Cambridge: Harvard University Press, 1990), 160.
85 Ladies' National Association, "The Garrison Towns of Kent, Third Letter from Mrs. Butler to the Editor. The 'Reclaiming and Elevating' Influences of the Acts," *Shield*, May 9, 1870, 79.

86 LNA, "The Ladies' Appeal and Protest."
87 See for instance Josephine Elizabeth Grey Butler (ed.), *Woman's Work and Woman's Culture: A Series of Essays* (London: Macmillan and Company, 1869); Butler, *The Education and Employment of Women*, on the importance of equality and cooperation between the sexes.
88 Butler, *Personal Reminiscences of a Great Crusade*, 90.
89 Josephine Elizabeth Grey Butler, "Ramah was there a voice heard, … Rachel weeping for her children, Storm-Bell [June 1898]," in *Josephine Butler and the Prostitution Campaigns: The Queen's Daughters in India* 5, eds. Jane Jordan and Ingrid Sharp (London: Routledge, Taylor and Francis, 2003), 585–90.
90 De Morsier, "Discours du 7 Dec 1883," *La mission de la femme*, 58. Author's translation.
91 Ibid.
92 Ibid.
93 Walkowitz, *City of Dreadful Delight*, 93.
94 Antoinette M. Burton, *Burdens of History: British Feminists, Indian Women, and Imperial Culture, 1865–1915* (Chapel Hill: University of North Carolina Press, 2000), 123.
95 Angelique Richardson, *Love and Eugenics in the Late Nineteenth Century: Rational Reproduction and the New Woman* (Oxford: Oxford University Press, 2003).
96 George Dangerfield, *The Strange Death of Liberal England* (London: Constable and Company Ltd, 1935), 139.
97 Ibid., 142.
98 Ibid., 143, 184.
99 Smith, *Berlin Coquette*, 80.
100 Walkowitz, *Prostitution and Victorian Society*, 225. This was also a practice in the American Women's suffrage movement with portraits of figures like Lucretia Mott and Susan B. Anthony.
101 Stephanie Forward, "Attitudes to Marriage and Prostitution in the Writings of Olive Schreiner, Mona Caird, Sarah Grand and George Egerton," *Women's History Review* 8, no. 1 (1999): 53.
102 Olive Schreiner to Karl Pearson, University College London Library, Special Collections, UCL, London, Olive Schreiner Letters Project transcription, July 19, 1885, Line 10.
103 Olive Schreiner to *Daily News*, 28 December 1885, Harry Ransom Research Center, University of Texas at Austin, Olive Schreiner Letters Project transcription.
104 Walkowitz, *City of Dreadful Delight*, 129.
105 It is worthwhile to note that she warned women against sentimental extravagance, believing them to be particularly susceptible to being carried away by their passions. This reflects a significant epistemological difference in terms of

emotionality between the eighteenth- and nineteenth-century feminists. For more on the eighteenth century, see Adela Pinch, *Strange Fits of Passion: Epistemologies of Emotion, Hume to Austen* (Stanford: Stanford University Press, 1996).
106 John Stuart Mill presented the House of Commons with a petition for women's mass suffrage complied by suffragettes Emily Davies and Elizabeth Garrett upon his election as Member of Parliament for the City of Westminster in 1865. Its failure was key to the development of the overall movement for women's liberation and led to the founding of the National Society for Women's Suffrage. By the time it saw success in 1918, the suffrage movement had changed immensely.
107 John Stuart Mill, *The Subjection of Women* (London: Longmans, Green, Reader, and Dyer, 1870), chapter 1.
108 Ibid., ch. 1.
109 Cited in Daggers and Neal, *Sex, Gender, and Religion: Josephine Butler Revisited*, 46.
110 For more on this, see Lisa Surridge, *Bleak Houses: Marital Violence in Victorian Fiction* (Columbus: Ohio University Press, 2005).
111 Mona Caird, *The Morality of Marriage: And Other Essays on the Status and Destiny of Woman* (London: G. Redway, 1897).
112 Dame Christabel Pankhurst, *The Great Scourge and How to End It* (London: E. Pankhurst, 1913).
113 Norma Clarke, "Feminism and the Popular Novel of the 1890s: A Brief Consideration of a Forgotten Feminist Novelist," *Feminist Review* 20, no. 1 (1985): 99–100.
114 Ibid.
115 Ibid.
116 Special Correspondent, "Brussels Conference of Social Hygiene (Concluded)," *The British Medical Journal* 2, no. 2020 (September 16, 1899): 676–8.
117 Albert Fournier, *Ligue contre la syphilis, Société française de prophylaxie sanitaire et morale* (Paris: C. Delagrave, 1904), 7. Author's translation.
118 Kristin Luker, "Sex, Social Hygiene, and the State: The Double-Edged Sword of Social Reform," *Theory and Society* 27, no. 5 (1998): 601–34.
119 Julia Roos, *Weimar through the Lens of Gender: Prostitution Reform, Woman's Emancipation, and German Democracy, 1919–33* (Ann Arbor: University of Michigan Press, 2010), 109.
120 She was legal guardian to a girl who had been raped and infected with venereal disease by her stepfather. Cited in Roos, *Weimar through the Lens of Gender*, 109.
121 The 1927 Law for Combating Venereal Diseases instituted new penalties for venereal disease infectors, as well as lifted a ban on advertising prophylactics. In terms of prostitution, it repealed the regulation system, banned brothels, decriminalized prostitution, and improved prostitutes' working conditions.
122 Roos, *Weimar through the Lens of Gender*, 110.

123 Levine, *Prostitution, Race and Politics: Policing Venereal Disease in the British Empire*.
124 Stephen Legg, "An Intimate and Imperial Feminism: Meliscent Shephard and the Regulation of Prostitution in Colonial India," *Environment and Planning D: Society and Space* 28, no. 1 (2010): 84.
125 Gusfield, *Contested Meanings: The Construction of Alcohol Problems*, 21.
126 Cited in David J. Oriel, *The Scars of Venus: A History of Venereology* (Berlin: Springer Science and Business Media, 2012), 196.
127 Fournier, *Ligue contre la syphilis*, 51. Author's translation.
128 Judith Große, "Der Kampf gegen Prostitution: Zwischen Sittlichkeitsreform, Feminismus und Medizin, 1864–1914," in *Biopolitik und Sittlichkeitsreform: Kampagnen gegen Alkohol, Drogen und Prostitution 1880–1950*, eds. Judith Große, Francesco Spöring and Jana Tschurenev (Frankfurt: Campus Verlag, 2014), 177–215.
129 Sarah Grand, *The Beth Book: Being a Study from the Life of Elizabeth Caldwell Maclure, a Woman of Genius* (Portsmouth: Heinemann, 1898), 442.
130 Richardson, *Love and Eugenics in the Late Nineteenth Century*, 72–5.
131 Ellice Hopkins, *The Present Moral Crisis: An Appeal to Women* (London: Dyer Brothers, 1886).
132 Anne L. Scott, "Physical Purity Feminism and State Medicine in Late Nineteenth-Century England," *Women's History Review* 8, no. 4 (1999): 644.
133 Antoinette Louisa Brown Blackwell, *The Sexes throughout Nature* (New York: GP Putnam, 1875), 123.
134 Charles Darwin and Clémence-Auguste Royer, *De l'origine des espèces ou des lois du progrès chez les êtres organisés par Charles Darwin* (Paris: Guillaumin et Cie, Victor Masson et Fils, 1862).
135 Darwin, *The Descent of Man*, 642.
136 Ibid., 643.
137 Ibid.
138 Ibid.
139 Romanes, "Mental Differences between Men and Women," 390.
140 Ibid.
141 Ibid.
142 Ibid.
143 Helen Wilson, "Evidence to the Royal Commission on Venereal Diseases in the United Kingdom," *British Medical Journal* 2, no. 2761 (November 29, 1913), 1442–3. https://www.ncbi.nlm.nih.gov/pmc/articles/PMC2345925/.
144 Carol Miller, "The Social Section and Advisory Committee on Social Questions of the League of Nations," in *International Health Organisations and Movements, 1918–1939*, eds. Paul Weindling, Charles Rosenberg and Colin Jones (Cambridge: Cambridge University Press, 1995), 163.

145 As a result of the International Convention for the Suppression of the Traffic in Women and Children, the Committee consisted of representatives from Denmark, France, Great Britain, Italy, Japan, Poland, Romania, Spain, and Uruguay, and from non-governmental organizations like the International Bureau.

146 For details, see Paul Knepper, "The Investigation into the Traffic in Women by the League of Nations: Sociological Jurisprudence as an International Social Project," *Law and History Review* 34, no. 1 (2016): 45–73. A summary version of the first reports of this study was published under the title *Human Merchandise: A Study of the International Traffic in Women* in 1928. Penned by H. Wilson Harris, it is sensationalist and moralizing, for instance, in its descriptions of prostitution as "sordid and repellant" (12) and of vice as a threat to the nation, thwarted only by engendering a moral force in the higher planes of truth and beauty (282).

147 Jessica R. Pliley, "Claims to Protection: The Rise and Fall of Feminist Abolitionism in the League of Nations: Committee on the Traffic in Women and Children, 1919–1936," *Journal of Women's History* 22, no. 4 (2010): 90–113.

148 Alison Neilans, "Woman, where are those thine accusers?" cited in Laite, *Common Prostitutes and Ordinary Citizens*, 2.

149 Josephine Elizabeth Grey Butler, *On the Moral Reclaimability of Prostitutes* (London: National Association for the Repeal of the Contagious Diseases Act, 1870).

150 Daniel Gorman, "Empire, Internationalism, and the Campaign against the Traffic in Women and Children in the 1920s," *Twentieth Century British History* 19, no. 2 (2008): 196.

151 Cited in Pliley, "Claims to Protection," 102.

152 Ibid.

Chapter 4

1 Stephen Legg, "'The Life of Individuals as Well as of Nations': International Law and the League of Nations' Anti-Trafficking Governmentalities," *Leiden Journal of International Law* 25, no. 3 (2012): 649–50.

2 United Nations, *Study on Traffic in Persons and Prostitution*, Department of Economic and Social Affairs, ST/SOA/SD/8, 1959, 14.

3 Cathy Faye, "12 – Social Psychology," in *The Cambridge Handbook of the Intellectual History of Psychology*, eds. Robert J. Sternberg and Wade E. Pickren (Cambridge: Cambridge University Press, 2019), 318.

4 Ana Antić, "Decolonizing Madness? Transcultural Psychiatry, International Order and Birth of a 'Global Psyche' in the Aftermath of the Second World War," *Journal of Global History* 17, no. 1 (2022): 20–41.

5 UNESCO, "Introducing Unesco," https://www.unesco.org/en/introducing-unesco.

6 Antić, "Decolonizing Madness?"
7 Eva Illouz, *Saving the Modern Soul. Therapy, Emotions, and the Culture of Self-Help* (Berkeley: University of California Press, 2008).
8 Jasper et al., *Public Characters*, 11.
9 Charles Taylor, *A Secular Age* (Cambridge, MA: The Belknap Press of Harvard University Press, 2007), 619.
10 Frank Mort, *Capital Affairs: London and the Making of the Permissive Society* (New Haven: Yale University Press, 2010).
11 Peter N. Stearns, *Sexuality in World History* (London and New York: Routledge, 2017), 93.
12 Ibid., 99,
13 Julia Laite, "A Global History of Prostitution: London," in *Selling Sex in the City: A Global History of Prostitution, 1600s–2000s*, eds. Magaly Rodríguez García, Lex Heerma van Voss, and Elise van Nederveen (Leiden: Brill, 2017), 115.
14 *Evidence for the Working Party on the Street Offences Acts 1959*, The Women's Library, GB 106 AMS/B/04/16/06.
15 Laite, "A Global History of Prostitution: London," 120.
16 Barbara Welter, "The Cult of True Womanhood: 1820–1860," *American Quarterly* 18, no. 2, part 1 (1966): 151–74.
17 Dana Becker, *The Myth of Empowerment: Women and the Therapeutic Culture in America* (New York: New York University Press, 2005), 14. She explains that women's interiority has been championed by men because "[i]f we continue fervently to privilege the inner world we will be less likely to foment trouble outside it."
18 Betty Friedan, *The Feminine Mystique* (New York: W. W. Norton, 1963).
19 Bruno Duriez, "La différenciation des engagements: l'Action catholique ouvrière entre radicalisme politique et conformisme religieux." Paper given at workshop *Porter les Évangiles au monde: les logiques religieuses d'engagements politiques des catholiques au XXème siècle,* AFSP, Toulouse, September 2007.
20 Lilian Mathieu, "Le mouvement abolitionniste français dans l'après-guerre," *Déviance et Société* 40, no. 1 (2016): 90..
21 Ibid.
22 Cited in ibid., 89.
23 Cited in ibid., 91. Author's translation.

Chapter 5

1 Jenna Basiliere, "Political is Personal: Scholarly Manifestations of the Feminist Sex Wars," *Michigan Feminist Studies* 22, no. 1 (2008). Available online: http://hdl.handle.net/2027/spo.ark5583.0022.101 (accessed March 19, 2019).

2. Kathryn Zoglin, "United Nations Action against Slavery: A Critical Evaluation," *Human Rights Quarterly* 8 (1986): 328.
3. Janet Halley, Prabha Kotiswaran, Hila Shamir and Chantal Thomas. "From the International to the Local in Feminist Legal Responses to Rape, Prostitution/Sex Work, and Sex Trafficking: Four Studies in Contemporary Governance Feminism," *Harvard Journal of Law and Gender* 29 (2006): 355.
4. For instance, sex workers were involved in the gay rights movement in the 1960s, such as Compton's Cafeteria riot and the Stonewall uprising. In Europe, French sex workers are often credited with launching the campaign through events such as the occupation of Saint-Nizier church in Lyon in protest of police and social harassment in 1975. This in any case inspired initiatives elsewhere, such as the English Collective of Prostitutes (ECP) formed that same year in the UK and similarly their own occupation of the Holy Cross Church, Kings Cross in 1982. For a recent and thorough study of this issue, see Chi Adanna Mgbako, "The Mainstreaming of Sex Workers' Rights as Human Rights," *Harvard Journal of Law and Gender* 43 (2020): 91–136.
5. National Organization for Women, *Statement of Purpose*, 1966. http://now.org/about/history/statement-of-purpose/.
6. Clare Hemmings, "Affective Solidarity: Feminist Reflexivity and Political Transformation," *Feminist Theory* 13, no. 2 (2012): 147–61.
7. Catherine A. MacKinnon, "Violence against Women: A Perspective," *Aegis: Magazine on Ending Violence Against Women* 33 (1982), 51.
8. Cited in Basiliere, "Political is Personal: Scholarly Manifestations of the Feminist Sex Wars."
9. Catharine A. MacKinnon, "Pornography, Civil Rights, and Speech," *Harvard Civil Rights-Civil Liberties Law Review* 20, no. 1 (1985), 299–311.
10. Audre Lorde, "The Uses of the Erotic: The Erotic as Power," in *The Lesbian and Gay Studies Reader*, ed. Henry Abelove (New York: Routledge, 1993), 339.
11. Ibid., 341.
12. Audre Lorde, *Sister Outsider: Essays and Speeches* (Berkeley: Crossing Press, 2012), 37.
13. Coalition for a Feminist Sexuality cited in Basiliere, "Political is Personal: Scholarly Manifestations of the Feminist Sex Wars."
14. Pierre Bourdieu, *Méditations pascaliennes* (Paris: Le Seuil, 2016).
15. Scheer, "Are Emotions A Kind of Practice …?"
16. Adrienne Rich, *Of Woman Born: Motherhood as Experience and Institution* (New York: W. W. Norton and Company, 1995), 283.
17. Demonstrating well the significance of tracing the epistemology of anger in all its forms within feminism, an increasingly large number of works have been produced on its politicization—past, present, and future—by feminists, especially in the

wake of #MeToo and Black Lives Matter. See Carla Kaplan, Sarah Haley, and Durba Mitra, "Outraged/Enraged: The Rage Special Issue," *Signs: Journal of Women in Culture and Society* 46, 4 (2021): 785–800.

18 Julia Lesage, "Women's Rage," in *Marxism and the Interpretation of Culture*, eds., Cary Nelson and Lawrence Grossberg (Urbana: University of Illinois, 1988), 421.

19 They were inspiring to second-wave white feminists—Catharine MacKinnon's use of Audre Lorde's notion of the erotic as discussed later is one example—yet the criticism that this has resulted in the neutralization of the racial politics of these works is vital to note.

20 This wording comes from Lilian Mathieu, "Des monstres ordinaires. La construction du problème public des clients de la prostitution," *Champ pénal/Penal field* 12 (2015) Available online: https://halshs.archives-ouvertes.fr/halshs-01326668.

21 Andrea Dworkin, *Our Blood: Prophecies and Discourses on Sexual Politics* (New York: Harper and Row, 1976), 103.

22 Andrea Dworkin, "Prostitution and Male Supremacy," *Michigan Journal of Gender & Law* 1 (1993): 12.

23 Ibid., 6.

24 Cecilie Høigård and Liv Finstad, *Backstreets: Prostitution, Money, and Love* (University Park: Penn State Press, 1992), 180.

25 Dorchen Leidholdt, "Prostitution: A Violation of Women's Human Rights," *Cardozo Women's Law Journal* 1 (1993): 135.

26 Dworkin, "Prostitution and Male Supremacy," 6.

27 Johanna Walters, "Gloria Steinem: 'Fewer people will say we live in a post-racist, post-feminist world,'" *The Guardian*, December 11, 2016. https://www.theguardian.com/books/2016/dec/11/gloria-steinem-feminism-womens-rights-donald-trump.

28 Yet the extent to which radical feminists sympathize with other victims varies, as exemplified by the existing split on the inclusion of transgendered people, with those who adopt a biological determinist view and ban their participation dubbed "TERFs": Trans-Exclusionary Radical Feminists.

29 Christina Hoff Sommers, *Who Stole Feminism?: How Women Have Betrayed Women* (New York: Simon and Schuster, 1994), 200.

30 Kathleen Barry, *Female Sexual Slavery* (Hoboken: Prentice Hall, 1979), 14.

31 Ibid., 215.

32 Kathleen Barry, "Female Sexual Slavery: Understanding the International Dimensions of Women's Oppression," *Human Rights Quarterly* 3 (1981): 44.

33 Geoffroy Clavel, "Les Femen contre la prostitution et pour la criminalisation des clients: une campagne choc," *The Huffington Post*, October 11, 2013. https://www.huffingtonpost.fr/2013/10/11/femen-prostitution-criminalisation-clients-campagne-choc_n_4080208.html. Author's translation.

34 Ibid. Author's translation.
35 Melissa Farley and Vanessa Kelly, "Prostitution: A Critical Review of the Medical and Social Sciences Literature," *Women and Criminal Justice* 11, no. 4 (2000): 29.
36 For more on how this becomes internalized, see the discussion of panopticon disciplinary practices which produce the "female figure" in Sandra L. Bartky, "Foucault, Femininity, and the Modernization of Patriarchal Power," in *Feminism and Foucault: Reflections on Resistance*, eds. Irene Diamond and Lee Quinby, 61–86 (Boston: Northeastern University Press, 1988).
37 See Andrea Dworkin and Catherine A. MacKinnon, *Pornography and Civil Rights: A New Day for Women's Equality* (Minneapolis: Organizing Against Pornography, 1988).
38 Memorandum to Minneapolis City Council cited in Winifred Ann Sandler, "The Minneapolis Anti-Pornography Ordinance: A Valid Assertion of Civil Rights," *Fordham Urban Law Journal* 13 (1984): 909–46.
39 Ibid.
40 Basiliere, "Political is Personal: Scholarly Manifestations of the Feminist Sex Wars".
41 Wendy Brown, *States of Injury: Power and Freedom in Late Modernity* (Princeton: Princeton University Press, 1995).
42 Ibid. Sara Ahmed, "The Organisation of Hate," *Law and Critique* 12, 3 (2001): 345–65. Jo Doezema, "Ouch! Western Feminists' 'Wounded Attachment' to the 'Third World Prostitute," *Feminist Review* 67, no. 1 (2001): 16–38.
43 Aya Gruber, "Rape, Feminism, and the War on Crime," *Washington Law Review* 8, no. 4 (2009): 583.
44 Term from Elizabeth Bernstein, "Militarized Humanitarianism Meets Carceral Feminism: The Politics of Sex, Rights, and Freedom in Contemporary Antitrafficking Campaigns," *Signs: Journal of Women in Culture and Society* 36, no. 1 (2010): 45–71.; Elizabeth Bernstein, "Carceral Politics as Gender Justice? The 'Traffic in Women' and Neoliberal Circuits of Crime, Sex, and Rights," *Theory and Society* 41, no. 3 (2012): 233–59.
45 Jonathan Simon, *Governing through Crime: How the War on Crime Transformed American Democracy and Created a Culture of Fear* (Oxford: Oxford University Press, 2007).
46 Roger Lancaster, "Punishment," in *A Companion to Moral Anthropology*, ed. Didier Fassin (Hoboken: John Wiley and Sons, 2012), 530.
47 Marie Gottschalk, *The Prison and the Gallows: The Politics of Mass Incarceration in America* (Cambridge: Cambridge University Press, 2006).
48 Ibid.
49 Brown, *States of Injury*.
50 Respectively the arguments made by Kristin Bumiller, *In an Abusive State: How Neoliberalism Appropriated the Feminist Movement against Sexual Violence*

(Durham, NC: Duke University Press, 2009), and Rose Corrigan, *Up against a Wall: Rape Reform and the Failure of Success* (New York: New York University Press, 2013).

51 Janie A. Chuang, "Exploitation Creep and The Unmaking of Human Trafficking Law," *American Journal of International Law* 108, no. 4 (2014): 613.
52 Bernstein, "Carceral Politics as Gender Justice?"; Jo Doezema, "Ouch! Western Feminists' 'Wounded Attachment' to the 'Third World Prostitute.'"
53 Wylie, *The International Politics of Human Trafficking*, 62.
54 Ibid., 612.
55 Bernstein, "Militarized Humanitarianism meets Carceral Feminism," 46–7.

Chapter 6

1 United Nations, *International Meeting of Experts on the Social and Cultural Causes of Prostitution and Strategies for the Struggle against Procuring and Sexual Exploitation of Women*, SHS-85/CONF.608/14, Madrid, Spain, Division of Human Rights and Peace, March 18–21, 1986, 5. http://unesdoc.unesco.org/images/0007/000715/071520EB.pdf
2 Ibid.
3 Ibid., 12.
4 Ibid., 8–9.
5 For example, contentions between the General Secretariat Hélène Sackstein in Geneva and the President of the International Committee Brigitte Polonovski culminated in the latter holding a Crisis Committee held in Paris on May 17, 1996, to force the former to relocate to Paris. See IAF, *Correspondence and Reports on Extraordinary Committee*, The Women's Library, 3AMS/E/37, November 30, 1996; IAF, *Rapport du comité de crise au Comité International de la FAI,* The Women's Library, 3AMS/E/37, 1996.
6 Malka Marcovich, *Resignation Letter from the International Abolitionist Federation*, The Women's Library, 3AMS/E/39, February 15, 1998. Author's translation. She identifies four French and Belgian associations to blame: *Le Mouvement du Nid*, *Le Mouvement du Cri, L'Association Contre la Prostitution Enfantine, L'Association Dauphinoise d'Aide aux Femmes.*
7 Ronald Weitzer, "Moral Crusade against Prostitution," *Society* 43, no. 3 (2006): 38.
8 Don Kulick,"Sex in the New Europe: The Criminalization of Clients and Swedish Fear of Penetration," *Anthropological Theory* 3, no. 2 (2003): 201.
9 Grainne Healy and Monica O'Connor, *The Links between Prostitution and Sex Trafficking: A Briefing Handbook*, CATW and EWL Project on Promoting Preventative Measures to Combat Trafficking in Human Beings for Sexual

Exploitation, Coalition Against Trafficking in Women, July 25, 2006. http://www.catwinternational.org/Home/Article/175-the-links-between-prostitution-and-sex-trafficking-a-briefing-handbook.

10 Max Waltman, "Sweden's Prohibition of Purchase of Sex: The Law's Reasons, Impact, and Potential," *Women's Studies International Forum* 34, no. 5 (2011): 449–74.

11 Cited in Gunilla Ekberg, "The Swedish Law that Prohibits the Purchase of Sexual Services: Best Practices for Prevention of Prostitution and Trafficking in Human Beings," *Violence Against Women* 10, no. 10 (2004): 1214.

12 Term from Prabha Kotiswaran, *Dangerous Sex, Invisible Labor: Sex Work and the Law in India* (Princeton: Princeton University Press, 2011), 32.

13 Halley et al., "From the International to the Local in Feminist Legal Responses to Rape, Prostitution/Sex Work, and Sex Trafficking," 411–12.

14 For a comprehensive work, see Janet Halley, Prabha Kotiswaran, Rachel Rebouché, and Hila Shamir, *Governance Feminism: An Introduction* (Minneapolis: University of Minnesota Press, 2018).

15 For instance, see Laure Bereni, "De la cause à la loi, Les mobilisations pour la parité politique en France (1992–2000)" (PhD Thesis, Université Panthéon-Sorbonne - Paris I, 2007).

16 Brown, *States of Injury*, ix–xx.

17 Mouvement du Nid Belgium, *Les Nouvelles du Nid*, Bibliothèque Royale de Belgique, BD 45793, no. 3. Author's translation.

18 Mouvement du Nid Belgium, *Les Nouvelles du Nid*, no. 1. Author's translation.

19 Mouvement du Nid Belgium, *Les Nouvelles du Nid*, no. 2, 8.

20 Mouvement du Nid Belgium, *Les Nouvelles du Nid*, no. 7.

21 Catherine Coutelle, Assemblée Nationale, *Session ordinaire de 2013–2014, Compte rendu intégral, Deuxième séance du vendredi 29 novembre 2013*. Author's translation.

22 Guy Geoffroy, Assemblée Nationale, *Compte rendu intégral, Séance du mercredi 6 avril 2016*, April 6, 2016. http://www.assemblee-nationale.fr/14/cri/2015-2016/20160170.asp. Author's translation.

23 Marie-Louise Fort, Assemblée Nationale, *Session ordinaire de 2013–2014, Compte rendu intégral, Deuxième séance du vendredi 29 novembre 2013*. Author's translation.

24 Bereni, "De la cause à la loi," 22.

25 Assemblée Nationale, *Déclaration des Droits de l'Homme et du Citoyen*, 1789. https://www.legifrance.gouv.fr/Droit-francais/Constitution/Declaration-des-Droits-de-l-Homme-et-du-Citoyen-de-1789. Author's translation.

26 Boistard, Sénat, *Séance du 14 octobre 2015*. Author's translation.

27 Assemblée Nationale, *Déclaration des Droits de l'Homme et du Citoyen*, article 6.

28 Laurence Rossignol, Sénat, *Séance du 10 mars 2016*. Author's translation.
29 Assemblée Nationale, *Loi n° 94-653 du 29 juillet 1994 relative au respect du corps humain*, 1994. https://www.legifrance.gouv.fr/affichTexte.do?cidTexte=JORFTEXT000000549619. Author's translation.
30 Laurence Rossignol, Sénat, *Séance du 10 mars 2016*. Author's translation.
31 Assemblée Nationale, *Rapport de M. Phillippe Gosselin, N° 3812 fait au nom de la commission des lois constitutionnelles, de la législation et de l'administration générale de la République, sur la proposition de loi constitutionnelle n° 1354*, 8 June 2016. http://www.assemblee-nationale.fr/14/rapports/r3812.asp.
32 Ibid. Author's translation.
33 Jean-Michel Arnaud, "Pourquoi la loi bioéthique devrait autant marquer le quinquennat d'Emmanuel Macron," *The Huffington Post*, August 26, 2018, https://www.huffingtonpost.fr/jeanmichel-arnaud/pourquoi-la-loi-bioethique-devrait-autant-marquer-le-quinquennat-demmanuel-macron_a_23507826/.
34 Claire Fenton-Glynn, "International Surrogacy before the European Court of Human Rights," *Journal of Private International Law* 13, no. 3 (2017): 546–67.
35 Laurence Rossignol, Assemblée Nationale, *Compte rendu intégral, Séance du mercredi 6 avril 2016*. Author's translation.
36 Lev Semenovich Vygotsky, "Problems of the Theory and Methods of Psychology," in *The Collected Works of LS Vygotsky* 3, eds. Robert W. Rieber and Jeffrey Wollock (Berlin: Springer Science and Business Media, 1997), 35–146.
37 European Women's Lobby, *18 Myths on Prostitution*, 2014. https://www.womenlobby.org/18-myths-on-prostitution-read-and-share-EWL-awareness-raising-tool?lang=en.
38 European Women's Lobby and Black Moon Production, "For a Change of Perspective," 2011. https://www.womenlobby.org/EWL-campaign-clip-For-a-change-of-perspective-2011?lang=en.
39 Nordic Model Now, "How the Swedish Sex Purchase Law Moved the Shame of Prostitution from Women to the Punters." Interview with Simon Häggström by Francine Sporenda, July 20, 2018. https://nordicmodelnow.org/2018/07/20/how-the-swedish-sex-purchase-law-moved-the-shame-of-prostitution-from-the-women-to-the-punters/.
40 Ekberg, "The Swedish Law That Prohibits the Purchase of Sexual Services." 1205.
41 Ibid.
42 See Leif Lenke and Börje Olsson, "Sweden: Zero Tolerance Wins the Argument?," In *European Drug Policies and Enforcement*, ed. Nicholas Dorn, Ernesto Savona, and Jorgen Jepse, 106–18 (London: Palgrave Macmillan UK, 1996).
43 Mouvement du Nid and McCann Paris, *Girls of Paradise*, 2016, http://www.mouvementdunid.org/Girls-of-paradise-quand-la-realite-s-impose-aux-clients-de-la-prostitution.

44 Lilian Mathieu, "De l'objectivation à l'émotion. La mobilisation des chiffres dans le mouvement abolitionniste contemporain." *Mots. Les langages du politique* 100 (2013): 173–85.
45 Snippets of these conversations were also played on Radio France.
46 Mouvement du Nid and McCann Paris, *Girls of Paradise*. Author's translation.
47 Mathieu, "De l'objectivation à l'émotion." 180.
48 Statement by secretary-general Christine Blec, appearing on their website article presenting this video, Mouvement du Nid and McCann Paris, *Girls of Paradise*. Author's translation.
49 James M. Jasper, "The Emotions of Protest: Affective and Reactive Emotions in and Around Social Movements," *Sociological Forum* 13, no. 3 (1998): 406.
50 Rutvica Andrijasevic, "Beautiful Dead Bodies: Gender, Migration and Representation in Anti-Trafficking Campaigns," *Feminist Review* 86, no. 1 (2007): 24–44.
51 Stanley Cohen, *Folk Devils and Moral Panics* (New York: Routledge, 2011).
52 Mouvement du Nid, *Les Bourreaux*, 2016. http://www.mouvementdunid.org/Les-Bourreaux-Le-Mouvement-du-Nid.
53 Erich Goode and Nachman Ben-Yehuda, *Moral Panics: The Social Construction of Deviance* (Chichester: John Wiley and Sons, 2010), 27.
54 Amnesty International, *Policy Background Document on Decriminalization of Sex Work,* 2014, 3. https://fr.scribd.com/doc/202126121/Amnesty-Prostitution-Policy-document.
55 EWL, *EWL's call to Amnesty International: Protect the Human Rights of ALL Women and Girls to Build a Society Based on Equality, Justice and Respect*, August 5, 2015. https://www.womenlobby.org/EWL-s-call-to-Amnesty-International-protect-the-human-rights-of-ALL-women-and?lang=en.
56 Ibid.
57 Ibid.
58 CATW, *Vote NO to Decriminalizing Pimps, Brothel Owners, and Buyers of Sex*, July 17, 2015, https://www.change.org/p/amnesty-international-vote-no-to-decriminalizing-pimps-brothel-owners-and-buyers-of-sex.
59 Amnesty International, *The Human Cost of 'Crushing' the Market,* 2016, https://www.amnesty.org/en/documents/eur36/4034/2016/en/.
60 Mathieu, *La fin du tapin*.
61 An argument of the "no" campaign during the European Union debates was that women would lose their voice and influence, see Zenia Hellgren and Barbara Hobson, "Gender and Ethnic Minority Claims in Swedish and EU Frames," in *Gender Politics in the Expanding European Union: Mobilisation, Inclusion, Exclusion*, ed. Silke Roth (New York: Berghahn Books, 2008), 211–36.
62 Susanne Dodillet and Petra Östergren, *The Swedish Sex Purchase Act: Claimed Success and Documented Effects,* International Workshop: Decriminalizing Prostitution and Beyond: Practical Experiences and Challenges, The Hague,

March 2011, 24–5. https://www.nswp.org/sites/nswp.org/files/Impact%20of%20 Swedish%20law.pdf.
63 Lars Trägårdh, *Sweden and the EU: Welfare State Nationalism and the Spectre of 'Europe'* (London: Routledge, 2002), 171.
64 Hellgren and Hobson, "Gender and Ethnic Minority Claims in Swedish and EU Frames."
65 Joyce Gelb, *Feminism and Politics: A Comparative Perspective* (Berkeley: University of California Press, 1986), 137.
66 Carina Gallo and Robert Elias, "Punishment or Solidarity: Comparing the US and Swedish Victim Movements," in *Reconceptualizing Critical Victimology. Interventions and Possibilities*, eds. Dale Spencer and Sandra Walklate (Thousand Oaks: SAGE, 2016), 80.
67 Barbara Hobson, "Recognition Struggles in Universalistic and Gender Distinctive Frames: Sweden and Ireland," in *Recognition Struggles and Social Movements*, ed. Barbara Hobson (Cambridge: Cambridge University Press), 2003, 64–92.
68 Hobson, "Recognition Struggles in Universalistic and Gender Distinctive Frames: Sweden and Ireland."
69 Hellgren and Hobson, "Gender and Ethnic Minority Claims in Swedish and EU Frames," 219.
70 Sverigeskvinnolobby http://sverigeskvinnolobby.se/en/about/about-the-organization/.
71 Simon Häggström, *Shadow's Law: The True Story of a Swedish Detective Inspector Fighting Prostitution* (Los Angeles: SCB Distributors, 2016), 1.
72 Of course, the local translation and application of the Nordic Model into different national settings, however, demonstrates varying degrees of faithfulness due to existing local practices and structures. For instance, in Northern Ireland those selling sex in groups of more than one person can be prosecuted for brothel-keeping.
73 European Parliament, *Resolution of 26 February 2014 on Sexual Exploitation and Prostitution and its Impact on Gender Equality. Ep P7_TA(2014)0162,* 2014. http://www.europarl.europa.eu/sides/getDoc.do?pubref=-//ep//text+ta+p7-ta-2014-0162+0+doc+xml+v0//en.
74 Eilis Ward and Gillian Wylie, *Feminism, Prostitution and the State: The Politics of Neo-Abolitionism* (New York: Routledge/Taylor and Francis, 2017).
75 Ward and Wylie, *Feminism, Prostitution and the State,* 14.
76 European Parliament, *Treaty of Lisbon,* December 13, 2007, article 10. https://eur-lex.europa.eu/legal-content/EN/TXT/?uri=celex%3A12007L%2FTXT.
77 European Economic and Social Committee, *Active Citizenship, for a Better European Society,* QE-32-11-790-EN-C, 2012. https://www.eesc.europa.eu/en/our-work/publications-other-work/publications/active-citizenship.

78 Greggor Mattson, *The Cultural Politics of European Prostitution Reform: Governing Loose Women* (New York: Palgrave Macmillan, 2016).
79 Janice Raymond, *Not a Choice, Not a Job: Exposing the Myths about Prostitution and the Global Sex Trade* (Dulles: Potomac Books, Inc., 2013).
80 European Parliament, *On the Consequences of the Sex Industry in the European Union, 2003/2107INI,* Committee on Women's Rights and Equal Opportunities, Marianne Eriksson, April 15, 2004. http://www.europarl.europa.eu/sides/getDoc.do?type=REPORT&reference=A5-2004-0274&language=GA.
81 Mattson, *The Cultural Politics of European Prostitution Reform*, 46.
82 International Committee on the Rights of Sex Workers in Europe, *The Declaration on the Rights of Sex Workers in Europe*, 2005. http://www.sexworkeurope.org/resources/declaration-rights-sex-workers-europe; International Committee on the Rights of Sex Workers in Europe, *Sex Workers in Europe Manifesto*, European Conference on Sex Work, Human Rights, Labour and Migration, Brussels, Belgium, October 15–17, 2005. http://www.sexworkeurope.org/resources/sex-workers-europe-manifesto.
83 ICRSWE, *Sex Workers in Europe Manifesto*, 1.
84 Ibid., 2.
85 Rutvica Andrijasevic, "Acts of Citizenship as Methodology," in *Enacting European Citizenship*, eds. Egin F. Isin and Michael Saward (Cambridge: Cambridge University Press, 2013), 49. For more on sex workers' mobilizations, see also International Committee on the Rights of Sex Workers in Europe, *Nothing About Us Without Us! Ten Years of Sex Workers' Rights Activism and Advocacy in Europe*, 2015. http://www.sexworkeurope.org/sites/default/files/userfiles/files/ICRSE_10years%20report_April2016_photo_%282%29.pdf; Roberto Scaramuzzino and Gabriella Scaramuzzino, "Sex Workers' Rights Movement and the EU: Challenging the New European Prostitution Policy Model," in *EU Civil Society: Patterns of Cooperation, Competition and Conflict*, eds. Sara Kalm and Hakan Johansson (London: Palgrave Macmillan, 2015) 137–54.
86 Andrijasevic, "Acts of Citizenship as Methodology."
87 Patricia Mooney Nickel, *Public Sociology and Civil Society: Governance, Politics, and Power* (New York: Routledge, 2015), 13.
88 Swedish Institute, *The Ban against the Purchase of Sexual Services, An Evaluation 1999–2008*, Anna Skarhed, 2010, 9.
89 Laure Bereni and Anne Revillard, "Movement Institutions: The Bureaucratic Sources of Feminist Protest," *Politics and Gender* 14, no. 3 (2018): 422.
90 Mathieu, "Des monstres ordinaires."
91 EWL, *EWL's call to Amnesty* International.
92 European Women's Lobby, "Together for a Europe Free from Prostitution," 2012. https://www.womenlobby.org/IMG/pdf/brussels_call_layout5_en.pdf.

93 EWL, *18 Myths on Prostitution*.
94 European Women's Lobby, "MEPs call for a Europe free from prostitution and support the Brussels' Call signed by 200 NGOs," October 2, 2013. https://www.womenlobby.org/MEPs-call-for-a-Europe-free-from-prostitution-and-support-the-Brussels-Call?lang=en.
95 EWL, *Together for a Europe Free from Prostitution*.
96 Ibid.
97 European Women's Lobby, *Values and Principles*, June 17, 2011. https://www.womenlobby.org/Values-and-principles?lang=en.
98 Ward and Wylie, *Feminism, Prostitution and the State*.
99 Mary Honeyball, *The Honeyball Buzz*, https://maryhoneyballmep.wordpress.com/.
100 European Parliament, *Report on Sexual Exploitation and Prostitution and its Impact on Gender Equality*, 2013/2103(INI), Mary Honeyball, February 4, 2014. http://www.europarl.europa.eu/sides/getDoc.do?pubRef=-//EP//TEXT+REPORT+A7-2014-0071+0+DOC+XML+V0//EN.
101 European Parliament, *Directive on Preventing and Combating Trafficking in Human Beings and Protecting its Victims, and Replacing Council Framework Decision 2002/629/JHA*, 2011/36/EU, April 5, 2011. Available online: https://eur-lex.europa.eu/legal-content/EN/TXT/?uri=CELEX%3a32011L0036 (accessed March 21, 2019).

Chapter 7

1 Brenda Cossman, *The New Sex Wars: Sexual Harm in the #MeToo Era* (New York: NYU Press, 2021), 15.
2 See the discussion of thick versus thin solidarity in Roseann Liu and Savannah Shange, "Toward Thick Solidarity: Theorizing Empathy in Social Justice Movements," *Radical History Review* 131 (2018): 189–98.
3 Catharine A. MacKinnon and Andrea Dworkin eds, *In Harm's Way: The Pornography Civil Rights Hearings* (Cambridge: Harvard University Press, 1997), 65.
4 Lisa Brodyaga, *Rape and Its Victims: A Report for Citizens, Health Facilities, and Criminal Justice* (Washington: National Institute of Law Enforcement and Criminal Justice, Law Enforcement Assistance Administration, U.S. Department of Justice, 1974).
5 Arthur Kleinman, Veena Das and Margaret Lock, eds., *Social Suffering* (Berkeley: University of California Press, 1997).
6 Nils Christie, "The Ideal Victim," in *From Crime Policy to Victim Policy: Reorienting the Justice System*, ed. Ezzat A. Fattah (London: Palgrave Macmillan, 1986), 17–30.

7. Rebecca Stringer, *Knowing Victims: Feminism, Agency and Victim Politics in Neoliberal Times* (New York: Routledge, 2014), 10–11.
8. Nancy Berns, *Framing the Victim: Domestic Violence, Media, and Social Problems* (New York: Routledge, 2017), 1.
9. Stringer, *Knowing Victims*. Doezema, "Ouch! Western Feminists' 'Wounded Attachment' to the 'Third World Prostitute.'"
10. Alice M. Miller, "Sexuality, Violence against Women, and Human Rights: Women Make Demands and Ladies Get Protection," *Health and Human Rights* 7, no. 2 (2004): 22.
11. UN, *Charter*. http://legal.un.org/repertory/art1.shtml.
12. UN, *Universal Declaration of Human Rights*, 1948. http://www.un.org/en/udhrbook/pdf/udhr_booklet_en_web.pdf.
13. Maria Eriksson, "Defining Rape: Emerging Obligations for States under International Law?" (PhD dissertation, Örebro Universitet, 2010).
14. Catherine A. MacKinnon, "Reflections on Sex Equality under Law," *Yale Law Journal* 100, no. 5 (1991): 1301.
15. Eriksson, "Defining Rape," 349.
16. UN, *Convention on the Elimination of All Forms of Discrimination Against Women*, 1979. http://www.un.org/womenwatch/daw/cedaw/.
17. Miller, "Sexuality, Violence against Women, and Human Rights," 27.
18. Ibid.
19. For further reading on this issue, see Kelly D. Askin, "Prosecuting Wartime Rape and Other Gender-Related Crimes under International Law: Extraordinary Advances, Enduring Obstacles," *Berkeley Journal of International Law* 21 (2003): 288–349.
20. Miller, "Sexuality, Violence against Women, and Human Rights," 27.
21. Eriksson, "Defining Rape."
22. For instance, with post-traumatic stress disorder being medicalized. For violence against women as a public health issue, see also WHO, *Putting Women First: Ethical and Safety Recommendations for Research on Domestic Violence against Women*, 2001. https://www.who.int/publications/i/item/WHO-FCH-GWH-01.1.
23. Eriksson, "Defining Rape," 297. See also UN, *Rome Statute of the International Criminal Court* II-7-c 1998. http://legal.un.org/icc/statute/99_corr/cstatute.htm. It defines rape, sexual slavery, and "any other sexual violence of comparable gravity" as a crime against humanity (II-7-c).
24. See for instance two separate interviews conducted in 2017 with the abolitionists Rachel Moran from SPACE (Survivors of Prostitution Abuse Calling for Enlightenment) International - and Lorraine Spiteri from the Malta Confederation of Women's Organisations. Mariangela Mianiti, "Prostitution is Paid Rape, and Men Know It," *Il Manifesto*, October 11, 2017, https://global.ilmanifesto.it/prostitution-is-paid-rape-and-men-know-it/. Kevin Schembri Orland, "Prostitution Is Paid

Rape, Says MCWO Chairwoman Lorraine Spiteri," *The Malta Independent*, September 9, 2017. http://www.independent.com.mt/articles/2017-09-09/local-news/Prostitution-is-paid-rape-says-MCWO-chairwoman-Lorraine-Spiteri-6736178562.

25 Sara Meger, "The Fetishization of Sexual Violence in International Security," *International Studies Quarterly* 60, no. 1 (2016): 149–59.

26 Jacqui True, "The Political Economy of Violence against Women: A Feminist International Relations Perspective," *Australian Feminist Law Journal* 32, no. 1 (2010): 42.

27 Catharine A. MacKinnon, *Toward a Feminist Theory of the State* (Cambridge: Harvard University Press, 1989), 336–7.

28 For an excellent overview of the socio-philosophical positions in this debate, see Lilian Mathieu, *Prostitution, Quel est le problème?* (Paris: Textuel, 2016).

29 Sverigeskvinnolobby, "Surrogacy: A Global Trade in Women's Bodies?" October 31, 2014. https://www.womenlobby.org/Surrogacy-a-global-trade-in-women-s-bodies?lang=en.

30 Kajsa Ekis Ekman, *L'être et la marchandise: Prostitution, maternité de substitution et dissociation de soi* (Ville Mont-Royal: M Editeur, 2013).

31 Mathieu, *Prostitution*, 87.

32 Orland, "Prostitution Is Paid Rape, Says MCWO Chairwoman Lorraine Spiteri."

33 See for instance Andrijasevic, "Beautiful Dead Bodies."

34 Mathieu, "Des monstres ordinaires."

35 Swedish Institute, *Targeting the Sex Buyer, the Swedish Example: Stopping Prostitution and Trafficking Where It All Begins*, 2011.

36 Mianiti, "Prostitution is Paid Rape, and Men Know It."

37 Brown, *States of Injury*, 278.

38 Rachel Moran, *Paid For: My Journey through Prostitution* (New York: W. W. Norton and Company, 2015).

39 Ibid.

40 Ibid.

41 Ibid.

42 Ibid.

43 Rebecca Mott, "To All Punters," July 4, 2018. https://rebeccamott.net/.

44 Rebecca Bender, "7 Ways Your Organization Could Be Re-Exploiting Survivors," June 29, 2017. https://rebeccabender.org/2017-6-29-7-ways-your-organization-could-be-re-exploitating-survivors/.

45 Space International, *Testimonials*. http://www.spaceintl.org/about/testimonials/.

46 Nordic Model Now, "Survivors Speak Out about What Prostitution Is REALLY Like," September 8, 2018. https://nordicmodelnow.org/2018/09/08/survivors-speak-out-about-what-prostitution-is-really-like/.

47 Bender, "7 Ways Your Organization Could Be Re-Exploiting Survivors."
48 Linda Alcoff and Laura Gray, "Survivor Discourse: Transgression or Recuperation?" *Signs: Journal of Women in Culture and Society* 18, no. 2 (1993), 285.
49 Space International, *Testimonials*.
50 Ibid.
51 Rachel Moran, "The Life of an Anti-Prostitution Campaigner," *The Irish Times*, May 29, 2015. https://www.irishtimes.com/life-and-style/people/the-life-of-an-anti-prostitution-campaigner-1.2230971.
52 Melinda Tankardreist, "Sex Industry Tries to Recruit Prostitution Survivor Back into the Trade at Book Launch," 2016. http://melindatankardreist.com/2016/09/sex-industry-tries-to-recruit-prostitution-survivor-back-into-the-trade-at-book-launch/.
53 Peter G. van der Velden, Mauro Pecoraro, Mijke S. Houwerzijl, Erik van der Meulen, "Mental Health Problems among Whistleblowers: A Comparative Study," *Psychological Reports* 122, no. 2 (2019): 632–44.
54 Meghan Murphy, "PODCAST: Survivors Speak Out in New Book about the Prostitution Industry," *Feminist Current*, August 12, 2016. https://www.feministcurrent.com/2016/08/12/podcast-prostitution-narratives-stories-survival-sex-trade/

Conclusion

1 Decrim Now, "Open Letter opposing the Nordic Model," https://decrimnow.org.uk/open-letter-on-the-nordic-model/
2 Donna Haraway, "Situated Knowledges: The Science Question in Feminism and The Privilege of Partial Perspective," in *Turning Points in Qualitative Research: Tying Knots in a Handkerchief*, eds. Yvonna S. Lincoln and Norman K. Denzin (Lanham: Rowman Altamira, 2003), 21–46.
3 Teresa Langle de Paz, "A Golden Lever for Politics: Feminist Emotion and Women's Agency," *Hypatia* 31, no. 1 (2016): 187–203.
4 Sandra L. Bartky, *Femininity and Domination: Studies in the Phenomenology of Oppression* (New York: Routledge, 1990),85.
5 Sara Ahmed, "Feminist Killjoys (And Other Willful Subjects)," *Scholar and Feminist Online*, Summer 2010, no. 8.3. http://sfonline.barnard.edu/polyphonic/ahmed_04.htm.

Bibliography

Acton, William. *Prostitution, Considered in Its Moral, Social, and Sanitary Aspects, in London and Other Large Cities and Garrison Towns, With Proposals for The Mitigation and Prevention of Its Attendant Evils*. London: J. Churchill, 1857.
Acton, William. *Prostitution, Considered in Its Moral, Social, and Sanitary Aspects, in London and Other Large Cities and Garrison Towns, With Proposals for The Mitigation and Prevention of Its Attendant Evils*, Second Edition. London: J. Churchill, 1870.
Agustin, Laura Maria. "The New Abolitionist Model." *Jacobinmag*, 2017. Available online: https://www.jacobinmag.com/2017/12/sex-work-the-pimping-of-prostitution-review (accessed March 21, 2019).
Ahmed, Sara. *The Cultural Politics of Emotion*. Edinburgh and London: Edinburgh University Press and Routledge, 2013.
Ahmed, Sara. "Feminist Killjoys (and Other Willful Subjects)." *Scholar and Feminist Online*, Summer 2010, no. 8.3. Available online: http://sfonline.barnard.edu/polyphonic/ahmed_04.htm (accessed March 21, 2019).
Ahmed, Sara. "The Organisation of Hate." *Law and Critique* 12, no. 3 (2001): 345–65.
Ahmed, Sara. *The Promise of Happiness*. Durham, NC: Duke University Press, 2010.
Alcoff, Linda and Laura Gray. "Survivor Discourse: Transgression or Recuperation?." *Signs: Journal of Women in Culture and Society* 18, no. 2 (1993): 260–290.
Allain, Jean. "White Slave Traffic in International Law." *Journal of Trafficking and Human Exploitation* 11 (2017): 1–40.
Amnesty International. *The Human Cost of 'Crushing' the Market*, 2016. Available online: https://www.amnesty.org/en/documents/eur36/4034/2016/en/ (accessed March 21, 2019).
Amnesty International. *Policy Background Document on Decriminalization of Sex Work*, 2014. Available online: https://fr.scribd.com/doc/202126121/Amnesty-Prostitution-Policy-Document (accessed March 21, 2019).
Andrijasevic, Rutvica. "Acts of Citizenship as Methodology." In *Enacting European Citizenship*, edited by Egin F. Isin and Michael Saward, 47–65. Cambridge: Cambridge University Press, 2013.
Andrijasevic, Rutvica. "Beautiful Dead Bodies: Gender, Migration and Representation in Anti-Trafficking Campaigns." *Feminist Review* 86, no. 1 (2007): 24–44.
Antić, Ana. "Decolonizing Madness? Transcultural Psychiatry, International Order and Birth of a 'Global Psyche' in the Aftermath of the Second World War." *Journal of Global History* 17, no. 1 (2022): 20–41.

Aquinas, Thomas. *Summa Theologica*, 1702. Available online: http://www.
documentacatholicaomnia.eu/03d/1225-1274,_thomas_aquinas,_summa_
theologiae-supplementum,_fr.pdf (accessed March 21, 2019).

Arnaud, Jean-Michel. "Pourquoi la loi bioéthique devrait autant marquer le
quinquennat d'Emmanuel Macron." *The Huffington Post,* August 26, 2018,
https://www.huffingtonpost.fr/jeanmichel-arnaud/pourquoi-la-loi-bioethique-
devrait-autant-marquer-le-quinquennat-demmanuel-macron_a_23507826/.

Arnold, David. *Colonizing the Body: State Medicine and Epidemic Disease in Nineteenth-
Century India*. Berkeley: University of California Press, 1993.

Askin, Kelly D. "Prosecuting Wartime Rape and Other Gender-Related Crimes under
International Law: Extraordinary Advances, Enduring Obstacles." *Berkeley Journal of
International Law* 21 (2003): 288–349.

Assemblée Nationale. *Compte rendu intégral, Séance du mercredi 6 avril 2016*,
April 6, 2016. Available online: http://www.assemblee-nationale.fr/14/cri/2015-
2016/20160170.asp (accessed March 21, 2019).

Assemblée Nationale. *Déclaration des Droits de l'homme et du Citoyen de 1789*, 1789.
Available online: https://www.legifrance.gouv.fr/Droit-francais/Constitution/
Declaration-des-Droits-de-l-Homme-et-du-Citoyen-de-1789 (accessed
March 21, 2019).

Assemblée Nationale. *Loi n° 94-653 du 29 juillet 1994 relative au respect du corps
humain*, 1994. Available online: https://www.legifrance.gouv.fr/affichTexte.do?cidTe
xte=JORFTEXT000000549619 (accessed March 21, 2019).

Assemblée Nationale. *Rapport de M. Phillippe Gosselin, N° 3812 fait au nom de la
commission des lois constitutionnelles, de la législation et de l'administration générale
de la République, sur la proposition de loi constitutionnelle n° 1354*, June 8, 2016.
Available online: http://www.assemblee-nationale.fr/14/rapports/r3812.asp
(accessed March 21, 2019).

Assemblée Nationale. *Session ordinaire de 2013–2014, Compte rendu intégral, Deuxième
séance du vendredi 29 novembre 2013*, November 29, 2013. Available online:
http://www.assemblee-nationale.fr/14/cri/2013-2014/20140088.asp (accessed
March 21, 2019).

Association For Moral and Social Hygiene. *Evidence for the Working Party on the Street
Offences Acts 1959*, The Women's Library, Gb 106 Ams/B/04/16/06.

Backhouse, Constance. "The White Women's Labor Laws: Anti-Chinese Racism
in Early Twentieth-Century Canada." *Law and History Review* 14, no. 2 (1996):
315–68.

Balfour, Lady Francis. "The Travellers' Aid Society." *The Sentinel* 8, no. 5 (1886): 56–7.

Barnes, Djuna. "How It Feels to Be Forcibly Fed." *New York World Magazine*,
September 6, 1914. Available online: http://hdl.handle.net/1903.1/14687 (accessed
March 21, 2019).

Barnett, Michael. *Empire of Humanity: A History of Humanitarianism*. Ithaca:
Cornell University Press, 2011.

Barry, Kathleen. "Female Sexual Slavery: Understanding the International Dimensions of Women's Oppression." *Human Rights Quarterly* 3 (1981): 44–52.
Barry, Kathleen. *Female Sexual Slavery*. Hoboken: Prentice Hall, 1979.
Bartky, Sandra L. *Femininity and Domination: Studies in The Phenomenology of Oppression*. New York: Routledge, 1990.
Bartky, Sandra L. "Foucault, Femininity, and The Modernization of Patriarchal Power." In *Feminism and Foucault: Reflections on Resistance*, edited by Irene Diamond and Lee Quinby, 61–86. Boston: Northeastern University Press, 1988.
Bartley, Paula. *Prostitution: Prevention and Reform in England, 1860–1914*. London and New York: Routledge, 2012.
Basiliere, Jenna. "Political is Personal: Scholarly Manifestations of the Feminist Sex Wars." *Michigan Feminist Studies* 22, no. 1 (2008). Available online: http://hdl.handle.net/2027/spo.ark5583.0022.101 (accessed March 19, 2019).
Becker, Dana. *The Myth of Empowerment: Women and the Therapeutic Culture in America*. New York: New York University Press, 2005.
Becker, Howard S. *Outsiders: Studies in the Sociology of Deviance*. New York: The Free Press, 1963.
Bell, Enid Moberly. *Josephine Butler: Flame of Fire*. London: Constable, 1963.
Bender, Rebecca. "7 Ways Your Organization Could Be Re-Exploiting Survivors," June 29, 2017. Available online: https://rebeccabender.org/2017-6-29-7-ways-your-organization-could-be-re-exploitating-survivors/ (accessed March 21, 2019).
Bentham, Jeremy. *The Collected Works of Jeremy Bentham: An Introduction to the Principles of Morals and Legislation*. Oxford: Oxford University Press, 1996.
Bereni, Laure. "De la cause à la loi, les mobilisations pour la parité politique en France (1992–2000)." PhD thesis, Université Panthéon-Sorbonne. Paris I, 2007.
Bereni, Laure and Anne Revillard. "Movement Institutions: The Bureaucratic Sources of Feminist Protest." *Politics and Gender* 14, no. 3 (2018): 407–32.
Berns, Nancy. *Framing the Victim: Domestic Violence, Media, and Social Problems*. New York: Routledge, 2017.
Bernstein, Elizabeth. "Carceral Politics as Gender Justice? The 'Traffic in Women' and Neoliberal Circuits of Crime, Sex, and Rights." *Theory and Society* 41, no. 3 (2012): 233–59.
Bernstein, Elizabeth. "Militarized Humanitarianism Meets Carceral Feminism: The Politics of Sex, Rights, and Freedom in Contemporary Antitrafficking Campaigns." *Signs: Journal of Women in Culture and Society* 36, no. 1 (2010): 45–71.
Bewes, Wyndham Anstis. *Manual of Vigilance Law*. London: Office of the National Vigilance Association, 1888.
Bindel, Julie. *The Pimping of Prostitution: Abolishing the Sex Work Myth*. London: Palgrave Macmillan, 2017.
Blackwell, Antoinette Louisa Brown. *The Sexes throughout Nature*. New York: GP Putnam, 1875.
Blackwell, Elizabeth. *Essays in Medical Sociology*, 2. London: Ernest Bell, 1902.

Blackwell, Elizabeth. *The Human Element in Sex: Being a Medical Enquiry into the Relation of Sexual Physiology to Christian Morality*. Enlarged. London: J. and A. Churchill, 1884.
Blackwell, Elizabeth. *Medicine and Morality*. London: W. Speaight and Sons, 1881.
Blackwell, Elizabeth. *Wrong and Right Methods of Dealing with Social Evil, As Shewn by Lately-Published Parliamentary Evidence*. New York: A. Brentano and Co., 1883.
Bland, Lucy. *Banishing the Beast: Feminism, Sex and Morality*. London: Tauris Parke Paperbacks, 2001.
Bland, Lucy. "'Purifying' The Public World: Feminist Vigilantes in Late Victorian England." *Women's History Review* 1, no. 3 (1992): 397–412.
Boddice, Rob. "The Manly Mind? Revisiting The Victorian 'Sex in Brain' Debate." *Gender and History* 23, no. 2 (2011): 321–40.
Boddice, Rob. *The Science of Sympathy: Morality, Evolution, and Victorian Civilization*. Champaign: University of Illinois Press, 2016.
Book Depository. Available online: https://www.bookdepository.com/Pimping-Prostitution-Julie-Bindel/9781137558893 (accessed March 21, 2019).
Booth, William. *In Darkest England and the Way Out*. New York: Funk and Wagnalls, 1890.
Bourdieu, Pierre. "Décrire et prescrire." *Actes de la Recherche en Sciences Sociales* 38, no. 2 (1981): 69–73.
Bourdieu, Pierre. *Méditations pascaliennes*. Paris: Le Seuil, 2016.
Bristow, Edward J. *Vice and Vigilance: Purity Movements in Britain Since 1700*. Dublin: Gill and Macmillan, 1977.
Brockliss, Laurence and David Eastwood, eds. *A Union of Multiple Identities: The British Isles, c. 1750–c. 1850*. Manchester: Manchester University Press, 1997.
Brodyaga, Lisa. *Rape and Its Victims: A Report for Citizens, Health Facilities, and Criminal Justice*. Washington: National Institute of Law Enforcement and Criminal Justice, Law Enforcement Assistance Administration, U.S. Department of Justice, 1974.
Brown, Christopher Leslie. *Moral Capital: Foundations of British Abolitionism*. Chapel Hill: University of North Carolina Press Books, 2006.
Brown, Stewart J. *Providence and Empire: Religion, Politics and Society in The United Kingdom, 1815–1914*. London: Routledge, 2008.
Brown, Wendy. *States of Injury: Power and Freedom in Late Modernity*. Princeton: Princeton University Press, 1995.
Buchanan, Claudius. "The Star in The East," *The Works of The Rev. Claudius Buchanan*. New York: Whiting and Watson, 1812.
Buffon, George Louis Leclerc. *Natural History: Containing a Theory of the Earth, a General History of Man, of the Brute Creation, and of Vegetables, Minerals* 7. London: H. D. Symonds, 1807.
Bumiller, Kristin. *In an Abusive State: How Neoliberalism Appropriated the Feminist Movement Against Sexual Violence*. Durham, NC: Duke University Press, 2009.

Bureau International. *La Traite des Blanches: Bulletin du Bureau International*, December 1901, no. 4, The Women's Library, 4ibs/4/1.

Burton, Antoinette M. *Burdens of History: British Feminists, Indian Women, and Imperial Culture, 1865–1915*. Chapel Hill: University of North Carolina Press, 2000.

Butler, Josephine Elizabeth Grey. *Address Delivered in Craigie Hall, Edinburgh*. Manchester: Ireland and Co, Printers, 1871.

Butler, Josephine Elizabeth Grey. "Address Delivered at Croydon [1871]." In *Josephine Butler and The Prostitution Campaigns: The Ladies' Appeal and Protest* 2, edited by Jane Jordan and Ingrid Sharp, 155–67. London: Taylor & Francis, 2003.

Butler, Josephine Elizabeth Grey. *An Autobiographical Memoir*, edited by George W. and Lucy A. Johnson. Bristol: J. W. Arrowsmith Press, 1909.

Butler, Josephine Elizabeth Grey. *The Constitution Violated: An Essay*. Edinburgh: Edmonston and Douglas, 1871.

Butler, Josephine Elizabeth Grey. *The Education and Employment of Women*. London: Macmillan, 1868.

Butler, Josephine Elizabeth Grey. *A Few Words Addressed to True-Hearted Women*, The Women's Library, 3jbl/04/09, 13 March 1872.

Butler, Josephine Elizabeth Grey. *Government By Police*. London: T. Fisher Unwin, 1888.

Butler, Josephine Elizabeth Grey. *A Grave Question*. The Western Harem. London: Hatchards, 1886.

Butler, Josephine Elizabeth Grey. "'Laws for the Protection of Youth', Letter Addressed to the Editor of the *Sentinel* [1882]." In *Josephine Butler and the Prostitution Campaigns: Child Prostitution and the Age of Consent* 4, edited by Jane Jordan and Ingrid Sharp, 103–7. London: Taylor & Francis, 2003.

Butler, Josephine Elizabeth Grey. *Letter to Frederic Harrison*. Women's Library, GB 106 3jbl/02/20, May 9, 1868.

Butler, Josephine Elizabeth Grey. "Letter to her Niece Edith Leupold, 8 March 1867." In *Josephine Butler and the Prostitution Campaigns: The Moral Reclaimability of Prostitutes*, edited by Jane Jordan and Ingrid Sharp, 82–8. London: Taylor & Francis, 2003.

Butler, Josephine Elizabeth Grey. "A Letter to The Mothers of England: Commended also to The Attention of Fathers, Ministers of Religion, and Legislators [1881]." In *Josephine Butler and The Prostitution Campaigns: Child Prostitution and the Age of Consent* 4, edited by Jane Jordan and Ingrid Sharp, 80–94. London: Taylor & Francis, 2003.

Butler, Josephine Elizabeth Grey. "Letter from Josephine E. Butler to Dr. William Carter. 'Private' 1 April 1880." In *Josephine Butler and The Prostitution Campaigns: Child Prostitution and the Age of Consent* 4, edited by Jane Jordan and Ingrid Sharp, 17–20. London: Taylor & Francis, 2003.

Butler, Josephine Elizabeth Grey. "The Modern Slave Trade. Letter to the Editor of the *Shield*. 1 May 1880." In *Josephine Butler and the Prostitution Campaigns: Child Prostitution and the Age of Consent*, edited by Jane Jordan and Ingrid Sharp, 21–4. London: Taylor & Francis, 2003.

Butler, Josephine Elizabeth Grey. *On the Moral Reclaimability of Prostitutes*. London: National Association for the Repeal of the Contagious Diseases Act, 1870.

Butler, Josephine Elizabeth Grey. *Personal Reminiscences of a Great Crusade*. London: H. Marshall and Son, 1910.

Butler, Josephine Elizabeth Grey. "Ramah Was There a Voice Heard, … Rachel Weeping for Her Children, Storm-Bell [June 1898]." In *Josephine Butler and The Prostitution Campaigns: The Queen's Daughters in India* 5, edited by Jane Jordan and Ingrid Sharp, 585–90. London: Taylor and Francis, 2003.

Butler, Josephine Elizabeth Grey. *The Revival and Extension of the Abolitionist Cause, A Letter to the Members of the Ladies' National Association*. Winchester: John T. Doswell, The Women's Library, 3hjw/A/6/03, 1887.

Butler, Josephine Elizabeth Grey. *Social Purity, An Address Given to Students at Cambridge, Social Purity Alliance [1879]*. London: Dyer Bros, 1881.

Butler, Josephine Elizabeth Grey. *Une voix dans le désert*. Neuchâtel: Bureau Du Bulletin Continental, 1876.

Butler, Josephine Elizabeth Grey ed. *Woman's Work and Woman's Culture: A Series of Essays*. London: Macmillan and Company, 1869.

Caird, Mona. *The Morality of Marriage: And Other Essays on the Status and Destiny of Woman*. London: G. Redway, 1897.

Carey, Brycchan. *British Abolitionism and the Rhetoric of Sensibility: Writing, Sentiment and Slavery, 1760–1807*. New York: Palgrave, 2005.

Chadwick, Edwin. *Report on the Sanitary Condition of the Labouring Population of Great Britain: Supplementary Report on the Results of Special Inquiry into the Practice of Interment in Towns*, 1. London: HM Stationery Office, 1842.

Chant, Laura Ormiston. *Why We Attacked the Empire*. London: Horace Marshall and Son, 1895.

Christie, Nils. "The Ideal Victim." In *From Crime Policy to Victim Policy: Reorienting the Justice System*, edited by Ezzat A. Fattah, 17–30. London: Palgrave Macmillan, 1986.

Chuang, Janie A. "Exploitation Creep and the Unmaking of Human Trafficking Law." *American Journal of International Law* 108, no. 4 (2014): 609–49.

Clarke, Norma. "Feminism and the Popular Novel of the 1890s: A Brief Consideration of a Forgotten Feminist Novelist." *Feminist Review* 20, no. 1 (1985): 91–104.

Clarkson, Thomas. *The History of The Rise, Progress, and Accomplishment of the Abolition of the African Slave Trade by the British Parliament*. Farnham: John W. Parker, 1839.

Clavel, Geoffroy. "Les Femen contre la prostitution et pour la criminalisation des clients: une campagne choc." *The Huffington Post*, October 11, 2013. Available online: https://www.huffingtonpost.fr/2013/10/11/femen-prostitution-criminalisation-clients-campagne-choc_n_4080208.html (accessed March 21, 2019).

Coalition Against Trafficking in Women. "Vote NO to Decriminalizing Pimps, Brothel Owners, and Buyers of Sex," July 17, 2015. Available online: https://www.change.org/p/amnesty-international-vote-no-to-decriminalizing-pimps-brothel-owners-and-buyers-of-sex (accessed March 21, 2019).

Cobbe, Frances Power. *The Duties of Women, A Course of Lectures*. Boston: Geo. H. Ellis; London: Williams & Norgate, 1881.

Cobbett, William. *Cobbett's Parliamentary History of England: From the Norman Conquest, in 1066, to the Year, 1803*, 28. London: T. C. Hansard, 1816.

Cohen, Stanley. *Folk Devils and Moral Panics*. New York: Routledge, 2011.

Comte, Auguste. *Cours de philosophie positive par M. Auguste Comte*, 1. Paris: Rouen Frères, Bachelier, 1830.

Corbin, Alain, Courtine Jean-Jacques and Vigarello Georges, eds. *Histoire de la virilité, le triomphe de la virilité, le XIXe siècle* 2. Paris: Le Seuil, 2011.

Corbin, Alain. *Les filles de noces: Misère sexuelle et prostitution au XIXe et XXe siècles*. Paris: Aubier Montaigne, 1978.

Corrigan, Rose. *Up Against a Wall: Rape Reform and The Failure of Success*. New York: New York University Press, 2013.

Cossman, Brenda. *The New Sex Wars: Sexual Harm in the #MeToo Era*. New York: New York University Press, 2021.

Cott, Nancy. *The Grounding of Modern Feminism*. New Haven: Yale University Press, 1987.

Cox, David J., Kim Stevenson, Candida Harris, and Judith Rowbotham. *Public Indecency in England 1857–1960: 'A Serious and Growing Evil'*. London and New York: Routledge, 2015.

Daggers, Jenny. "Josephine Butler and Christian Women's Identity." In *Sex, Gender, and Religion: Josephine Butler Revisited*, edited by Jenny Daggers and Diana Neal, 97–112. American University Studies Series 242. New York and Oxford: Peter Lang, 2006.

Dangerfield, George. *The Strange Death of Liberal England*. London: Constable and Company LTD, 1935.

Darwin, Charles. *The Descent of Man, and Selection in Relation to Sex*. Reprinted From the Second English Edition, Revised, and Augmented. New York: Clarke, Given and Hooper, 1874.

Darwin, Charles and Clémence-Auguste Royer. *De l'origine des espèces ou des lois du progrès chez les êtres organisés par Charles Darwin*. Paris: Guillaumin Et Cie, Victor Masson Et Fils, 1862.

De Morsier, Émilie. *La Mission De La Femme: Discours Et Fragments*. Paris: Fischbacher, 1897.

Decrim Now. "Open Letter opposing the Nordic Model." Available online: https://decrimnow.org.uk/open-letter-on-the-nordic-model/ (accessed November 12, 2021).

de Sainte-Croix, Ghénia Avril. *Le Féminisme*. Paris: V. Giard and E. Brière, 1907.

de Vries, Petra. "Josephine Butler and the Making of Feminism: International Abolitionism in the Netherlands 1870–1914." *Women's History Review* 17, no. 2 (2008): 257–77.

Desmond, Adrian. *The Politics of Evolution: Morphology, Medicine, and Reform in Radical London*. Chicago: University of Chicago Press, 1992.

Dodillet, Susanne and Petra Östergren. *The Swedish Sex Purchase Act: Claimed Success and Documented Effects*, International Workshop: Decriminalizing Prostitution and Beyond: Practical Experiences and Challenges, The Hague, March 2011. Available online: https://www.nswp.org/sites/nswp.org/files/Impact%20of%20Swedish%20law.pdf (accessed March 21, 2019).

Doezema, Jo. "Loose Women or Lost Women? The Re-Emergence of The Myth of White Slavery in Contemporary Discourses of Trafficking in Women." *Gender Issues* 18, no. 1 (1999): 23–50.

Doezema, Jo. "Ouch! Western Feminists' 'Wounded Attachment' to the 'Third World Prostitute.'" *Feminist Review* 67, no. 1 (2001): 16–38.

Durbach, Nadja. *Bodily Matters: The Anti-Vaccination Movement in England, 1853–1907*. Durham, NC: Duke University Press, 2004.

Duriez, Bruno. "La différenciation des engagements: l'Action catholique ouvrière entre radicalisme politique et conformisme religieux." Paper given at workshop *Porter les Évangiles au monde: les logiques religieuses d'engagements politiques des catholiques au XXème siècle*, AFSP, Toulouse, September 2007.

Durnová, Anna. "Lost in Translation: Expressing Emotions in Policy Deliberation." In *Handbook of Critical Policy Studies*, edited by Frank Fischer, Douglas Torgerson, Anna Durnová, and Michael Orsini, 222–40. Cheltenham: Edward Elgar Publishing, 2015.

Dworkin, Andrea. *Men Possessing Women*. New York: Perigee, 1981.

Dworkin, Andrea. *Our Blood: Prophecies and Discourses on Sexual Politics*. New York: Harper and Row, 1976.

Dworkin, Andrea. "Prostitution and Male Supremacy." *Michigan Journal of Gender & Law* 1, no. 1 (1993): 1–12.

Dworkin, Andrea and Catherine A. MacKinnon. *Pornography and Civil Rights: A New Day for Women's Equality*. Minneapolis: Organizing against Pornography, 1988.

Dyer, Alfred. *The European Slave Trade in English Girls*. London: Dyer Brothers, Pasternoster Row, 1882.

Editor. "Houses of Commons." *John Bull*, February 28, 1825, 66–7.

Editor. "The National Vigilance Association." *The Echo*, October 13, 1888, London, no. 6174.

Editor. "Venereal Disease in The Army and Navy." *The Lancet*, March 19, 1864, 327–9.

Ekberg, Gunilla. "The Swedish Law That Prohibits the Purchase of Sexual Services: Best Practices for Prevention of Prostitution and Trafficking in Human Beings." *Violence Against Women* 10, no. 10 (2004): 1187–1218.

Ekman, Kajsa Ekis. *L'être et la marchandise. Prostitution, maternité de substitution et dissociation de soi*. Ville Mont-Royal: M Editeur, 2013.

Elston, Mary Ann. "Women and Anti-Vivisection in Victorian England, 1870–1900." In *Vivisection in Historical Perspective*, edited by Nicolaas A. Rupke, 259–94. London: Routledge, Kegan and Paul, 1987.

Eriksson, Maria. "Defining Rape: Emerging Obligations for States under International Law?." PhD dissertation, Örebro Universitet, 2010.

European Economic and Social Committee. *Active Citizenship, for a Better European Society*, QE-32-11-790-EN-C, 2012. Available online: https://www.eesc.europa.eu/en/our-work/publications-other-work/publications/active-citizenship (accessed March 21, 2019).

European Parliament. *Directive on Preventing and Combating Trafficking in Human Beings and Protecting its Victims, and Replacing Council Framework Decision 2002/629/JHA, 2011/36/EU*, April 5, 2011. Available online: https://eur-lex.europa.eu/legal-content/EN/TXT/?uri=CELEX%3a32011L0036 (accessed March 21, 2019).

European Parliament. *On the Consequences of the Sex Industry in the European Union, 2003/2107INI*, Committee on Women's Rights and Equal Opportunities, Marianne Eriksson, April 15, 2004. Available online: http://www.europarl.europa.eu/sides/getDoc.do?type=REPORT&reference=A5-2004-0274&language=GA (accessed March 21, 2019).

European Parliament. *Report on Sexual Exploitation and Prostitution and its Impact on Gender Equality*, 2013/2103(Ini), Mary Honeyball, February 4, 2014. Available online: http://www.europarl.europa.eu/sides/getDoc.do?pubref=-//EP//TEXT+REPORT+A7-2014-0071+0+DOC+XML+V0//EN (accessed March 21, 2019).

European Parliament. *Resolution of 26 February 2014 on Sexual Exploitation and Prostitution and its Impact on Gender Equality*, Ep P7_TA(2014)0162, 2014. Available online: http://www.europarl.europa.eu/sides/getDoc.do?pubref=-//ep//text+ta+p7-ta-2014-0162+0+doc+xml+v0//en (accessed March 21, 2019).

European Parliament. *Treaty of Lisbon*. December 13, 2007. Available online: https://eur-lex.europa.eu/legal-content/EN/TXT/?uri=celex%3A12007L%2FTXT (accessed March 21, 2019).

European Women's Lobby. "18 Myths on Prostitution," 2014. Available online: https://www.womenlobby.org/18-myths-on-prostitution-read-and-share-EWL-awareness-raising-tool?lang=en (accessed March 21, 2019).

European Women's Lobby. "EWL and the Brussels' Call Celebrate the Adoption of the French Law on the Abolition of Prostitution," April 6, 2016. Available online: https://www.womenlobby.org/ewl-and-the-brussels-call-celebrate-the-adoption-of-the-french-law-on-the?lang=en (accessed March 21, 2019).

European Women's Lobby. "EWL's Call to Amnesty International: Protect the Human Rights of All Women and Girls to Build a Society Based on Equality, Justice and Respect," August 5, 2015. Available online: https://www.womenlobby.org/EWL-s-call-to-Amnesty-International-protect-the-human-rights-of-ALL-women-and?lang=en (accessed March 21, 2019).

European Women's Lobby. "MEPs call for a Europe free from prostitution and support the Brussels' Call signed by 200 NGOs," October 2, 2013. Available online: https://www.womenlobby.org/MEPs-call-for-a-Europe-free-from-prostitution-and-support-the-Brussels-Call?lang=en (accessed March 21, 2019).

European Women's Lobby. "Together for a Europe Free from Prostitution," 2012. Available online: https://www.womenlobby.org/IMG/pdf/brussels_call_layout5_en.pdf (accessed March 21, 2019).

European Women's Lobby. "Values and Principles," June 17, 2011. Available online: https://www.womenlobby.org/Values-and-principles?lang=en (accessed March 21, 2019).

European Women's Lobby and Black Moon Production. "For a Change of Perspective," 2011. Available online: https://www.womenlobby.org/EWL-campaign-clip-For-a-change-of-perspective-2011?lang=en (accessed March 21, 2019).

Fallot, Tommy. *Communication sur l'organisation de la lutte contre la pornographie: faite au congrès de L'association protestante pour l'étude pratique des questions sociales. Marseille, 28 et 29 Octobre.* Nice: Impr. De V.-E. Gauthier, 1891.

Farley, Melissa. "#MeToo Must include Prostitution." *Dignity: A Journal on Sexual Exploitation and Violence* 3, no. 1 art. 9 (2018): 1–5.

Farley, Melissa and Vanessa Kelly. "Prostitution: A Critical Review of the Medical and Social Sciences Literature." *Women and Criminal Justice* 11, no. 4 (2000): 29–64.

Faulk, Barry J. *Music Hall and Modernity: The Late-Victorian Discovery of Popular Culture.* Athens: Ohio University Press, 2004.

Faye, Cathy. "12 – Social Psychology." In *The Cambridge Handbook of the Intellectual History of Psychology*, edited by Robert J. Sternberg and Wade E. Pickren. Cambridge: Cambridge University Press, 2019, 318–44.

Fenton-Glynn, Claire. "International Surrogacy Before the European Court of Human Rights." *Journal of Private International Law* 13, no. 3 (2017): 546–67.

Filmer, Robert. *Patriarcha, Or the Natural Power of Kings, Patriarcha and Other Political Works of Sir Robert Filmer.* Oxford: Basil Blackwell, 1949.

Fisher, Anna. "Josephine Butler: Pioneering Feminist Activist." Nordic Model Now, June 1, 2020. Available online: https://nordicmodelnow.org/2020/06/01/josephine-butler-pioneering-feminist-activist/ (accessed October 14, 2021).

Flanchon, Victor. "L'affaire Forissier." *La Lanterne*), July 13, 1903.

Fondation Scelles. "The Scelles Foundation in Mexico Promoting the Criminalization of the Demand for Prostitution." 2016. Available online: http://www.fondationscelles.org/en/prostitution/prostitution-by-country?id=128 (accessed March 21, 2019).

Forward, Stephanie. "Attitudes to Marriage and Prostitution in the Writings of Olive Schreiner, Mona Caird, Sarah Grand and George Egerton." *Women's History Review* 8, no. 1 (1999): 53–80.

Foucault, Michel. *L'archéologie du savoir.* Paris: Gallimard, 1969.

Foucault, Michel. *Naissance de la clinique une archéologie du regard médical.* Paris: Presses Universitaires De France, 1963.

Foucault, Michel. *Surveiller et punir. Naissance de la prison.* Paris: Éditions Gallimard, 2014.

Fournier, Alfred. *Ligue contre la syphilis, Société française de prophylaxie sanitaire et morale*. Paris: C. Delagrave, 1904.

Freedman, Estelle B. *Redefining Rape: Sexual Violence in the Era of Suffrage and Segregation*. Cambridge, MA: Harvard University Press, 2013.

Friedan, Betty. *The Feminine Mystique*. New York: W. W. Norton, 1963.

Gallo, Carina and Robert Elias. "Punishment or Solidarity: Comparing the US and Swedish Victim Movements." In *Reconceptualizing Critical Victimology. Interventions and Possibilities*, edited by Dale Spencer and Sandra Walklate, 79–94. Thousand Oaks: SAGE, 2016.

García, Magaly Rodríguez. "The League of Nations and the Moral Recruitment of Women." *International Review of Social History* 57, no. S20 (2012): 97–128.

Gammerl, Benno. "Emotional Styles: Concepts and Challenges." *Rethinking History* 16, no. 2 (2012): 161–75.

Gelb, Joyce. *Feminism and Politics: A Comparative Perspective*. Berkeley: University of California Press, 1989.

Goode, Erich and Nachman Ben-Yehuda. *Moral Panics: The Social Construction of Deviance*. Chichester: John Wiley and Sons, 2010.

Goodreads. Reader reviews. Available online: https://www.goodreads.com/book/show/34428143-the-pimping-of-prostitution (accessed March 21, 2019).

Goodrich, Chauncy A. et al. *Webster's Complete Dictionary of the English Language*. London: George Bell & Sons, 1886.

Gorman, Daniel. "Empire, Internationalism, and the Campaign against the Traffic in Women and Children in the 1920s." *Twentieth Century British History* 19, no. 2 (2008): 186–216.

Gospel Purity Association. *Licensed Plague Spots: India's Curse and Britain's Shame*. The Women's Library, 3ams/C/02/01, 1888.

Gottschalk, Marie. *The Prison and the Gallows: The Politics of Mass Incarceration in America*. Cambridge: Cambridge University Press, 2006.

Grand, Sarah. *The Beth Book: Being a Study from the Life of Elizabeth Caldwell Maclure, a Woman of Genius*. Portsmouth: Heinemann, 1898.

Graves, Lucia. "The Strange Alliance between #MeToo and the Anti-porn Movement." *The Guardian* (2018).

Gregg, Stephen H. "'A Truly Christian Hero': Religion, Effeminacy, and Nation in The Writings of The Societies for Reformation of Manners." *Eighteenth-Century Life* 25, no. 1 (2001): 17–28.

Grey, Maria Georgina. *Address to Women of All Classes*. Rome, The Women's Library, Gb 106 1bwe/B/2, January 1886.

Große, Judith. "Der Kampf gegen Prostitution: Zwischen Sittlichkeitsreform, Feminismus und Medizin, 1864–1914." In *Biopolitik und Sittlichkeitsreform: Kampagnen gegen Alkohol, Drogen und Prostitution 1880–1950*, edited by Judith Große, Francesco Spöring and Jana Tschurenev, 177–215. Frankfurt: Campus Verlag, 2014.

Gruber, Aya. "Rape, Feminism, and the War on Crime." *Washington Law Review* 8, no. 4 (2009): 581–658.
Gupta, Kat. *Representation of the British Suffrage Movement*. London: Bloomsbury Publishing, 2017.
Gusfield, Joseph R. *Contested Meanings: The Construction of Alcohol Problems*. Madison: University of Wisconsin Press, 1996.
Gusfield, Joseph R. *Symbolic Crusade: Status Politics and the American Temperance Movement*. Chicago: University of Illinois Press, 1986.
Häggström, Simon. *Shadow's Law: The True Story of a Swedish Detective Inspector Fighting Prostitution*. Los Angeles: SCB Distributors, 2016.
Halley, Janet, Prabha Kotiswaran, Hila Shamir and Chantal Thomas. "From the International to the Local in Feminist Legal Responses to Rape, Prostitution/Sex Work, and Sex Trafficking: Four Studies in Contemporary Governance Feminism." *Harvard Journal of Law and Gender* 29 (2006): 335–424.
Halley, Janet, Prabha Kotiswaran, Rachel Rebouché, and Hila Shamir, *Governance Feminism: An Introduction*. Minneapolis: University of Minnesota Press, 2018.
Halttunen, Karen. "Humanitarianism and the Pornography of Pain in Anglo-American Culture." *The American Historical Review* 100, no. 2 (1995): 303–34.
Haraway, Donna. "Situated Knowledges: The Science Question in Feminism and the Privilege of Partial Perspective." In *Turning Points in Qualitative Research: Tying Knots in a Handkerchief*, edited by Yvonna S. Lincoln and Norman K. Denzin, 21–46. Lanham: Rowman Altamira, 2003.
Harrington, Carol. *Politicization of Sexual Violence: From Abolitionism to Peacekeeping*. Farnham: Ashgate Publishing, Ltd., 2010.
Hay-Cooper, L. *Josephine Butler and Her Work for Social Purity*. London: Society for Promoting Christian Knowledge, 1922.
Healy, Grainne and Monica O'Connor. *The Links between Prostitution and Sex Trafficking: A Briefing Handbook*. CATW and EWL Project on Promoting Preventative Measures to Combat Trafficking in Human Beings for Sexual Exploitation. Coalition Against Trafficking in Women, July 25, 2006. Available online: http://www.catwinternational.org/Home/Article/175-the-links-between-prostitution-and-sex-trafficking-a-briefing-handbook (accessed March 21, 2019).
Hellgren, Zenia and Barbara Hobson. "Gender and Ethnic Minority Claims in Swedish and EU Frames." In *Gender Politics in the Expanding European Union: Mobilisation, Inclusion, Exclusion*, edited by Silke Roth, 211–36. New York: Berghahn Books, 2008.
Hemmings, Clare. "Affective Solidarity: Feminist Reflexivity and Political Transformation." *Feminist Theory* 13, no. 2 (2012): 147–61.
Herren, Madeleine. "Governmental Internationalism and the Beginning of a New World Order in the Late Nineteenth Century." In *The Mechanics of Internationalism: Culture, Society, and Politics from the 1840s To the First World War*, edited by Martin H. Geyer and Johannes Paulmann, 121–44. Oxford: Oxford University Press, 2001.

Hobson, Barbara. "Recognition Struggles in Universalistic and Gender Distinctive Frames: Sweden and Ireland." In *Recognition Struggles and Social Movements*, edited by Barbara Hobson, 64–92. Cambridge: Cambridge University Press, 2003.

Hodder, Edwin. *The Life and Work of The Seventh Earl of Shaftesbury, K.G.* London: Cassell, 1892.

Hodgkinson, Ruth G. *The Origins of the National Health Service: The Medical Services of the New Poor Law, 1837–1871*. Berkeley: University of California Press, 1967.

Høigård, Cecilie, and Liv Finstad. *Backstreets: Prostitution, Money, and Love*. University Park: Penn State Press, 1992.

Honeyball, Mary. *The Honeyball Buzz*. Available online: https://maryhoneyballmep.wordpress.com/ (accessed March 21, 2019).

Hopkins, Ellice. *The Present Moral Crisis: An Appeal to Women*. London: Dyer Brothers, 1886.

Hunt, Alan. *Governing Morals: A Social History of Moral Regulation*. Cambridge: Cambridge University Press, 1999.

Hunt, Margaret. "The De-Eroticization of Women's Liberation: Social Purity Movements and The Revolutionary Feminism of Sheila Jeffreys." *Feminist Review* 34, no. 1 (1990): 23–46.

Ichikawa, Chieko. "A Body Politic of Women's Own: Josephine Butler, Social Purity, and National Identity." *Victorian Review* 41, no. 1 (2015): 107–23.

Illouz, Eva. *Saving the Modern Soul: Therapy, Emotions, and the Culture of Self-Help*. Berkeley: University of California Press, 2008.

International Abolitionist Federation. *Correspondence and Reports on Extraordinary Committee*. The Women's Library, 3ams/E/37, November 30, 1996.

International Abolitionist Federation. *The New Abolitionists: A Narrative of a Year's Work: Being an Account of the Mission Undertaken to the Continent of Europe by Mrs. Josephine Butler, and of the Events Subsequent Thereupon / Published under the Direction of the British, Continental, and General Federation for the Abolition of Government Regulation of Prostitution*. London: Dyer Brothers, 1876.

International Abolitionist Federation. *Rapport du comité de crise au Comité International de la FAI*. The Women's Library, 3ams/E/37, 1996.

International Committee on the Rights of Sex Workers in Europe. *The Declaration on the Rights of Sex Workers in Europe*, 2005. http://www.sexworkeurope.org/resources/declaration-rights-sex-workers-europe

International Committee on the Rights of Sex Workers in Europe. *Nothing About Us Without Us! Ten Years of Sex Workers' Rights Activism and Advocacy in Europe*, 2015. http://www.sexworkeurope.org/sites/default/files/userfiles/files/ICRSE_10years%20report_April2016_photo_%282%29.pdf

International Committee on the Rights of Sex Workers in Europe. *Sex Workers in Europe Manifesto*. European Conference on Sex Work, Human Rights, Labour and Migration, Brussels, Belgium, October 15–17, 2005. http://www.sexworkeurope.org/resources/sex-workers-europe-manifesto.

Irwin, Mary Ann. "'White Slavery' as Metaphor Anatomy of a Moral Panic, Commercial Sex Information Service." *Ex Post Facto: The History Journal* 5 (1996). Available online: https://www.walnet.org/csis/papers/irwin-wslavery.html (accessed March 21, 2019).

Jackson, Louise A. *Child Sexual Abuse in Victorian England*. London and New York: Routledge, 2013.

Jasper, James M. "The Emotions of Protest: Affective and Reactive Emotions in and around Social Movements." *Sociological Forum* 13, no. 3 (1998): 397–424.

Jasper, James M., Michael P. Young, and Elke Zuern. *Public Characters: The Politics of Reputation and Blame*. Oxford: Oxford University Press, 2020.

Jeffreys, Sheila. *The Spinster and Her Enemies: Feminism and Sexuality, 1880–1930*. North Geelong: Spinifex Press, 1997.

Jordan, Jane. *Josephine Butler*. London: John Murray, 2001.

Jordan, Jane. "Prostitution and the Contagious Diseases Acts." 2016. Available online: https://www.routledgehistoricalresources.com/feminism/essays/prostitution-and-the-contagious-diseases-acts. Accessed April 19, 2020.

Kaplan, Carla, Sarah Haley, and Durba Mitra. "Outraged/Enraged: The Rage Special Issue." *Signs: Journal of Women in Culture and Society* 46, 4 (2021): 785–800.

Kent, Susan Kingsley. *Sex and Suffrage in Britain 1860–1914*. London: Routledge, 2005.

Kleinman, Arthur, Veena Das and Margaret Lock. *Social Suffering*. Berkeley: University of California Press, 1997.

Knepper, Paul. "The Investigation into the Traffic in Women by the League of Nations: Sociological Jurisprudence as an International Social Project." *Law and History Review* 34, no. 1 (2016): 45–73.

Knowles, Elizabeth M., and Angela Partington. *The Oxford Dictionary of Quotations*. Oxford: Oxford University Press, 1999.

Kotiswaran, Prabha. *Dangerous Sex, Invisible Labor: Sex Work and the Law in India*. Princeton: Princeton University Press, 2011.

Krug, Kate. "Women Ovulate, Men Spermate: Elizabeth Blackwell as a Feminist Physiologist." *Journal of The History of Sexuality* 7, no. 1 (1996): 51–72.

Kulick, Don. "Sex in the New Europe: The Criminalization of Clients and Swedish Fear of Penetration." *Anthropological Theory* 3, no. 2 (2003): 199–218.

Ladies' National Association. "The Garrison Towns of Kent, Third Letter from Mrs. Butler to the Editor. The 'Reclaiming and Elevating' Influences of the Acts." *Shield*, May 9, 1870.

Ladies' National Association. "The Ladies' Appeal and Protest." *Daily News*, London, January 1, 1870.

Laite, Julia A. "The Association for Moral and Social Hygiene: Abolitionism and Prostitution Law in Britain 1915–1959." *Women's History Review* 17, no. 2 (2008): 207–23.

Laite, Julia A. *Common Prostitutes and Ordinary Citizens: Commercial Sex in London, 1885–1960*. London: Palgrave, 2012.

Laite, Julia. "A Global History of Prostitution: London." In *Selling Sex in the City: A Global History of Prostitution, 1600s–2000s*, edited by Magaly Rodríguez García, Lex Heerma van Voss, and Elise van Nederveen Meerkerk, 111–37. Leiden: Brill, 2017.

Lammasniemi, Laura. "Anti-White Slavery Legislation and Its Legacies in England." *Anti-Trafficking Review*, no. 9 (2017): 64–76.

Lancaster, Roger. "Punishment." In *A Companion to Moral Anthropology*, edited by Didier Fassin, 519–39. Hoboken: John Wiley and Sons, 2012.

Langle De Paz, Teresa. "A Golden Lever for Politics: Feminist Emotion and Women's Agency." *Hypatia* 31, no. 1 (2016): 187–203.

Laqueur, Thomas. *Making Sex: Body and Sex from the Greeks to Freud*. Cambridge, MA: Harvard University Press, 1990.

Lecky, William Edward Hartpole. *History of European Morals, from Augustus to Charlemagne*, 2. Boston: D. Appleton and Company, 1897.

Legg, Stephen. "'The Life of Individuals as Well as of Nations': International Law and the League of Nations' Anti-Trafficking Governmentalities." *Leiden Journal of International Law* 25, no. 3 (2012): 647–64.

Legg, Stephen. "An Intimate and Imperial Feminism: Meliscent Shephard and the Regulation of Prostitution in Colonial India." *Environment and Planning D: Society and Space* 28, no. 1 (2010): 68–94.

Legg, Stephen. *Prostitution and the Ends of Empire*. Durham, NC: Duke University Press, 2014.

Legouvé, Ernest. *Histoire morale des femmes*. Paris: J. Hetzel, 1897.

Leidholdt, Dorchen. "Prostitution: A Violation of Women's Human Rights." *Cardozo Women's Law Journal* 1 (1993): 133–47.

Leneman, Leah. "The Awakened Instinct: Vegetarianism and the Women's Suffrage Movement in Britain." *Women's History Review* 6, no. 2 (1997): 271–87.

Lenke, Leif and Börje Olsson. "Sweden: Zero Tolerance Wins the Argument?" In *European Drug Policies and Enforcement*, edited by Nicholas Dorn, Ernesto Savona, and Jorgen Jepse, 106–18. London: Palgrave Macmillan UK, 1996.

Lesage, Julia. "Women's Rage." In *Marxism and the Interpretation of Culture*, edited by Cary Nelson and Lawrence Grossberg, 421. Urbana: University of Illinois, 1988.

Levine, Philippa. *Prostitution, Race and Politics: Policing Venereal Disease in the British Empire*. New York: Routledge, 2003.

Limoncelli, Stephanie A. *The Politics of Trafficking: The First International Movement to Combat the Sexual Exploitation of Women*. Stanford: Stanford University Press, 2010.

Liu, Roseann and Savannah Shange. "Toward Thick Solidarity: Theorizing Empathy in Social Justice Movements." *Radical History Review* 131 (2018): 189–98

Locke, John. *Two Treatises of Government*. London: Whitmore and Fenn and C. Brown, 1821.

Lodge, Carey. "10 Inspirational Quotes from William Wilberforce." *Christian Today*, July 30, 2015. Available online: https://www.christiantoday.com/article/10-inspirational-quotes-from-william-wilberforce/60570.htm (accessed March 21, 2019).

Lombroso, Cesare and Guglielmo Ferrero. *The Female Offender*. New York: D. Appleton, 1895. Available online: http://brittlebooks.library.illinois.edu/brittlebooks_open/books2009-08/lombce0001femoff/lombce0001femoff.pdf (accessed March 21, 2019).

London Anti-Vivisection Society. "The Growth of the Vivisection Evil." Speech Delivered April 26, 1899 by Mrs. Charles Mallet, London, London Anti-Vivisection Society, 1899.

Lorde, Audre. *Sister Outsider: Essays and Speeches*. Berkeley: Crossing Press, 2012.

Lorde, Audre. "The Uses of the Erotic: The Erotic as Power." In *The Lesbian and Gay Studies Reader*, edited by Henry Abelove, 339–43. New York: Routledge, 1993.

Luker, Kristin. "Sex, Social Hygiene, and the State: The Double-Edged Sword of Social Reform." *Theory and Society* 27, no. 5 (1998): 601–34.

Lupton, Deborah. *Medicine as Culture: Illness, Disease and the Body*. Thousand Oaks: SAGE, 2012.

Lytton, Constance. *Prisons and Prisoners: Some Personal Experiences*. Peterborough: Broadview Press, 2008.

Macfarlane, Bruce A. *Historical Development of the Offence of Rape*. Canadian Bar Association, 1992. https://archive.org/stream/413655-hist-devel-of-offence-of-rape/413655-hist-devel-of-offence-of-rape_djvu.txt

Machiels, Christine. *Les féminismes et la prostitution 1860–1960*. Rennes: Presses universitaires de Rennes, 2016.

Machiels, Christine. "The 'Truth about White Slavery.' Présentation d'une enquête réalisée par Teresa Billington-Greig pour *The English Review* (juin 1913)." *Recherches sociologiques et anthropologiques* 39, no. 1 (2008): 27–40.

MacKinnon, Catherine A. "Pornography, Civil Rights, and Speech." *Harvard Civil Rights-Civil Liberties Law Review* 20, no. 1 (1985): 299–311.

MacKinnon, Catherine A. "Reflections on Sex Equality under Law." *Yale Law Journal* 100, no. 5 (1991): 1281–328.

MacKinnon, Catherine A. *Toward a Feminist Theory of the State*. Cambridge, MA: Harvard University Press, 1989.

MacKinnon, Catherine A. "Violence against Women: A Perspective." *Aegis: Magazine on Ending Violence Against Women* 33 (1982): 51–7.

MacKinnon, Catherine A. and Andrea Dworkin (eds.) *In Harm's Way: The Pornography Civil Rights Hearings*. Cambridge: Harvard University Press, 1997.

Mantena, Karuna. *Alibis of Empire: Henry Maine and the Ends of Liberal Imperialism*. Princeton: Princeton University Press, 2010.

Marcovich, Malka. *Resignation Letter from the International Abolitionist Federation*, The Women's Library, 3ams/E/39, February 15, 1998.

Mathieu, Lilian. "De l'objectivation à l'émotion. La mobilisation des chiffres dans le mouvement abolitionniste contemporain." *Mots. Les langages du politique* 100 (2013): 173–85.

Mathieu, Lilian. "Des monstres ordinaires, la construction du problème public des clients de la prostitution." *Champ Pénal/Penal Field* 12 (2015). Available online: https://halshs.archives-ouvertes.fr/halshs-01326668 (Accessed March 21, 2019).

Mathieu, Lilian. "Le mouvement abolitionniste français dans l'après-guerre." *Déviance Et Société* 40, no. 1 (2016): 79–100.

Mathieu, Lilian. *La fin du tapin. Sociologie de la croisade pour l'abolition de la prostitution*. Paris: François Bourin, 2014.

Mathieu, Lilian. *Prostitution, quel est le problème?* Paris: Textuel, 2016.

Mattson, Greggor. *The Cultural Politics of European Prostitution Reform: Governing Loose Women* New York Palgrave Macmillan, 2016.

McConnaughy, Corrine M. *The Woman Suffrage Movement in America: A Reassessment*. Cambridge: Cambridge University Press, 2013.

McElroy, Wendy. "The Contagious Disease Acts." *Freedom Daily*, March 2000. Available online: https://www.fff.org/explore-freedom/article/contagious-disease-acts/ (Accessed October 28, 2021).

McGrigor, James Allen. "On the Real Differences in the Minds of Men and Women." *Journal of The Anthropological Society* 7 (1869): cxcv–ccxix.

Meger, Sara. "The Fetishization of Sexual Violence in International Security." *International Studies Quarterly* 60, no. 1 (2016): 149–59.

Mgbako, Chi Adanna. "The Mainstreaming of Sex Workers' Rights as Human Rights." *Harvard Journal of Law and Gender* 43 (2020): 91–136.

Mianiti, Mariangela. "Prostitution is Paid Rape, and Men Know It." *Il Manifesto*, October 11, 2017. Available online: https://global.ilmanifesto.it/prostitution-is-paid-rape-and-men-know-it/ (accessed March 21, 2019).

Midgley, Clare. "Anti-Slavery and Feminism in Nineteenth-Century Britain." *Gender and History* 5, no. 3 (1993): 343–62.

Milburn, Colin. "Science from Hell: Jack the Ripper and Victorian Vivisection." In *Science Images and Popular Images of the Sciences*, edited by Hüppauf Bernd-Rüdiger and Peter Weingart, 125–58. New York: Routledge, 2008.

Mill, John Stuart. *The Collected Works of John Stuart Mill, Volume XVII—The Later Letters of John Stuart Mill 1849–1873 Part IV [1869]*, edited by Francis E. Mineka and Dwight N. Lindley. Toronto: University of Toronto Press, London: Routledge & Kegan Paul, 1972. Available online: http://oll.libertyfund.org/titles/254 (accessed March 21, 2019).

Mill, John Stuart. *On Liberty*. London: Longmans, Green, Reader, and Dyer, 1869.

Mill, John Stuart. *The Subjection of Women*. London: Longmans, Green, Reader, and Dyer, 1870.

Miller, Alice M. "Sexuality, Violence against Women, and Human Rights: Women Make Demands and Ladies Get Protection." *Health and Human Rights* 7, no. 2 (2004): 16–47.

Miller, Carol. "The Social Section and Advisory Committee on Social Questions of the League of Nations." In *International Health Organisations and Movements*,

1918–1939, edited by Paul Weindling, Charles Rosenberg and Colin Jones, 154–75. Cambridge: Cambridge University Press, 1995.

Miller, Ian. "Necessary Torture? Vivisection, Suffragette Force-Feeding, and Responses to Scientific Medicine in Britain c. 1870–1920." *Journal of The History of Medicine and Allied Sciences* 64, no. 3 (2009): 333–72.

Moran, Rachel. "The Life of an Anti-Prostitution Campaigner." *The Irish Times*, May 29, 2015. Available online: https://www.irishtimes.com/life-and-style/people/the-life-of-an-anti-prostitution-campaigner-1.2230971 (accessed March 21, 2019).

Moran, Rachel. *Paid For: My Journey through Prostitution*. New York: W. W. Norton and Company, 2015.

Mort, Frank. *Capital Affairs: London and the Making of the Permissive Society*. New Haven: Yale University Press, 2010.

Mort, Frank. *Dangerous Sexualities: Medico-Moral Politics in England since 1830*. New York: Routledge, 2002.

Moscucci, Ornella. *The Science of Woman: Gynaecology and Gender in England, 1800–1929*. Cambridge: Cambridge University Press, 1993.

Mothersole, Brenda. "Female Philanthropy and Women Novelists of 1840–1870." PhD dissertation." Brunel University School of Sport and Education, 1989.

Mott, Rebecca. "To All Punters," July 4, 2018. Available online: https://rebeccamott.net/ (accessed March 21, 2019).

Mouvement du Nid. *Les Bourreaux*, 2016. Available online: http://www.mouvementdunid.org/Les-Bourreaux-Le-Mouvement-du-Nid (accessed March 21, 2019).

Mouvement du Nid Belgium. *Les Nouvelles Du Nid*, no. 1–12, Bibliothèque royale de Belgique, BD 45793, 1982–1985.

Mouvement du Nid and McCann Paris. *Girls of Paradise*. 2016. Available online: http://www.mouvementdunid.org/Girls-of-paradise-quand-la-realite-s-impose-aux-clients-de-la-prostitution (accessed March 21, 2019).

Murphy, Meghan. "Podcast: Survivors Speak out in New Book about the Prostitution Industry." *Feminist Current*, August 12, 2016. Available online: https://www.feministcurrent.com/2016/08/12/podcast-prostitution-narratives-stories-survival-sex-trade/ (accessed March 21, 2019).

Murray, James A. H. ed. *A New English Dictionary of Historical Principles* 5. Oxford: Clarendon Press, 1901.

National Association for the Repeal of the CD Acts. "An Address to Working Men and Women, Relative to a Recent Distressing Case of Suicide, at Aldershot, under Cruel, Oppressive, and Immoral Acts of Parliament." In *Josephine Butler and the Prostitution Campaigns: The Constitution Violated: The Parliamentary Campaign* 3, edited by Jane Jordan and Ingrid Sharp, 30–7. London: Taylor & Francis, 2003.

National Association for the Repeal of the CD Acts. *Summary of the Evil Principles and Revolting Practices of the Immoral Laws Known as the Contagious Diseases Acts*, Leaflet D, The Women's Library, 3ams/B/01/02, 1877.

National Organization for Women. *Statement of Purpose*. 1966. Available online: http://now.org/about/history/statement-of-purpose/ (accessed March 21, 2019).

National Vigilance Association. *The White Slave Trade: Transactions of the International Congress on the White Slave Trade, 21–23 June 1899*. London: Office of the National Vigilance Association, 1899.

Nickel, Patricia Mooney. *Public Sociology and Civil Society: Governance, Politics, and Power*. New York: Routledge, 2015.

Nordic Model Now. "How the Swedish Sex Purchase Law Moved the Shame of Prostitution from Women to the Punters." Interview with Simon Häggström by Francine Sporenda, July 20, 2018. Available online: https://nordicmodelnow.org/2018/07/20/how-the-swedish-sex-purchase-law-moved-the-shame-of-prostitution-from-the-women-to-the-punters/ (accessed March 21, 2019).

Nordic Model Now. "Survivors Speak out about What Prostitution Is Really Like," 8 September 2018. Available online: https://nordicmodelnow.org/2018/09/08/survivors-speak-out-about-what-prostitution-is-really-like/ (accessed March 21, 2019).

Nordic Model Now. "What is the Nordic Model?" https://nordicmodelnow.org/what-is-the-nordic-model/.

Offen, Karen M. *European Feminisms, 1700–1950: A Political History*. Stanford: Stanford University Press, 2000.

Oriel, David J. *The Scars of Venus: A History of Venereology*. Berlin: Springer Science and Business Media, 2012.

Orland, Kevin Schembri. "Prostitution Is Paid Rape, Says MCWO Chairwoman Lorraine Spiteri," *The Malta Independent*. September 9, 2017. Available online: http://www.independent.com.mt/articles/2017-09-09/local-news/Prostitution-is-paid-rape-says-MCWO-chairwoman-lorraine-spiteri-6736178562 (accessed March 21, 2019).

Pankhurst, Dame Christabel. *The Great Scourge and How to End It*. London: E. Pankhurst, 1913.

Parent-Duchâtelet, Alexandre. *De la prostitution dans la ville de Paris considérée sous le rapport de l'hygiène publique, de la morale et de l'administration*. Paris: J.-B. Baillière Et Fils, 1836.

Parliament. *Report of the Royal Commission on Alien Immigration* 1. London, Royal Commission on Alien Immigration, H. M. Stationery Office, 1903.

Parliament. *The Parliamentary Debates: Official Reports, 36, Comprising the Period From 29 October 1801 to 12 August 1803*. London: T. C. Hansard, 1820.

Parliament. *Vagrancy Act of 1824*. Available online: http://www.legislation.gov.uk/ukpga/geo4/5/83/contents/enacted (accessed March 21, 2019).

Parliament. *Vagrancy Act of 1824 Amendment Bill*, Revised 1898. Available online: https://api.parliament.uk/historic-hansard/bills/vagrancy-act-amendment-bill (accessed March 21, 2019).

Patmore, Coventry. *The Angel in The House*, 1854. Available online: https://www.bl.uk/collection-items/coventry-patmores-poem-the-angel-in-the-house (accessed March 21, 2019).

Pearson, Michael. *The Age of Consent: Victorian Prostitution and its Enemies*. Newton Abbot: David and Charles, 1972.

Pinch, Adela. *Strange Fits of Passion: Epistemologies of Emotion, Hume to Austen*. Stanford: Stanford University Press, 1996.

Pitts, Jennifer. *A Turn to Empire: The Rise of Imperial Liberalism in Britain and France*. Princeton: Princeton University Press, 2009.

Pliley, Jessica R. "Any Other Immoral Purpose: The Mann Act, Policing Women, and the American State, 1900–1941." PhD dissertation, The Ohio State University, 2010.

Pliley, Jessica R. "Claims to Protection: The Rise and Fall of Feminist Abolitionism in the League of Nations: Committee on the Traffic in Women and Children, 1919–1936." *Journal of Women's History* 22, no. 4 (2010): 90–113.

Porter, Bernard. *The Origins of the Vigilant State: The London Metropolitan Police Special Branch Before the First World War*. Woodbridge: Boydell and Brewer, 1987.

Raymond, Janice. *Not a Choice, Not a Job: Exposing the Myths about Prostitution and the Global Sex Trade*. Dulles: Potomac Books, Inc., 2013.

Reid, Donald. "In The Name of the Father: A Language of Labour Relations in Nineteenth-Century France." *History Workshop Journal* 38, no. 1 (1994): 1–22.

Rich, Adrienne. *Of Woman Born: Motherhood as Experience and Institution*. New York: W. W. Norton and Company, 1995.

Richardson, Angelique. *Love and Eugenics in the Late Nineteenth Century: Rational Reproduction and the New Woman*. Oxford: Oxford University Press, 2003.

Ricord, Philippe. *Traité pratique des maladies vénériennes*. Paris: Librairie Des Sciences Médicales De Just Rouvier et E. Le Bouvier, 1838.

Rimke, Heidi and Alan Hunt. "From Sinners to Degenerates: The Medicalization of Morality in the 19th Century." *History of the Human Sciences* 15, no. 1 (2002): 59–88.

Roberts, F. David. *The Social Conscience of the Early Victorians*. Stanford: Stanford University Press, 2002.

Roberts, F. David. *Paternalism in Early Victorian England*. New York: Routledge, 1979.

Romanes, George John. "Mental Differences between Men and Women." *The Nineteenth Century* 13, January/June 1887.

Roos, Julia. *Weimar through the Lens of Gender: Prostitution Reform, Woman's Emancipation, and German Democracy, 1919–33*. Ann Arbor: University of Michigan Press, 2010.

Rosenwein, Barbara H. *Anger: The Conflicted History of an Emotion*. New Haven: Yale University Press, 2020.

Rosenwein, Barbara H. *Emotional Communities in the Early Middle Ages*. Ithaca: Cornell University Press, 2006.

Royal Commission on the Contagious Diseases Acts. *Report of Royal Commission upon the Administration and Operation of the Contagious Diseases*. London, Printed by George Edward Eyre and William Spottiswoode, for Her Majesty's Stationery Office, 1871.

Saint-Simon, C. H. D. *Oeuvres De Saint-Simon*. Paris: E. Dentu. Iv, 1868.

Sandler, Winifred Ann. "The Minneapolis Anti-Pornography Ordinance: A Valid Assertion of Civil Rights." *Fordham Urban Law Journal* 13 (1984): 909–46.

Scaramuzzino, Roberto and Gabriella Scaramuzzino. "Sex Workers' Rights Movement and the EU: Challenging the New European Prostitution Policy Model." In *EU Civil Society: Patterns of Cooperation, Competition and Conflict,* edited by Sara Kalm and Hakan Johansson, 137–54. London: Palgrave Macmillan, 2015.

Scheer, Monique. "Are Emotions a Kind of Practice and Is That What Makes Them Have a History? A Bourdieuian Approach to Understanding Emotion." *History and Theory* 51, no. 2 (2012): 193–220.

Scott, Anne L. "Physical Purity Feminism and State Medicine in Late Nineteenth-Century England." *Women's History Review* 8, no. 4 1999: 625–53.

Sénat. *Séance du 10 mars 2016 (compte rendu intégral des débats)*, March 10, 2016. Available online: https://www.senat.fr/seances/s201605/s20160510/s20160510_mono.html (accessed March 21, 2019).

Sénat. *Séance du 14 octobre 2015 (compte rendu intégral des débats)*, October 14, 2015. Available online: http://www.senat.fr/seances/s201510/s20151014/st20151014000.html (accessed March 21, 2019).

Sharpe, Jenny. *Allegories of Empire: The Figure of Woman in the Colonial Text*. Minneapolis: University of Minnesota Press, 1993.

Schreiner, Olive. *Olive Schreiner Daily News, 28 December 1885*, Harry Ransom Research Center, University of Texas at Austin, Olive Schreiner Letters Project transcription.

Schreiner, Olive. *Olive Schreiner to Karl Pearson, 15 September 1885*, University College London Library, Special Collections, UCL, London, Olive Schreiner Letters Project transcription.

Simon, Jonathan. *Governing through Crime: How the War on Crime Transformed American Democracy and Created a Culture of Fear*. Oxford: Oxford University Press, 2007.

Smith, Jill Suzanne. *Berlin Coquette: Prostitution and the New German Woman*. Cornell: Cornell University Press, 2014.

Smith, Jonathan. "The Huxley-Wilberforce 'Debate' on Evolution, 30 June 1860." In *Extension of Romanticism and Victorianism on The Net. Branch: Britain, Representation and Nineteenth-Century History*, edited by Dino Franco Felluga, February 2013. Available online: http://www.branchcollective.org/?ps_articles=jonathan-smith-the-huxley-wilberforce-debate-on-evolution-30-june-1860 (accessed March 21, 2019).

Smolak, Alex. "White Slavery, Whorehouse Riots, Venereal Disease, and Saving Women: Historical Context of Prostitution Interventions and Harm Reduction in New York City during the Progressive Era." *Social Work in Public Health* 28, no. 5 (2013): 496–508.

Society of Friends. *Petition from London Yearly Meeting of the Society of Friends, Presented to Parliament on 16 June 1783*, 1783. Available online: http://abolition.e2bn.org/source_34.html (accessed March 21, 2019).

Solomon, Claire. "Reconsidering Anti-Semitism and White Slavery in Contemporary Historical Fiction about Argentina." *Comparative Literature* 63, no. 3 (2011): 307–27.

Sommers, Christina Hoff. *Who Stole Feminism?: How Women Have Betrayed Women*. New York: Simon and Schuster, 1994.

Space International. *Testimonials*. Available online: http://www.spaceintl.org/about/testimonials/ (accessed March 21, 2019).

Special Correspondent. "Brussels Conference of Social Hygiene (Concluded)." *The British Medical Journal* 2, no. 2020 (September 16, 1899): 739–41.

Stanton, Elizabeth Cady. *A History of Woman Suffrage* 1. Rochester, NY: Fowler and Wells, 1889.

Stead, William T. "The Maiden Tribute of Modern Babylon." *Pall Mall Gazette*, 1885.

Stead, William T. "The Steamy Side of Empire." *Pall Mall Budget*, February 3, 1887.

Stearns, Peter N. *Global Outrage: The Impact of World Opinion on Contemporary History*. Oxford: Oneworld Publications Limited, 2005.

Stearns, Peter N. *Sexuality in World History*. London and New York: Routledge, 2009.

Stringer, Rebecca. *Knowing Victims: Feminism, Agency and Victim Politics in Neoliberal Times*. New York: Routledge, 2014.

Summers, Anne. "Which Women? What Europe? Josephine Butler and the International Abolitionist Federation." *History Workshop Journal* 62, no. 1 (2006): 214–31.

Surridge, Lisa. *Bleak Houses: Marital Violence in Victorian Fiction*. Columbus: Ohio University Press, 2005.

Survivors' Agenda. "The Survivors' Agenda." Available online: https://survivorsagenda.org/agenda/full-agenda/ (Accessed November 21, 2021).

Sverigeskvinnolobby. "Surrogacy: A Global Trade in Women's Bodies?," October 31, 2014. Available online: https://www.womenlobby.org/Surrogacy-a-global-trade-in-women-s-bodies?lang=en (accessed March 21, 2019).

Swedish Institute. *Targeting the Sex Buyer. The Swedish Example: Stopping Prostitution and Trafficking Where It All Begins*. 2011.

Swedish Institute. *The Ban against the Purchase of Sexual Services, An Evaluation 1999–2008*. Anna Skarhed, 2010.

Tait, Lawson. *Diseases of Women and Abdominal Surgery* 1. Philadelphia: Lea, 1889.

Tankardreist, Melinda. "Sex Industry Tries to Recruit Prostitution Survivor Back into the Trade at Book Launch," 2016. Available online: http://melindatankardreist.

com/2016/09/sex-industry-tries-to-recruit-prostitution-survivor-back-into-the-trade-at-book-launch/ (accessed March 21, 2019).

Taylor, Barbara. *Mary Wollstonecraft and the Feminist Imagination*. Cambridge: Cambridge University Press, 2003.

Taylor, Charles. *A Secular Age*. Cambridge, MA: The Belknap Press of Harvard University Press, 2007

Thorne, Susan. *Congregational Missions and the Making of an Imperial Culture in Nineteenth-Century England*. Stanford: Stanford University Press, 1999.

Todorov, Tzvetan. *Imperfect Garden: The Legacy of Humanism*. Trans. C. Cosman. Princeton: Princeton University Press, 2002.

Trägårdh, Lars. *Sweden and the EU: Welfare State Nationalism and the Spectre of 'Europe'*. London: Routledge, 2002.

Traïni, Christophe. *The Animal Rights Struggle*. Amsterdam: Amsterdam University Press, 2016.

True, Jacqui. "The Political Economy of Violence against Women: A Feminist International Relations Perspective." *Australian Feminist Law Journal* 32, no. 1 (2010): 39–59.

Trumble, Kelly Lynn. "'Her Body is Her Own': Victorian Feminists, Sexual Violence, and Political Subjectivity." PhD dissertation, English Department, The Florida State University, 2004.

Turda, Marius. *Modernism and Eugenics*. Berlin: Springer, 2010.

United Nations Educational, Scientific, and Cultural Organization. "Introducing UNESCO." Available online: https://www.unesco.org/en/introducing-unesco (accessed November 2, 2021).

United Nations. *Charter*. Available online: http://legal.un.org/repertory/art1.shtml (accessed March 21, 2019).

United Nations. *Convention on the Elimination of All Forms of Discrimination Against Women*. 1979. Available online: http://www.un.org/womenwatch/daw/cedaw/ (accessed March 21, 2019).

United Nations. *International Meeting of Experts on the Social and Cultural Causes of Prostitution and Strategies for the Struggle Against Procuring and Sexual Exploitation of Women*. Shs-85/Conf.608/14, Madrid, Spain, Division of Human Rights and Peace, March 18–21, 1986. Available online: http://unesdoc.unesco.org/images/0007/000715/071520EB.pdf (accessed March 21, 2019).

United Nations. *Platform for Action at Beijing*, Fourth World Conference on Women, 1995. Available online: http://www.un.org/womenwatch/daw/beijing/platform/ (accessed March 21, 2019).

United Nations. *Rome Statute of the International Criminal Court* II-7-c, 1998. http://legal.un.org/icc/statute/99_corr/cstatute.htm

United Nations. *Study on Traffic in Persons and Prostitution*, Department of Economic and Social Affairs, St/Soa/Sd/8, 1959.

United Nations. *Universal Declaration of Human Rights*, 1948. Available online: http://www.un.org/en/udhrbook/pdf/udhr_booklet_en_web.pdf (accessed March 21, 2019).

van der Velden Peter G., Mauro Pecoraro, Mijke S. Houwerzijl, and Erik van der Meulen, "Mental Health Problems among Whistleblowers: A Comparative Study." *Psychological Reports* 122, no. 2 (2019): 632–44.

Vigarello, Georges. *Histoire du viol: XVIe–XXe Siècle*. Paris: Editions du Seuil, 1998.

Vigarello, Georges. *Le propre et le sale, L'hygiène du corps depuis le Moyen Age*. Paris, Éditions du Seuil, 1985.

Vygotsky, Lev Semenovich. "Problems of the Theory and Methods of Psychology." In *The Collected Works of LS Vygotsky* 3, edited by Robert W. Rieber and Jeffrey Wollock, 35–146. Berlin: Springer Science and Business Media, 1997.

Wahrman, Dror. "'Middle-Class' Domesticity Goes Public: Gender, Class, and Politics from Queen Caroline to Queen Victoria." *Journal of British Studies* 32, no. 4 (1993): 396–432.

Walkowitz, Judith. *City of Dreadful Delight: Narratives of Sexual Danger in Late-Victorian London*. Chicago: University of Chicago Press, 1992.

Walkowitz, Judith. *Prostitution and Victorian Society: Women, Class, and the State*. Cambridge: Cambridge University Press, 1980.

Walters, Johanna. "Gloria Steinem: 'Fewer People Will Say We Live in a Post-Racist, Post-Feminist World.'" *The Guardian*, December 11, 2016. Available online: https://www.theguardian.com/books/2016/dec/11/gloria-steinem-feminism-womens-rights-donald-trump (accessed March 21, 2019).

Waltman, Max. "Sweden's Prohibition of Purchase of Sex: The Law's Reasons, Impact, and Potential." *Women's Studies International Forum* 34, no. 5 (2011): 449–74.

Wanrooij, Bruno. "Josephine Butler and Regulated Prostitution in Italy." *Women's History Review* 17, no. 2 (2008), 153–71.

Ward, Eilis and Gillian Wylie, eds. *Feminism, Prostitution and The State: The Politics of Neo-Abolitionism*. New York: Routledge/Taylor & Francis, 2017.

Weeks, Jeffrey. Sex, *Politics and Society: The Regulation of Sexuality since 1800*. London: Longman, 1981.

Weitzer, Ronald. "Moral Crusade against Prostitution." *Society* 43, no. 3 (2006): 33–8.

Welter, Barbara. "The Cult of True Womanhood: 1820–1860." *American Quarterly* 18, no. 2 part 1 (1966): 151–74.

Wilkinson, James John Garth. *The Forcible Introspection of Women for the Army and Navy by the Oligarchy, Considered Physically*. London: J. Pitman, 1870.

Wilson, Helen. "Evidence to the Royal Commission on Venereal Diseases in the United Kingdom." *British Medical Journal*, November 29, 1913, 2, no. 2761, 1442–3. https://www.ncbi.nlm.nih.gov/pmc/articles/PMC2345925/.

Wollstonecraft, Mary. *A Vindication of the Rights of Men, in A Letter to the Right Honourable Edmund Burke: Occasioned by His Reflections on the Revolution in France*. Cambridge: Cambridge University Press, 1790.

Worboys, Michael. *Spreading Germs: Disease Theories and Medical Practice in Britain, 1865–1900*. Cambridge: Cambridge University Press, 2000.

World Health Organization. *Putting Women First: Ethical and Safety Recommendations for Research on Domestic Violence against Women*, 2001. https://www.who.int/publications/i/item/WHO-FCH-GWH-01.1.

Worth, Jennifer. *Farewell to the East End*. London: Hachette UK, 2009.

Wylie, Gillian. *The International Politics of Human Trafficking*. London: Palgrave Macmillan, 2016.

Yeo, Eileen Janes. "Social Motherhood and the Sexual Communion of Labour in British Social Science, 1850–1950." *Women's History Review* 1, no. 1 (1992): 63–87.

Zoglin, Kathryn. "United Nations Action against Slavery: A Critical Evaluation." *Human Rights Quarterly* 8 (1986): 306–39.

Index

#MeToo 1–2, 133, 153–4

ACT UP 134
Acton, William 13–14, 26, 28
Allan, James McGrigor 36
American Woman Suffrage Association 83
Amicale du Nid 113, 143
Amnesty International 33, 122–3, 129, 137
anger 21, 26, 113, 134, 148, 154–6
 feminist 75–80, 101–4, 140, 151
 survivor 140–2
animal welfare movement 43, 57, 69
anti-pornography movement 99, 133–4, 149, 154
antislavery movement 16–20, 30, 34–5, 42–3, 54, 69, 78, 127, 148, 153
anti-trafficking movement 38, 106–8, 111, 123, 128, 140
anti-vaccination movement 28–9, 148, 151
anti-vivisection movement 29, 32–3, 35, 53, 69–70, 148, 151
Association for Moral and Social Hygiene 80–1, 84–5, 91
Australia 1, 145
Austria 1, 130

Baker, Annie 85
Barnes, Djuna 71
Barry, Kathleen 3, 99, 104, 109–10, 139
Belgium 36, 39
Bentham, Jeremy 59–60
Bérenger, René 24, 55
Bieber-Böhm, Hanna 55, 79
Bindel, Julie 2–3, 7, 151–2
Blackwell, Antoinette Brown 83
Blackwell, Elizabeth 32, 48, 50, 70, 83
Booth, Bramwell 37
Booth, Florence 45
Booth, William 50
British Social Hygiene Council 80–1

Bush, George W. 108
Butler, Josephine 15–21, 23, 30, 53, 58, 61, 73–6, 91, 95, 98, 148–9
 and social purity 37–9, 45
 Legacy of 3, 6–8, 55, 76, 150–1
 On the aristocracy 25–6
 On the double moral standard 2, 65
 On the police 24–5
 On scientific medicine 32–4, 66–7
 On women's public role 65–8, 74, 78

Canada 1, 47
Carlyle, Thomas 60
Cartel d'action morale et sociale 95
Cauer, Minna 55
Chadwick, Edwin 60
Chant, Laura Ormiston 48, 52
civil rights 28, 55, 68, 99, 106
civil rights movement 97, 134
civilizing mission 41, 61, 65, 68, 73, 75, 151, 153
Coalition Against Trafficking in Women 105, 111, 126, 149
Cobbe, Frances Power 69–70
compassion 7, 11, 15–20, 30, 38, 44, 48, 69, 71–2, 74, 86, 89, 95, 114, 128, 140, 142, 144, 148, 153
 economy of 18, 34
Conseil de salubrité 13
Consent, age of 39, 77
Contagious Diseases Acts 2, 13–14, 21, 23, 27–8, 31, 44, 46, 55, 66, 69
 campaign to repeal 15–16, 20, 35, 56, 58, 73, 77–8
 suspension of 36
Coote, William Alexander 40, 46, 51
Criminal Law Amendment Act 39, 47
Crowdy, Dame Rachel 84–5
Cust, Harry 47

Darwin, Charles 49, 52, 57, 64, 83
Darwinism 29, 44, 52, 64, 83–4, 148

de Morsier, Émilie 32, 55, 74
de Sainte-Croix, Ghénia Avril 67, 76, 85, 95
Despard, Charlotte 71
disgust 5, 17, 21, 30, 96, 119, 152–3, 156
domestic violence 98, 103, 107, 121, 124, 128, 134–5, 138, 149
Dworkin, Andrea 99, 102–3, 106, 139

Ekberg, Gunilla 120
Ekman, Kajsa Ekis 139
Elmy, Elizabeth Wolstenholme 20, 68
Enlightenment 19, 58
Eugenics 46, 49, 64–5, 75, 77, 81–3, 86, 148
European Parliament 112, 123, 125–7, 129–30, 150
European Union 111–12, 124–30, 154
European Women's Lobby 112, 118, 122, 124, 126–30, 139
  For a Change in Perspective 119, 129
  For a Europe Free from Prostitution 124, 129

Falco, Denise Pouillon 109–10
Falco, Marcelle Legrand 55
Fallot, Tommy 47
Farley, Melissa 130
Fawcett, Millicent Garrett 45, 47
fear 17, 28–9, 34, 37, 39–40, 43–4, 71, 86, 90, 122, 153, 155
  culture of 104, 107, 134–5
  of degeneracy 64, 114, 151
  of government and police 21, 23, 26, 148, 153
  of humiliation 118
  of scientific medicine 27, 32
  providentialist 39–40, 44, 47, 114
FEMEN 105
Fiaux, Louis 80
Fondation Scelles 129–30, 143
Fournier, Alfred 79, 81, 143
France 1, 59, 76, 90, 94–5, 110, 114–15, 139
French National Assembly 116–17
French Revolution 59
Friedan, Betty 93, 99

Galton, Francis 64
Gaskell, Elizabeth 62
Germany 1, 10, 36, 40, 55, 76, 80, 88, 130

Global Alliance Against Traffic in Women 108
Grand, Sarah 76, 82
Great Britain 2, 15, 21, 24, 36, 39, 53, 62, 72, 77, 88, 92, 111, 147
guilt 19, 89–90, 119, 141, 153
Guyot, Yves 24

Häggström, Simon 119, 125
happiness 18–19, 59, 99
hate 47, 113, 142
Hicher, Rosen 143
Hoggan, Frances 83
Hopkins, Ellice 82
human rights 98, 116, 122, 128–9, 136–8, 153
humanitarianism 17, 42, 51, 74, 118, 128, 147, 150–1
  imperialist 86
  militarized 108, 150
humiliation 10, 118, 154
Hungary 40

Iceland 1
imperialism 9, 63, 65, 74, 89, 94, 148, 151
  liberal 51
India 19, 36, 81
indignation 114, 117, 151, 154
  righteous 11, 15–18, 20–1, 28, 30, 32–3, 38, 75, 77
industrial revolution 59
International Abolitionist Federation 36–8, 40, 55, 66, 80, 87, 98, 109
International Bureau 40, 46, 84, 85, 87
International Council of Women 84
International Women's Suffrage Alliance 36
Ireland 1
Israel 1
Italy 36, 55, 139

Josephine Butler Society 7, 152

Kingsford, Anna 83

Ladies' National Association 20, 22, 36, 80, 85
League of Nations 81, 84, 87
Ligue contre la syphilis 81
Lorde, Audre 100–1, 159

love 75, 90, 93, 95, 100, 113
  compassionate 16, 152
  fatherly 58
  motherly 56–8, 61–2, 69
Lovelace, Linda 137

MacKinnon, Catherine 99–100, 106–7, 134–5, 138–9, 149
Manif pour tous 116–17
Marcovich, Malka 110, 123
Mill, John Stuart 21–2, 77
moral shock 9, 121
Moran, Rachel 140–1, 143, 145
Mott, Lucretia 54
Mouvement du Nid 113–14, 120, 129
  Girls of Paradise 121–2
  Les Bourreaux 122

National Organization for Women 93
National Vigilance Association 39–40, 42, 44–6, 48
Neilans, Alison 85–6
Netherlands 10, 36, 110, 130
Neville-Rolfe, Sybil 81
New Left movement 94
New Zealand 1, 144
Nordic Model 1–2, 105, 111–12, 114–15, 117, 119, 123–5, 128, 130–1, 150, 152
Nordic Model Now 7, 123, 143
Northern Ireland 1
Norway 1, 123

outrage 37, 75, 77, 79, 121, 128
  moral 113–15, 117, 120, 142, 153

Pape, Pierrette 129
Pappritz, Anna 55, 76, 80
Parent-Duchâtelet, Alexandre 13–14
pity 6, 74, 118, 121
police des mœurs 22–4, 36, 55
Portugal 40
pride 5, 7, 20–1, 24–5, 65, 121
Proclamation Society 42

Rape 31, 38, 72–3, 98, 105, 107, 135–8, 149, 154
  Medical 30–4, 71–3
  Paid 138–9

Raymond, Janice 98, 126
Reformation of Manners 48
resentment 75–6, 104, 107, 142
Rich, Adrienne 99, 101, 152
Ricord, Philippe 14, 31, 79
Romanes, George John 84
Royal Commission on Venereal Disease 84
Royer, Clémence 83
Ruskin, John 60

Salvation Army 37, 50
Scarlet Alliance 145
Scharlieb, Dame Mary 84
Scheven, Katharina 76, 80
sex workers' rights 3, 97, 99, 108
shame 19–20, 26, 29, 31, 34, 65, 69, 95, 122, 134, 150, 153, 156
  male 118–20, 122
  survivor 141
silence, breaking of 16, 21, 23, 81, 134, 137, 142, 145
smallpox 28, 148
Snow, William F. 85
social hygiene 49, 80, 86, 151
Social purity 9, 20, 23, 37, 40–1, 44–5, 55, 73, 148
Social Purity Alliance 48
Société française de prophylaxie sanitaire et morale 79
solidarity 54, 75–6, 99, 101, 103–4, 107, 114, 120–1, 124, 133, 152
Somerset, Lady Henry 45, 49
Space International 133, 143
Spain 40, 130, 139
Spencer, Herbert 64
Spinoza, Baruch 118
Stanton, Elizabeth Cady 54
Stead, William T. 7, 17, 37, 77
Steinem, Gloria 99, 103
Stopes, Marie 82
Suffrage movement 54, 63, 70–1, 73, 75–7, 148
surrogacy 116–17, 139
Survivor movement
Sweden 1, 10, 92, 111, 120, 123–5, 127, 139
Switzerland 10, 36, 53
sympathy 15, 17–18, 48, 52, 54, 64, 103, 153

Travellers' Aid Society 46

UNESCO 89, 109–10
Union contre la traite des Êtres Humains 109
Union temporaire contre la prostitution réglementée et la traite des femmes 55
United Kingdom 1, 82, 152
United Nations 87, 98, 104, 109, 125, 136, 138, 154
United Nations Working Group on Slavery 109, 149

United States 1, 17, 47, 53–4, 80, 88–9, 92–3, 107–8, 111, 140, 142
utilitarianism 21, 59–60

white slavery 9, 37, 39, 40, 46–7, 51, 55, 77, 98, 110, 140, 148, 150–1
Wilberforce, William 19, 29, 43, 61–2
Wilson, Helen 84
Wollstonecraft, Mary 68, 77, 83
women's rights movement 2, 6, 53–4, 73, 78, 86, 93, 112, 130, 149
World Health Organization 154

www.ingramcontent.com/pod-product-compliance
Lightning Source LLC
Chambersburg PA
CBHW062222300426

44115CB00012BA/2185